DEMOSTHENES OLYNTHIACS

Edited with Introduction, Commentary & Vocabulary by

E.I. McQueen
Lecturer in Classics, University of Bristol
(using text and some introductory material
from the edition by J.M. MacGregor)

Published by Bristol Classical Press
General Editor: John H. Betts
(text and some introductory material by arrangement
with the Syndicate of the Cambridge University Press)

This impression 2003
First published in 1986 by
Bristol Classical Press
an imprint of
Gerald Duckworth & Co. Ltd.
61 Frith Street, London W1D 3JL
Tel: 020 7434 4242
Fax: 020 7434 4420
inquiries@duckworth-publishers.co.uk
www.ducknet.co.uk

© 1986 by E.I. McQueen

All rights reserved. No part of this publication
may be reproduced, stored in a retrieval system, or
transmitted, in any form or by any means, electronic,
mechanical, photocopying, recording or otherwise,
without the prior permission of the publisher.

A catalogue record for this book is available
from the British Library

ISBN 0 86292 073 6

CONTENTS

Preface v
INTRODUCTION

I The Story of Demosthenes

    1 Birth, Education and Early Manhood   1
    2 The Rise of Macedonia   6
    3 Olynthus and the Olynthian War   13
    4 From the Fall of Olynthus to Chaeronea   19
    5 The Triumph of Macedon and the Final Effort   29

II The Oratory of Demosthenes

    1 The Three Categories of Speech   36
    2 The Divisions of Ancient Speeches   36
    3 Analysis of the Olynthiacs   37
    4 Demosthenes' Use of Rhetorical Devices   41

III The Sources of the Text 49

Appendix A: The Order of the Olynthiac Speeches   51

Appendix B: The Theoric Fund   53

Select Bibliography 58

ΟΛΥΝΘΙΑΚΟΣ Α 61

ΟΛΥΝΘΙΑΚΟΣ Β 69

ΟΛΥΝΘΙΑΚΟΣ Γ 79

COMMENTARY

    First Olynthiac 90
    Second Olynthiac 125
    Third Olynthiac 161

VOCABULARY 203

Map of Greece 226

Map of Northern Greece 227

PREFACE

This edition of Demosthenes' *Olynthiacs* is in part a new work, and partly a revised and expanded version of the Pitt Press edition by J.M. MacGregor (Cambridge University Press, 1915).

The Introduction is largely based on that of MacGregor, considerable portions of which have been repeated verbatim, though some pruning of the more long-winded parts has been attempted and his division into sections has been overhauled. I have revised much of it and added a good deal of fresh material in the light of work on the history of the period which has been published since MacGregor wrote; in particular a section on Olynthus and the Chalcidian League seemed to be desirable. I have added, to fill an obvious gap, a mostly new section (II: pp.36ff.) on the oratory of Demosthenes; within it part 3, analysis of the speeches (pp.37ff.) has been taken over from MacGregor verbatim; and the same holds true for section III on the sources of the text (pp.49f.). The Bibliography (pp.58f.) I have compiled myself.

The text of Demosthenes' speeches is fortunately in a good state of preservation. That printed by MacGregor, itself based on the edition of F. Blass, has been retained in this edition, but the few places where it differs to any meaningful extent from that of S.H. Butcher's Oxford Text (1903) have been indicated in the notes.

The Commentary, though greatly indebted to those of MacGregor and of J.E. Sandys (Macmillan, 1924), and to the various translations listed in the bibliography, is completely new. While providing, where relevant, information on history, geography and political institutions of ancient Greece, it is intended primarily to help students who find themselves face to face with Demosthenes for the first time. It therefore concerns itself largely with matters grammatical and syntactical, as an aid to understanding the meaning of the Greek. Bearing in mind that little emphasis is placed nowadays on the learning of the principal parts of verbs, I have sought to explain all such cases in which the student is likely to be in any doubt. On points of syntax, I have attempted to cater for those students who may lack the time to consult works of grammar by providing some assistance in the notes wherever it seemed to me to be desirable. I have also supplied, for the benefit of those who may wish to pursue a more detailed investigation of syntax, references to relevant sections of W.W. Goodwin's *Greek Grammar* (Macmillan, 1879, new edition 1894).

The two Appendices, *The Order of the Olynthiac Speeches* and *The Theoric Fund*, which replace the corresponding sections of MacGregor's edition, have been completely rewritten to take account of modern works on the subject.

I would like to thank John Betts for editorial assistance and Frances Bond who has undertaken lay-out. Jean Bees produced the cover drawing and Elizabeth Induni the two new maps.

E.I.M.
Bristol, 1986.

INTRODUCTION

I

THE STORY OF DEMOSTHENES

1 *Birth, Education and Early Manhood*

Demosthenes, the son of Demosthenes of the deme Paeania, situated to the south of Athens on the eastern slope of Mt. Hymettus, was born about the year 384 B.C. His father was a man of good standing and considerable wealth, the owner of two factories, the one for the manufacture of cutlery¹ and the other for that of couches. His mother was Cleobule, daughter of a certain Gylon, who had fled from Athens to escape death for treason and had married a Scythian woman.² The elder Demosthenes died when his son was seven years old, leaving him, together with a sister two years younger, in the charge of three guardians, Aphobus his sister's son, Demophon the son of his brother Demon, and his friend Therippides.

A thin and sickly child, the future orator was not, it is said, subjected to the regular physical exercises of the free-born Greek boy; but he himself assures us that he received the liberal training proper to one in his position.³ His ambition to become an orator was, the story runs, fired by a *cause celebre* of the day at which he contrived to be present. Callistratus, the distinguished statesman and orator, was on trial for his life⁴ and Demosthenes heard his *paedagogus* arranging with others to witness the scene in court. He succeeded in gaining permission to accompany them, and the servants to the court, who were intimate with the *paedagogus* and his

---

¹Hence the orator was nicknamed 'the cutler' (ὁ μαχαιροποιός).
²This is the account of Aeschines (3.171-2), the opponent of Demosthenes. The offence of Gylon was the betrayal, while *phrurach* of Nymphaeum, a Milesian colony in the Crimea, probably to the ruler of the Bosporus Kingdom. The fiery vehemence of Demosthenes has been ascribed to the northern strain in his blood, but it is equally possible that Aeschines is biased, and that Gylon's wife was Greek, since Cepi, the city he received as the reward of his treachery and where he married, was itself a Milesian colony.
³*On the Crown* 312 ἐμοὶ μὲν τοίνυν παιδὶ μὲν ὄντι φοιτᾶν εἰς τὰ προσήκοντα διδασκαλεῖα. Elsewhere, however, (*1st Against Aphobus* 46) he complains that his guardians' peculations had deprived him of his proper advantages. Cf. Plutarch *Dem*. 4.
⁴Plutarch (*Dem*. 5) states that the trial was 'concerned with Oropus', i.e. presumably with his role in the negotiations that led to the loss of Oropus to the Boeotians in 366 B.C.

friends, provided them with a good position. The boy's heart was stirred by the glory attendant upon the accused's successful defence, but still more impressed was he by the power of an eloquence which could thus charm hostility and dominate opposition. Abandoning all other pursuits, he devoted himself to the study of oratory, taking for his teacher Isaeus,[5] a master of cogent reasoning and a vigorous style, whose influence can be clearly traced in the early speeches of his pupil.[6]

At his death the elder Demosthenes had left an estate estimated as worth more than fourteen talents. With good management, the orator insists, its value might have been doubled, but owing to the neglect and fraud of the trustees, the son received but a fractional part of the amount bequeathed by the father. Smarting under this injustice, Demosthenes sought to vindicate his rights at law and found himself frustrated by the subterfuges of his guardians in a series of prosecutions he brought against them. But his talent for forensic argument found employment not on his own behalf alone, for Attic practice required that the plaintiff and defendant in a suit should appear in person. Accordingly one who was himself without ability to plead his cause to the best effect had recourse to another whose inclination and training fitted him for such a task, and procured from him a speech in which to present his case to the jury. The profession of speech-writing (λογογράφειν), which Demosthenes pursued throughout his career, not only afforded him a source of income but provided in his early days an opportunity for the exercise and development of his powers of reasoning and expression. Since a political issue at Athens was often involved in the trial of an individual, a writer of speeches (*logographos*) naturally became interested in the political questions of the day. It was moreover the position of a prominent politician, influencing the votes of the citizens and controlling the policy of the city in the assembly, which formed the object of Demosthenes' ambition.

His early efforts at addressing the sovereign body of the Athenians were however attended with failure. Inexperienced as he was, he was confounded by the clamour of the populace,

---

[5] It is suggested (Plutarch *Dem*. 5) that Demosthenes did not have recourse to Isocrates, the most famous teacher of the day, because of inability to pay the high fee.
[6] These speeches are the three against Aphobus and the two against Onetor (numbers 27-31 in the extant Demosthenic corpus), which are greatly influenced by Isaeus' speech *On the Estate of Ciron*. (Compare Dem. 27.2-3 with Isae. 8.5; Dem. 27.47ff. with Isae 8.25; Dem. 28.23 with Isae. 8.45; Dem. 30.37 with Isae. 8.12).

while certain physical disabilities under which he laboured
as a speaker now revealed themselves all too clearly and
brought about his discomfiture. His voice was weak, his articulation indistinct;[7] his shortness of breath interfered
with the even flow of his speech and rendered his delivery
rough and broken. Disheartened by his lack of success, he
is said to have complained on one occasion, that while ignorant and besotted sailors[8] could obtain a hearing, he himself
failed to secure their attention in spite of an industry and
pains that had come near to ruining his physical health. Yet
encouragement was not wholly lacking. A certain Eunomus, who
had in his boyhood listened to Pericles, compared the young
speaker's oratory to that of the great statesman, and ascribed his failure to his lack of hardihood both of mind and body.
The distinguished actor Satyrus exhibited how much a speech
could gain or lose through the manner of its delivery, by
causing Demosthenes to recite a passage of poetry and then
himself repeating it in a tone and manner suitable to the
character to whom it belonged and the circumstances in which
it was uttered.[9] Demosthenes set himself resolutely to work
with a view to remedying his defects. He built, so the story
runs, a subterranean chamber, wherein he practised speaking
for two or three months together, and in order to prevent in-
terrruption of his studies, he would shave the half of his
head, so that shame should make him unable to appear in public, even if he were to desire to do so. Demetrius of
Phalerum[10] heard Demosthenes himself in his later years re-
counting how he endeavoured to improve his articulation by
reciting speeches with pebbles in his mouth; how he sought to
strengthen his voice and gain control of his breathing by
speaking while running and ascending hills and by delivering
passages of poetry and prose without pausing to respire; and
how with a view to securing a suitable posture he used to

---

[7] Hence the nickname Battalus ('stammerer') to which his
enemies gave a more offensive significance. Cf. Aeschines
1.126 and 131; Dem. 18.180.
[8] The allusion was perhaps to his fellow demesman and political adversary Demades.
[9] The importance which Demosthenes himself attached to this
is shown by an anecdote told in Plutarch (*Dem.* 11) and
by the story related in many authors (e.g. Cicero *De Orat.*
3.56 and [Plutarch] *Moralia* 845B) that, in answer to the
question what was most important in oratory, Demosthenes
replied 'Delivery'; and then in response to further questions ascribed to 'Delivery' the second and third places
in importance also.
[10] A distinguished orator, poet, philosopher and statesman,
who ruled Athens on behalf of Cassander from 317-307 B.C.

practice the delivery of his orations before a large mirror.[11]

The elaborate care which Demosthenes bestowed upon his speeches was actually made a reproach against him. Like Pericles, he hardly ever spoke *ex tempore*, but carefully selected the times and the subjects of his harangues. In this he offered a striking contrast to his contemporary Demades and it was remarked that, while the latter often came on the spur of the moment to the assistance of Demosthenes, when he was assailed by an outcry in the assembly, similar service was never rendered by Demosthenes to Demades. Yet at times Demosthenes delivered an impromptu oration with convincing effect.[12] One such occasion is recorded by Plutarch.[13] A certain sophist, by name Lamachus, had written in praise of Philip and Alexander a composition containing a violent attack on the Thebans and Olynthians. This he proceeded to read to the Greeks assembled at the Olympian Festival, probably in 324, when Demosthenes intervened and expounded at length the services rendered to Greece by the peoples attacked by Lamachus, and the evils wrought by those who endeavoured to carry favour for themselves with the Macedonian monarchs.

The public career of Demosthenes is said by Plutarch to have begun in the year of the outbreak of the Phocian War (355 B.C.). But it was not until some time later that he became politically prominent. During the four years 355 - 352 B.C. he was chiefly concerned with the composition of law court speeches which had a political bearing, and which were written for a series of prosecutions inspired by the ris-

---

[11] Similarly it is said ([Plutarch] *Moralia* 844E) that, in order to habituate himself to the tumult of the Athenian assembly, Demosthenes used to practise beside the breaking waves at Phalerum. To his success as a speaker there is abundant testimony; most striking is the story of Demosthenes' rival Aeschines, who, when his recital of of Demosthenes' speech *On the Crown* was received by the Rhodians with the liveliest admiration, is said to have exclaimed, 'What would you have said if you had heard the beast himself?' (Pliny *Epist.* 2.3.10; cf. Cicero *De Orat.* 3.56 and 213; Quintilian 11.3.7).

[12] He was moreover on occasion responsible for a happy repartee. Pytheas, an opponent of Demosthenes and a notorious evil-liver, declared that Demosthenes' reflections 'smelt of the lamp'. 'The lamp', replied Demosthenes, 'sees you and me at different work'. When Epicles complained that Demosthenes was 'always considering', the other retorted that he would be ashamed to advise so great a people without consideration.

[13] Plutarch *Dem.* 9.1-2.

ing conservative statesman Eubulus and his supporters.[14] Though Eubulus was subsequently to become one of Demosthenes' opponents, at this stage they appear to have worked in harmony. Even if Demosthenes did not associate himself closely with Eubulus' group, he certainly had no objections to accepting employment as a speech writer in their cause. He also embarked on a political career of his own at this time, and addressed to the assembly the orations *On the Symmories* (354 B.C.), *For the Megalopolitans* (353 B.C.) and *For the Liberty of the Rhodians* (traditionally and perhaps rightly assigned to 351 B.C.). It was however as the champion of Athens against the rise of Macedon under its able but unscrupulous ruler Philip that "he quickly won reputation, and was lifted by his speeches and outspokeness into a conspicuous place, with the result that he excited the admiration of the Greeks and the attentions of the Great King, while Philip regarded him more seriously than he did any other statesman, and even those who hated him admitted that they had to deal with a man of distinction.[15] It becomes necessary therefore to direct our attention for a time to that new power which arose in the Greek world in the 350s B.C. For with the history of Macedonia the career of Demosthenes is inextriably associated.

---

[14] The speeches in question are *Against Androtion* (355 B.C.), *Against the Proposal of Leptines* (354), *Against Timocrates* (353) and *Against Aristocrates* (352 B.C.). Only the speech *Against the Proposal of Leptines* was delivered by Demosthenes in person.

[15] Plutarch *Dem.* 12.3-4.

2 The Rise of Macedonia

Stretched along the northern frontier of Thessaly, from Thrace in the east to Illyria in the west, Macedonia had played hitherto but little part in the affairs of Greece. At the time of the Persian invasion the Macedonian king, Alexander I, had openly sided with Xerxes, while at the same time he sought in secret to secure his position with the Greeks by furnishing them advantageous information. During the Peloponnesian War Perdiccas II, who then occupied the Macedonian throne, found his best means of preservation was to play off the Athenians against the Spartans and accordingly constantly switched sides, without in the end lending any effective aid to either. His successor, Archelaus, following the example of the tyrants of an earlier age such as Hiero of Syracuse and Peisistratus of Athens, had gathered to his court a number of men skilled in letters and the fine arts.[16] He had also erected buildings and constructed roads, but despite his efforts which merited an appreciative comment from Thucydides,[17] Macedonia still remained outside the strict confines of the Greek world.

The City-State (*polis*), that distinguishing mark of Greek political organisation, was replaced in the case of Macedonia by the tribal association (*ethnos*); the people were rude and wild, drinking deep and devoting themselves to hunting and fighting; and although their language was a form of the Greek speech and the ruling house had had its Greek birthright acknowledged at Olympia, the Macedonians were regarded by the Greeks in general as barbarians.[18] The element of 'Greekness" was probably much weaker in Upper Macedonia, the wild mountainous regions of the interior, than it was in Macedonia proper, 'Lower Macedonia' of the central plain.[19]

---

[16] Among these were Euripides and Agathon the tragedians, Timotheus the lyric poet, Zeuxis the painter, Choerilus the epic poet and Hellanicus the logographer.

[17] Thucydides 2.100.2.

[18] See especially Demosthenes 3 (*3rd Olynthiac*) 16 and 9 (*3rd Philippic*) 31. Even an admirer of Philip like Isocrates makes a clear distinction between Greeks and Macedonians; if they were not to him wholly barbarian, they weren't really Greek either and formed a sort of imtermediate category. In his *Philip* Isocrates says, 'I say that you should serve as a benefactor for Greeks, a king for Macedonians and a master for barbarians; if you do so, the Greeks will be grateful for your benefits, the Macedonians if you rule over them like a king rather than as a tyrant, and other nations if you free them from barbarian despotism and bring them under Greek protection' (Isoc. 5.154 and cf. 107-8).

[19] The upper Macedonian peoples inhabiting the cantons of Pelagonia, Orestis, Paraevaea, Elymiotis and Stymphaea are all regarded by Strabo (7.7.5) as ethnically Epirot and so presumably having at least some Illyrian blood in their veins.

Beset by turbulent neighbours - the Illyrians to the west,
the Paeonians to the north, the Thracians to the east, to
say nothing of the Chalcidians and Thessalians to the south
- disturbed by frequent faction and by revolt of the tribes
subject to her sway, Macedonia seemed unlikely to develop
within the short space of half a century into the mightiest
power, not in Greece alone, but in the world. Nevertheless
she did possess undoubted advantages. A large country with
fertile soil in the central plain, Macedonia was well populated and well supplied with both agricultual and natural resources. The soil was capable of raising domestic animals,
corn in large quantities and horses for military use, while
the vast tracts of forest provided timber and pitch. Silver
and some gold were obtained from mines in various parts of the
country. Macedonia was, in fact, a potentially strong state,
both militarily and economically, if only her resources could
be developed; all that was needed was the emergence of a strong
king capable of doing so.

However such was her weakness in 368 B.C. that when the
Boeotian Pelopidas, in retaliation for Macedonian interference
in Thessaly, invaded the country, he had little difficulty in
imposing a settlement. As part of that settlement, he carried
away with him to Thebes thirty youths of noble birth as hos-
tages for the future good behaviour of Macedonia, amongst whom
was Philip, brother of the young king, Alexander II. He remained there for four years till his release in 364 B.C., at a
time when, through the political skill and military genius of
Epameinondas, Thebes became the leading city in Greece. Philip
did not disregard the opportunity thus afforded him, and events
were to prove that he had learned well his lessons in state-
craft and the art of war.

In 359 B.C. King Perdiccas III fell in battle against the Illyrians, and Philip, a young man of twenty-three or twenty-four,
became ruler of Macedonia. His position was a difficult one.
On the west, he was threatened by the Illyrians, on the north
by the Paeonians. On the east, the Thracians were ready to
advocate in arms the claims of Pausanias, a pretender to the
throne, while another aspirant, Argaeus, had the active support
of the Athenians, who despatched a fleet to his aid. In this
early crisis the conduct of Philip was marked by the energy and
shrewdness for which he was afterwards to become famous.[20]
Gold, a weapon in which he always placed great confidence[21]
secured immunity, at least for a time, from the Thracians and
Paeonians. Argaeus was defeated, but to escape, if possible,

---

[20] *Olynthiac* 1.12ff and 2.15
[21] See, e.g. Diodorus 16.8.7, 53.3 and 54.3-5; Plutarch *Aemil-
ius Paulus* 12.6 and *Moralia* 178B; Cicero *Ad Att.* 1.16.7;
Horace *Odes* 3.16.13-15; Valerius Maximus 7.2.10.

Athenian resentment, Philip allowed the Athenians who were
captured during Argaeus' invasion to depart unharmed, and
formally renounced all claims to Amphipolis, a mercantile and
strategic city of great importance on the river Strymon and
a lost possession of Athens which she earnestly desired to
recover.[22] Relieved from the most insistent perils, Philip
devoted the winter to reconstituting and training his troops,
then turning with reorganised forces first against the Paeonians and then against the Illyrians, he secured in both campaigns a signal success.

    The natural direction for the expansion of Macedonian power
was southwards and eastwards. The possession of Chalcidice
and its harbours promised control of the Thermaic Gulf and
Northern Aegean; the mountain range of Pangaeum to the east of
Macedonia offered bounteous store of gold and silver wherewith
to pay troops and to ensure diplomatic successes; while in the
Thracian Chersonese, commanding the entrance to the Propontis
and the Euxine, was to be found a position of which the strategic value was generally recognised and which was, in fact, of
no less importance in ancient than in modern times. But there
were obstacles in the way. The passage eastward across the
Strymon was barred by Amphipolis, to which Philip had abandoned his claim. The shores of the Thermaic Gulf and Chalcidice
were fringed with cities, either autonomous, like Olynthus and
the other members of the Chalcidic Confederacy, or controlled
by Athens, like Potidaea. Amphipolis was first attacked. She
appealed for aid to Athens, but in vain. The Athenians were
fully occupied with restoring their influence in Euboea and in
the Chersonese. In addition negotiations were conducted with
Philip, as a result of which the Athenians were led to believe
he would hand the city over to them.[23] Amphipolis fell, followed closely by Pydna in 357 B.C., and though it soon became
clear that he intended to retain Amphipolis himself, the Athenians were unable to take any steps against him because of the
outbreak of the Social War, in which Chios, Cos, Rhodes and
Byzantium, important members of the Athenian Confederacy, revolted, abetted by Mausolus, hereditary satrap of Caria. After
two years of warfare Athens was both weakened in resources and
compelled to acknowledge their independence. Meanwhile an
attempt by the Chalcidian Confederacy to achieve a rapproch-
ment with Athens was frustrated when Philip induced the Chalcidians to conclude an alliance with himself, offering as a
bribe possession of the Athenian controlled city of Potidaea.
The City fell to Philip in 356 B.C., and was duly handed over

---

[22] Amphipolis was founded as an Athenian colony in 436 B.C.
In 424, it fell into the hands of Brasidas and was never
regained by Athens. In the 360's it had been garrisoned by
Perdiccas III but was currently independent and in alliance
with the Chalcidian Confederacy.

[23] See *Olynthiac* 2.6 and Commentary *ad loc*.

as promised.

The tone of Demosthenes' references to Philip in his earlier speeches betrays no grave apprehension of that monarch's growing power. In the speech *Against the Proposal of Leptines* (354 B.C.) mention is made of the capture of Pydna and Potidaea[24]; in that *On the Symmories* (354 B.C.) the passages which allude to the enemies of Athens[25] *may* refer to Philip, although it is far from certain that they do so. In the speech *For the Liberty of the Rhodians* there is a passing warning against treating Philip as beneath contempt, but there is no grave insistence upon the admonition.[26] In the speech *Against Aristocrates* (352 B.C.) the name of the Macedonian King is mentioned more frequently and with a greater seriousness.[27] This oration was delivered against a proposal made in favour of Charidemus of Oreus, the brother-in-law of the Thracian king Cersobleptes, whereby the person of that leader was rendered inviolable, apparently a move to secure Cersobleptes' aid against Philip. Such had been the course of events that it might well suggest to thinking men what a formidable power Macedonia had by now become.

Under the influence of the Thessalian and Boeotian Leagues, the members of the Delphian Amphictyony had condemned the Phocians to pay a heavy fine as indemnity for an alleged sacrilege (356 B.C.). The Phocians retaliated by seizing Delphi. By means of the treasures accumulated there they readily gathered to their support a large number of mercenary soldiers, and took the field against their foes under the leadership of Philomelus, thereby inaugurating the so-called Third Sacred War (355 B.C.). After vanquishing a joint Boeotian and Locrian army, they suffered a severe defeat at the hands of the Boeotians at Neon (354 B.C.) where Philomelus perished. His successor Onomarchus, however, by his military skill and freehanded use of the wealth at his command, reduced his adversaries to such straits that the Thessalian League, also under pressure from the hostility of the ruling family of Pherae currently headed by Lycophron and Peitholaus, called in assistance from its northern neighbour Philip. He had been engaged in taking Methone, the last of the possessions of Athens on the Thermaic Gulf, and had lost an eye in the attack (354 B.C.). In the campaigns of 353 B.C. Philip defeated a Phocian force command-

---

[24] Demosthenes 20.61
[25] Demosthenes 14.11 and 41.
[26] Demosthenes 15.24 ὁρῶ δ' ὑμῖν ἐνίους Φιλίππου μὲν ὡς ἄρ' οὐδένος ἀξίου ὀλιγωροῦντας, βασιλέα δ' ὡς ἰσχυρὸν ἐχθρὸν οἷς ἂν προέληται φοβουμένους.
[27] Demosthenes 23.107, 111, 116 and 121 (ὁ μάλιστα δοκῶν νῦν ἡμῖν ἐχθρὸς εἶναι Φίλιππος οὑτοσί).

ed by Onomarchus' brother Phayllus while Onomauchus himself
was operating in Boeotia, then faced Onomarchus in person in
two battles, of which the first was indecisive, the second a
clear Phocian victory. Philip retired to Macedonia for the
winter to reorganise his army, then reappeared in Thessaly
the following year to avenge his defeat. Philip's overwhelming victory at the Battle of the Crocus Field (352 B.C.)
resulted in the death of Onomarchus in the field, the expulsion of Lycophron and his brother from Pherae, the ending
of factionalism within Thessaly and the siege and capture of
Pagasae, the port of Pherae, which held out against Philip
even after Lycophron's departure. It was probably now that
Philip secured his extraordinary election as *Archon* of the
Thessalian League, a position held by all subsequent Macedonian kings. The office gave him *inter alia* the right to
summon the Thessalian army (its cavalry was very important and
played a large part in the subsequent victories of both Philip
and Alexander), to levy certain dues and taxes, presumably to
help defray the cost of running the League[28] and to exercise
some measure of direct control over the Thessalian *perioecesis*,[29] together with some authority over the Thessalian constitution with which he interfered on more than one occasion
in the way best calculated to suit his interests.[30] In addition, his control of Thessaly enabled him to pass through the
country without hindrance while on campaigns, and a decisive
voice on the Amphictyonic Council where the voting system had
always been rigged to ensure that Thessaly and its *perioecesis*
were in a majority.

Ever ready to press an advantage home, Philip now moved
southward, intending to strike a decisive blow at his Phocian
enemies in their own territory. But his advance had roused
the fears of the allies of Phocis. Reinforced by five thousand
Athenians under Nausicles, and by troops from Sparta and Achaea, the Phocians barred his way at Thermopylae. Philip, recognising that the time was not yet ripe for him, withdrew.
Six years were to pass before the success now denied him was to
be achieved. Frustrated in Greece, he turned his attention
to Thrace, where he laid siege to Heraeum Teichus, a fortified
post of Cersobloptes.[31] The alarm which Philip's advance to

---

[28] Harbour and market dues are mentioned by Demosthenes (*1st Olynthiac* 22; *2nd Philippic* 22).
[29] This comprised all the outlying districts subject to Thessaly, such as Perrhaebia in the north and Magnesia in the east.
[30] See, e.g. *2nd Philippic* 22 and *3rd Philippic* 26.
[31] This place cannot be located with any degree of certainty, but it may perhaps be identified with a Heraeum said by Herodotus (4.90) to be 'near Perinthus'.

Thermopylae had created at Athens was intensified by the menace of his presence in the neighbourhood of the Athenian cleruchies in the Chersonese.

The situation afforded Demosthenes his opportunity. He had had already a considerable experience of public life and its activities; study and practice had confirmed and established his natural talent for oratory. He now came forward as a political leader, the advocate of a policy the keynote of which was opposition to Philip and the restoration to Athens of her old imperial position. Animated by the ideal of Athens as she had existed in the days of Pericles,[32] he believed that the attainment of that ideal involved a fundamental change in the character of his contemporaries.[33] But he had courage enough not to despair of being able to effect such a change. 'Pay your war tax' and 'serve youselves in the army' (instead of relying on mercenary forces) became the regular slogans of Demosthenes' speeches during the next decade.[34]

The speech which marks Demosthenes' advance into the position of a leading politician is known as the *First Philippic* (351 B.C.). The orator begins with an apology for addressing the assembly before the recognised leaders of public opinion have expressed their views. His hearers, he declares, may be encouraged not only by Athens' inaction in the past but also by the history[35] of her struggle with Sparta[36] to hope that

---

[32] Cf. *3rd Olynthiac* 21-26
[33] Cf. *2nd Olynthiac* 13 πολλὴν δὴ τὴν μετάστασιν καὶ μεγάλην δεικτέον τὴν μεταβολήν
[34] *1st Olynthiac* 6 χρήματ' εἰσφέροντας προθύμως καὶ αὐτοὺς ἐξιόντας; *2nd Olynthiac* 13 εἰσφέροντας, ἐξιόντας, ἅπαντα ποιοῦντας ἑτοίμως; *2nd Olynthiac* 30 τριηραρχεῖν, εἰσφέρειν, στρατεύεσθαι; *3rd Olynthiac* 34 στρατιώτης αὐτὸς ὑπάρχων ἀπὸ τῶν αὐτῶν λημμάτων; *1st Philippic* 19 δύναμιν φημὶ προχειρίσασθαι δεῖν ὑμᾶς ... μὴ ξένους ... ἀλλ' ἡ τῆς πόλεως ἔσται; *On the Chersonese* 21 ἡμεῖς οὔτε χρήματ' εἰσφέρειν βουλόμεθ' οὔτ' αὐτὸ! στρατεύεσθαι (cf. 23); *On the Chersonese* 46 τί οὖν εὖ φρονούντων ἀνθρώπων ἐστιν; ... χρήματα δ' εἰσφέρειν; *On the Cheronese* 76 χρήματ' εἰσφέρειν φημὶ δεῖν; *4th Philippic* 19 αὐτοὶ δ' εἰσφέροντες ... καὶ κατασκευαζόμενοι στράτευμα.
[35] A characteristic touch. Demosthenes found inspiration in the past. His favourite reading is said to have been Thucydides' *History*, which, according to Lucian (*Adversus Indoctum* 4), he copied out no less than eight times. Cf. *3rd Olynthiac* 23 οὐ γὰρ ἀλλοτρίοις ὑμῖν χρωμένοις παραδείγμασιν ἀλλ' οἰκείοις, ὦ ἄνδρες 'Αθηναῖοι, εὐδαίμοσιν ἔξεστι γενέσθαι.
[36] The reference is presumably to the war begun in alliance with the Thebans in 378 B.C.

when action *is* taken against Philip, success will speedily follow, and surely the time for action has arrived. Even if fortune, 'always more solicitous for us than we are for ourselves'[37] were to add to her past favours a fatal termination of Philip's present illness, the Athenians, 'with their schemes and preparations far away'[38] would be unable even to accept what opportunity had offered to them. A definite proposition follows. The city should aim at a force of fifty triremes and a sufficient number of transports for half the cavalry. As a preliminary measure, Demosthenes urges the provision of a force of 2000 men (1500 mercenaries and 500 citizens, these latter serving in rotation for a short period), ten swift triremes and 200 cavalry with a suitable fleet of transports. He adds his reasons for not embarking upon a more ambitious scheme and for insisting on the presence of citizens among the troops, as well as a financial statement[39] showing how the expenses involved in this scheme might be discharged. The establishment of a standing force would enable Athens to seize opportunities for striking at Philip, would afford protection to commerce, and would prevent the success of those sudden expeditions which had already brought so much profit to their enemy. The speech concludes with an urgent appeal for organised action and personal service in the field in place of the fault-finding and the tittle-tattle with which the Athenians concerned themselves. Throughout there is a grave apprehension of the peril, warning is not neglected, but the spirit of hope predominates.

The speech however failed. The amount suggested as payment for the proposed force,[40] well below that normally given troops on active service, and below even the average labourer's wage, must have been considered unacceptable. In the interests of making his scheme attractive to the Treasury through its cheapness, Demosthenes over-estimated his fellow citizens' patriotism; the Athenians were not prepared to fight for chicken feed, however much the orator felt it to be their duty. Moreover, as Philip had fallen sick in Thrace, they must have hoped that the disease would rid them of their troublesome foe. But the Macedonian king recovered, contrary to their expectations, and was soon engaged in fresh schemes of conquest, this time in Chalcidice.

---

[37] ἥπερ ἀεὶ βέλτιον ἢ ἡμεῖς ἡμῶν αὐτῶν ἐπιμελούμεθα (§12).
[38] ἀπηρτημένοι καὶ ταῖς παρασκευαῖς καὶ ταῖς γνώμαις (§12).
[39] This statement was comprised in a separate document, read to the assembly, but not embodied in the speech.
[40] 2 obols per day for infantry and marines and 6 obols per day for cavalry, as subsistence allowance (*siteresion*), with no actual wage (*misthos*). Presumably Demosthenes intended that plunder should bring the amount up to a respectable sum.

3 *Olynthus and the Olynthian War*

The city of Olynthus was at the time of Philip's attack the administrative centre and largest city of the Chalcidian Confederacy. Chalcidice was a peninsula jutting into the north Aegean, cut off from Macedonia by a mountain range and itself running into three smaller and narrower peninsulas, named from west to east, Pallene, Sithonia and Acte. Olynthus was situated on the main body of the peninsula about two miles from the Toronic Gulf that separates Pallene from Sithonia. The Chalcidians were Greek immigrants to the area, mainly of Ionic descent, from the Aegean Island of Andros and from the Euboean cities of Eretria and Chalcis. Since the latter city provided the largest number of settlers, it gave its name to the entire territory.

Olynthus was, prior to 479 B.C. inhabited by Bottiaeans, a non-Greek people who had settled in the inland portion of the Chalcidian peninsula. Suspected of disloyalty to the Persian cause, these Bottiaeans were expelled by Artabazus and the city was handed over to the still loyal Chalcidians.[41] After the expulsion of the Persians from Europe, the various Chalcidian cities, Olynthus included, joined the Delian League. If any federal state existed at this time, the Athenians disregarded it and assessed the various cities individually. The comparative insignificance of Olynthus at this period may be seen by contrasting its 2 talents per year assessment with the larger sums paid by some other Chalcidian cities: Mende was assessed at 8 talents per year, Scione and Torone at 6, Sermylia at 5 and even Aphytis at 3.

In 432 B.C., just prior to the outbreak of the Peloponnesian War, and with pressure from the Corinthians and Perdiccas II of Macedonia, some of the Chalcidian cities, Olynthus included, revolted from Athens. On the advice of Perdiccas, the rebels destroyed the existing cities which, lying on the coast, were particularly vulnerable to Athenian counter-attacks, and moved inland. The more easily defensible Olynthus was selected as the capital of the state, and it is from this period that it became both populous and important. In the Peloponnesian War, the Chalcidians succeeded in keeping their independence and by the time the war ended they had absorbed most, though not all, of the cities of the area that had remained loyal to Athens in 432. With the threat of Athenian attack removed, the cities which had been destroyed at the time of the synoecism of Olynthus were rebuilt. The existence of populated centres outside Olynthus necessitated the strengthening of the federal institutions; while we know little about these, it is clear that there were federal magistrates who exercised control over trade with other states and had the right to impose customs

---

[41] Herodotus 8.127

duties and export and import dues.[42] Moreover citizens of all member cities had the right to own property and to contract legal marriages within all the states of the confederacy.[43] We also hear of a federal law code and a federal treasury.

In the early fourth century B.C. the Confederacy was an influential state, described in a speech in Xenophon's *Hellenica* as a 'power that is growing strong both by land and by sea, with an abundance of timber for shipbuilding and plentiful revenues from harbours and trading-posts, possessing a large population and well supplied with corn'.[44] At this time the Chalcidians were more than a match for a Macedonia weakened by civil wars, dynastic struggles and barbarian inroads, and concluded an alliance with king Amyntas III in which the latter was very much the junior partner.[45] In the 380s B.C. the Confederacy began to recruit new members by coercion, and in 383 was considerably enlarged when Amyntas, expelled from his kingdom by the Illyrians, entrusted to it for temporary safeguarding a portion of adjacent Macedonian territory.[46] When Amyntas recovered his throne, the Chalcidians refused to return the land entrusted to them and in the ensuing war expanded at Amyntas' expense by incorporating further pieces of his territory, including Pella, his capital city. A subsequent attempt by the Chalcidians to incorporate forcibly the Greek cities of Acanthus and Apollonia led to an appeal from the victims and from Amyntas to Sparta, currently the leading power in Greece.[47] The Spartans, eager to crush a potentially powerful threat to their hegemony and having as a pretext the clause in the King's Peace guaranteeing the automony of all participating states,[48] sent out successively Eudamidas, Teleutias the half-brother of king Agesilaus, king Agesipolis I and, finally Polybiadas to conduct the war, which lasted from 382 to 379 B.C. Despite inflicting one major defeat on Sparta

---

[42] Tod, *Greek Historical Inscriptions* (hereafter *GHI*) Vol.II no.111, line 10ff.
[43] Xenophon *Hellenica* 5.2.19
[44] Xenophon *Hellenica* 5.2.16
[45] Tod, *GHI* no.111. For what remains of the terms of the alliance, Amphipolis, Acanthus, Mende and the Bottiaeans are clearly designated as the enemy against whom the alliance is aimed.
[46] Diodorus 15.19.2. Amyntas may already have done the same in the course of an earlier Illyrian invasion ten years previously (Diodorus 14.92.3), unless the two passages are doublets.
[47] Xenophon *Hellenica* 5.2.11ff.; Diodorus 15.19.3.
[48] Macedonia was in all probability not a party to the King's Peace, but Acanthus and Apollonia, as well as the Chalcidian Confederacy, certainly were.

and her allies,[49] the Chalcidians were greatly outnumbered, and obliged in the end to conclude peace on unfavourable terms. Olynthus was obliged to become an ally of Sparta and, though no source specifically says so, the Spartans are likely to have dissolved the Confederacy on the grounds that its existence infringed the autonomy of its member states, as was done in the analogous case of the Boeotian Confederacy in 387/6 B.C. In this way the one state that might have proved capable of curbing Macedonian expansionism in the reign of Philip was seriously weakened and the Confederacy, though eventually resurrected, never succeeded in regaining its previous strength.

In the 360s B.C., the revived Confederacy became embroiled in hostilities with the old enemy Athens[50] in a clash of interests in the Thermaic Gulf area, where each sought to increase its influence. In the course of this struggle in which the Chalcidians were supported by Perdiccas III of Macedonia, Athens gained Pydna and Methone, possibly from Macedonia, and Potidaea and Torone, probably at Chalcidian expense (366-364 B.C.). Amphipolis remained outside both the Chalcidian and the Athenian Confederacies, though she was in alliance with the former. The accession of Philip in 359 led to a temporary Macedonian rapprochement with Athens, whose claim to Amphipolis he recognised, but when he himself besieged and captured the city in 357, Athens declared war. The Chalcidians, alarmed at the capture of Amphipolis, took the unprecedented step of making overtures to the Athenians, but they, distracted by the outbreak of the Social War and by trouble in Euboea, and unable to shake off the long-standing animosity they felt towards the Chalcidians, rebuffed them. Philip, seeing his opportunity, stepped in with the offer of an alliance on favourable terms, whereby, in return for Chalcidian support in the war against Athens, he would acknowledge their claim to the Athenian cleruchy of Potidaea. A mutilated inscription[51] preserves the Chalcidian oath, though unfortunately not the details of the text of the alliance. By the insertion of a clause forbidding either party to make peace with Athens without the consent of the other, Philip firmly linked the Chalcidians to his side in the struggle

---

[49] Xenophon *Hellenica* 5.3.3-6
[50] 'Chalcidians from Thrace' are mentioned as members of the Second Athenian Confederacy in the 370s B.C. (Tod, *GHI* no.123, lines 101-2) but it is doubtful if these should be identified with the Chalcidian Confederacy, which was weak after its defeat by Sparta. No other source indicates that the Confederacy became an Athenian ally at this time, and if it did, we must postulate an otherwise unattested secession soon afterwards.
[51] Tod, *GHI* no.158.

with Athens, or such at least was his hope.

That the Chalcidians benefitted from the Alliance was clear to all, when Potidaea was duly annexed (356 B.C.), but many elements within the Confederacy were nevertheless unhappy. The alliance was scarcely an equal partnership, the power of Macedonia was increasing rapidly and as a neighbour Philip was likely to prove more of a threat than were the Athenians. A large number of Chalcidians came to feel that the continuation of the war was no longer in their interests, and in 352 B.C. their numbers had grown to such an extent that they induced the Confederacy, contrary to the terms of its alliance with Philip, to make peace with Athens.[52] This breach of faith led Philip to demonstrate his displeasure by making a raid on Chalcidian territory,[53] a show of strength perhaps designed to bring the Chalcidians to heel. Perhaps the raid succeeded in its intention at least in part if the expulsion of the pro-Athenian politician Apollonides[54] is connected with this event; but the Chalcidians soon reverted to their anti-Macedonian stance by offering refuge to Arrhidaeus and Menelaus, two half-brothers of Philip and sons of Amyntas III by Gygaea, who were pretenders to the Macedonian throne.[55] This action in particular led Philip to conclude that his allies could no longer be trusted, and, in order to remove any possibility of a disaffected Chalcidice offering a base of operations against his territory to a hostile state like Athens, he declared war in 349 B.C., offering as a pretext the refusal of the Chalcidians to hand over the two pretenders.

Philip spent the campaigning season of 349 B.C. attacking and capturing one by one the smaller members of the Confederacy, in order to weaken Olynthus. The Confederacy in alarm appealed to Athens for an alliance and urgent assistance. The request was granted, and the Athenians sent a force consisting of 2000 mercenary peltasts and 38 ships under Chares (autumn 349 B.C.).[56] However by the time of its arrival, little remained of the campaigning season, and the smallness of the force must have disappointed Chalcidian expectations. In the spring of 348 B.C. a second Chalcidian appeal led to the despatch of a force of 4000 peltasts, 150 Athenian cavalry and 18 ships under Charidemus, who joined up with the Chalcidian army to attack

---

[52] Demosthenes 23.109; Libanius, *Hypothesis to 1st Olynthiac*, section 2.
[53] Demosthenes 4 (*1st Philippic*) 17.
[54] Demosthenes 9 (*3rd Philippic*) 56.
[55] A third half-brother, Archelaus, had been eliminated by Philip early in his reign (Justin 8.3.10 and cf. 7.4.5).
[56] For details of the three Athenian forces sent to Chalcidice, see Philochorus (fgts.49-51, Jacoby), and for an interpretation, see G.L. Cawkwell, *The Defence of Olynthus* in *CQ* 12 (1962) 122ff., esp. 129-131.

and plunder some of the territory Philip had annexed in the course of the previous year.

With the arrival of Philip on the field however, the situation of the Chalcidians rapidly deteriorated. Their army suffered two defeats, which Philip followed up by the capture of the important city of Torone and of Mecyberna the Olynthian port, thereby cutting off Olynthus from the sea. The Chalcidian cause sustained a further blow when 500 cavalry, encouraged by their commanders, the pro-Macedonian leaders Euthycrates and Lasthenes, allegedly in Philip's pay,[57] defected without striking a blow. Olynthus itself, its morale shattered, was now besieged (summer 348 B.C.) and a last desperate appeal to Athens for a full-scale expedition of citizen troops was answered by the despatch of 2000 Athenian hoplites, 300 cavalry and 17 ships under Chares. However by the time the Athenian force arrived in autumn of the same year, the city had already fallen. Philip's reply to earlier Chalcidian moves for peace to the effect that either the Olythians must abandon Olynthus or he Macedonia[58] was now implemented: Olynthus was razed to the ground, its inhabitants were enslaved and the proceeds from the sale were used to defray the cost of the war. The land was divided up to provide estates for yet more of Philip's rapidly growing number of *hetairoi*, and the Chalcidian Confederacy ceased to exist.[59]

Despite Demosthenes' best endeavours, the Athenians did remarkably little to aid the Chalcidians. Only the third expedition included citizen hoplites, while of the 38 ships of the first expedition, perhaps only 8 involved any extraordinary preparation.[60] Various explanations for the inadequacy of the Athenian aid may be suggested. Firstly, the Chalcidians' past record of hostility to Athens, and particularly their support for Amphipolis in the face of repeated Athenian attempts

---

[57] Demosthenes *De Falsa Legatione* 266-7; *On the Chersonese* 40; *3rd Philippic* 66.
[58] Demosthenes *3rd Philippic* 11.
[59] According to Demosthenes (*3rd Philippic* 26) Philip destroyed thirty-two πόλεις ἐπὶ Θρᾴκης, some of them presumably in the course of the Olynthian War, but the statement seems exaggerated: apart from Olynthus (Diodorus 16.53.3; Justin 8.3.11), the only Chalcidian cities definitely known to have been destroyed at this time were Stageira (Plutarch *Alexander* 7.3 and *Moralia* 1126F), and a place (? Zereia) whose name has been corrupted in the manuscripts of Diodorus 16.52.9.
[60] See Cawkwell (*loc. cit.* cf. n.56 above), who argues that thirty of the thirty-eight ships sent with the first expedition were the regular squadron stationed in the northern Aegean, while only 8 were manned in response to an appeal for volunteer trierarchs.

to recover it had not been entirely forgotten. Nor were the
Athenians convinced that Chalcidice was likely to prove a reliable ally in future, especially when they reflected on the
manifest instability of its internal politics and the bitter
factional strife within the state.[61] Such doubts made the
Athenians reluctant to commit much in the way of troops and resources in support of a dubious ally whose ability to sustain
the war was highly suspect. In addition, there were those
who welcomed the outbreak of war between Philip and the Chalcidians but had no wish for Athens to become involved. If
they had no firm grasp of political realities, they might hope
that each side would wear out the other to the lasting benefit
of Athens, while the more politically aware would realise that
Athens had no realistic hope of achieving more than a temporary respite for Chalcidice were she to intervene. It would be
difficult, if not impossible, for the Athenians to keep Philip
out of Chalcidice permanently, when his own power base was adjacent and their lines of communication were fully stretched.
Though Demosthenes kept insisting that if Athens did not fight
Philip in the north, she would have to fight him in Greece,[62]
there were others who believed no less passionately that only
by fighting Philip in Greece would Athens have any hope of
victory. These preferred that she should preserve her resources for use in areas where her lines of communication were
manageable, as for instance at Thermopylae, where Philip had
already been stopped short in 352 B.C.[63] Finally the outbreak of trouble in Euboea in the winter of 349/8 made it difficult for the Athenians, even had they wished, to agree to the
despatch of an adequate force to Olynthus in 348. Though Demosthenes was opposed to intervention in Euboea,[64] presumably
because it would detract from the scale of aid he wished to
send to the Chalcidians, the Athenians decided that the strategically important Euboea should have priority. In the circumstances, the reluctance of the Athenians to commit large scale
forces to the defence of Olythus at a time when they were faced
with a critical situation nearer home is understandable. For a
variety of reasons therefore the Athenians remained at best
lukewarm in their support of the Chalcidians, and Demosthenes'
efforts to procure effective action signally failed. For the
timing and order of his Olynthiac orations, see Appendix A
below.

---

[61] For internal divisions within Olynthus, see Demosthenes *De Falsa Legatione* 264ff. and *3rd Philippic* 56 and 63ff.
[62] Demosthenes *1st Philippic* 50, *1st Olynthiac* 12,14,25 and *On the Chersonese* 18.
[63] Diodorus 16.38.2.
[64] Demosthenes *On the Peace* 5.

4 From the Fall of Olynthus to Chaeronea

Demosthenes must have been sorely tried by his inability to rouse the Athenians to effective action. To add to his misfortune he had suffered a personal affront which clearly excited in him strong feelings of anger and resentment. In the theatre, on the occasion of the Great Dionysia of 348 B.C. at which Demosthenes was acting as *choregus* for his tribe, one of his enemies, a wealthy and objectionable man named Meidias, struck the orator a blow. Owing to the position held by Demosthenes and the time and place at which the blow was dealt him, the act was capable of being construed as impiety (ἀσεβεία) rather than outrage (ὕβρις). It is plain from the language used by Demosthenes that he was deeply moved by the insult, but Aeschines informs us that in the end he compromised the action for thirty minae[65] owing to the strong position in which wealth and powerful friends had placed his adversary.

The capture and destruction of Olynthus, together with the loss of Euboea, created a deep impression on the minds of the Athenians and, in order to consolidate the forces of Greece against Philip, overtures were made to the Peloponnesian cities. A speaker who emerged into prominence in connection with these unsuccessful embassies was Aeschines, Demosthenes' future rival, whose attitude towards Philip at this period was one of pronounced hostility.

Meanwhile the Sacred War was being waged against Phocis by the Boeotians and Thessalians, who, unable to bring the conflict to a satisfactory conclusion, sought assistance again from Philip as they had done six years before. Now, as then, Philip readily acceded to their request, while the Phocians on their side appealed to Athens and Sparta for help. In response to the call, both the Spartans and the Athenians ('The Decree of Eubulus') sent troops to Thermopylae, which was in the hands of the Phocian leader Phalaecus. But the situation was complicated by faction among the Phocians themselves. Phalaecus was at variance with the party which had sent the appeal to Athens and Sparta. Having already intrigued with the enemies of Athens in Euboea in 348, he now refused to allow either the Athenians or the Spartans to enter the pass. A policy of active resistance to Philip now became impossible, and if Phalaecus and his mercenaries were to make terms with Philip, as they eventually did, the city might be confronted by an overwhelming force on the borders of Attica itself. Philip, on the other hand, was not unready to come to terms. It was in his present interest to reduce, so far as he might, the resistance to his progress into central Greece.

---

[65] Aeschines *Against Ctesiphon* 52. The same assertion is made by Plutarch (*Dem.* 12.3) and is not contradicted by Demosthenes himself.

On the proposition of Philocrates from whom the peace which followed has taken its name, an embassy, including amongst its members both Demosthenes and Aeschines, was despatched to Philip in 347 B.C. The terms which were arranged amounted to a recognition by both parties of the *status quo* at the time of the final ratification of the peace, and an alliance, as well as peace, was to be concluded between Philip and Athens. Philip, however, desiring to deal as he wished with the Phocians and with Halus, a perioecic city in revolt from the Thessalian League, insisted on their exclusion from the treaty. There was some reluctance on the part of the Athenians about accepting an arrangement which did not explicitly secure the safety of these allies outside her Confederacy but, as Philip through his agents had let it be known that he was not ill-disposed toward Phocis but on the contrary would prefer to reduce the power of Thebes, a city towards which the Athenians in general entertained no very friendly feelings, they set aside their misgivings and agreed. A second embassy now left Athens for Pella in the spring of 346 B.C. for the purpose of securing Philip's sworn adherence to the treaty. This they succeeded in obtaining only after considerable delay, for Philip had employed himself during the interval in making additions to his Thracian conquests, which under the terms arranged thus remained in his hands.

After returning to Pella and taking the oath required from him, Philip advanced southward into Thessaly. Having subjugated Halus and returned it to the control of Pharsalus, he proceeded on his way against Phocis. Phalaecus surrendered the pass of Thermopylae into his hands on condition that he and his troops were allowed to depart unmolested. The Athenian assembly passed a decree summoning the Phocians to place the sanctuary of Delphi in the hands of the Amphictyons, on whose behalf Philip was avowedly acting. Thus betrayed by their military leader and deserted by Athens, the Phocians were left to the mercy of their ancient enemies, the Thessalians and Boeotians, who possessed a predominant influence in the Council of the Amphictyons. That body decided that all the Phocian cities, with the exception of Abae, should be broken up into village communities; the sacred treasure which the Phocians had appropriated was to be repaid at the rate of sixty talents per year (subsequently reduced to thirty, then ten talents); and the votes formerly assigned to Phocis in the Amphictyonic Council were now to be given to Philip. In addition he was elected President of the League for the purpose of celebrating the Pythian Games of 346 B.C. Athens marked her displeasure by refusing to send representatives to the festival. The fate of the Phocians, whom she had been led to believe Philip would treat with consideration, had filled her with resentment and alarm. There was even talk of war, but Demosthenes dissuaded his countrymen from so rash a project in his speech *On the Peace*. Recognising the present weakness of Athens[66] and the combination against her,[67] he did not allow the bitterness of his hostility to Philip to blind him to the exigence of the situation; for he was realistic enough to know that, with Philip in control of Thermopylae and Athens destitute of allies, resistance was futile. However so great was the unpopularity of the Peace that, though both Demosthenes and Aeschines had been involved in the negotiations, each sought to endeavour to dissociate himself from it and to blame the other for its failure.

Philip for his part, perhaps already considering a Persian campaign[68] which would require Athenian cooperation and Athenian ships, sought to make the peace and alliance work and did his best to assure the Athenians of his goodwill. He showed this by avoiding any direct interference in Greece for the next few years, despite considerable provocation, but appeals from his partisans, which provided opportunities that he could not afford to lose, were answered indirectly. Such indirect interference tended to discredit his professions of sincerity, and played into the hands of his opponents at Athens who had no interest in making a success of the alliance but were simply biding their time. For them, the peace was accepted only for so long as it was convenient.

An early example of indirect interference came in 345 B.C. when the Messenians appealed to Philip for assistance against the Spartans, who had never recognised their independence. Philip was able to turn Spartan unpopularity in the Peloponnese to his own advantage by strengthening his existing links with the Argives and Megalopolitans, as well as with the Messenians. Demosthenes, viewing this development with alarm, and seeing that his city might be confronted with foes from the south as well as from the north, induced the Athenians

---

[66] *On the Peace* 13 πολλὰ γὰρ προείμεθα, ὧν ὑπαρχόντων τότ' ἂν ἦ νῦν ἀσφαλέστερος καὶ ἐάων ἦν ἡμῖν ὁ πόλεμος.

[67] *On the Peace* 14 ὅπως μὴ προαξόμεθα ... τοὺς συνεληλυθότας τούτους καὶ φάσκοντας 'Αμφικτύονας νῦν εἶναι εἰς ἀνάγκην καὶ πρόφασιν κοινοῦ πολέμου πρὸς ἡμᾶς.

[68] That Philip had made up his mind to attack Persia by 346 B.C. is stated by Diodorus (16.60.5) and supported by Isocrates, who writes (*Epistle* 3.3) that his previous letter of 346 B.C. to Philip was sent to a man who had already made his mind up. However his intentions were not a matter of public knowledge till 341 B.C. when Persia for the first time took action against him at Perinthus; the earliest passages of Demosthenes showing knowledge of his plan belong to the same year (see *3rd Philippic* 27 οὔθ' ἡ 'Ελλὰς οὔθ' ἡ βάρβαρος τὴν πλεονεξίαν χωρεῖ τἀνθρώπου. cf. *3rd Philippic* 71 and *4th Philippic* 31-34).

in 344 B.C. to despatch embassies to the cities of the Peloponnese in order to counteract the efforts of the agents of Philip. He himself undertook the role of ambassador, and so antagonised both Philip and the Peloponnesians that both sent representatives to Athens. Philip's envoys asserted his peaceful intentions and protested against Demosthenes' misconstruction of his actions, while the Peloponnesians complained of the orator's interference in their internal affairs. It was on the occasion of the arrival of these envoys that Demosthenes delivered the *Second Philippic*. In characteristic fashion he invites his audience to consider the fate of other peoples such as the Olynthians, to whom Philip had come with fair words and gracious benefactions, and draws from their history the lesson that 'the nature of the wise possesses within itself one universal safeguard, which ensures safety and well-being to all, and especially to democracies in their dealings with tyrants'. This safeguard is 'Mistrust'. 'Treasure it, cling to it' he adjures the Athenians; 'if you keep it intact, no harm will ever befall you'.[69] What reply the Athenians made to the Macedonian and Peloponnesian envoys is unknown, but Demosthenes' attempt to obtain Peloponnenian allies had failed.

In 343 B.C. the battle between the faction which wished to keep the peace and the faction hostile to Philip was fought out in the Athenian lawcourts. In this year Demosthenes revived against Aeschines a charge of misconduct in connection with the second embassy to Philip. This charge he had brought three years before, but his opponent had then countered the attack by prosecuting Timarchus, a friend of Demosthenes associated with him in the prosecution, for profligacy and debauchery (345 B.C.). Now however the accusation of misconduct was renewed; Demosthenes persisted with the prosecution and Aeschines, despite a skilful defence and an impressive number of distinguished character witnesses called to his support, only managed to escape condemnation by the narrow margin of thirty votes. Eubulus' faction was clearly still sufficiently influential to secure acquittal, nor was Demosthenes able to prove his case beyond all manner of doubt, but the smallness of the majority greatly strengthened his position. A second important political trial this year was the prosecution of Philocrates, now made the scapegoat for the unpopularity of the Peace to which he gave his name, for treason and corruption by the anti-Macedonian statesman and orator Hyperides. Philocrates fled from the city without even standing trial and, as we have no reason to suspect that he was any more corrupt than the other envoys, his action may be interpreted as a gesture of despair and recognition that the anti-Macedonian faction was now on top. The results of the two trials

---

[69] *2nd Philippic* 24

do indicate that a majority of Athenians were now coming
to believe that hostilities against Philip would sooner or
later be resumed. Certainly there was more than one issue
which might serve as a pretext for a declaration of war when
the time was ripe.

The two issues of 343 B.C. were the outbreak of a pro-
Macedonian revolution in Elis, which gave Philip a new ally
in the Peloponnese, and an attempted *coup de'état* in Megara,
in which Macedonian complicity was suspected.[70] To both
events, the Athenian reaction was vigorous: at Megara
Phocion intervened to prevent the city going over to Macedon
and arranged an alliance with Athens; in the Peloponnese
Demosthenes once again undertook an embassy, accompanied by
Polyeuctus, Hegesippus and Lycurgus. On this occasion (342
B.C.) he met with rather more success than he had had two
years previously, to the extent of concluding alliances with
Argos, Messenia, Megalopolis and Mantinea. However as these
states were all already allies of Philip and did not repudi-
ate their alliances with him, Demosthenes' efforts brought
only moderate results: at best, he had neutralised Philip's
influence in the Peloponnese.

Philip now (342 B.C.) sent troops to Euboea, to shore up
the pro-Macedonian factions in Eretria and Oreus. His intervention aroused the hostility of Callias of Chalcis, an old
enemy of Athens, who was now obliged to reverse his policies
and call in Athenian help. With this assistance the pro-Macedonian regimes in Eretria and Oreus were overthrown and an
anti-Macedonian Euboean League embracing all three cities
was established. This new League, with Callias at its head,
now concluded an alliance with Athens, and Philip's diplomacy
suffered a severe setback. Meanwhile, Philip himself was active
in Epirus, where he expelled the Molossian king Arybbas and
replaced him with his nephew Alexander, who was the brother
of Philip's wife Olympias. Arybbas had been too sympathetic
to Athens and Philip desired the establishment of a friendly
power in the north-west to facilitate the expansion of his
own influence in the area. He now incorporated into Alexander's
kingdom several autonomous Greek cities (spring 342 B.C.) but
his activities were seen as a threat by Corinth, which had
traditional links with the area, and by her colonies Leucas
and Ambracia. These turned increasingly towards Athens, with
whom they eventually concluded an alliance.

Meanwhile, the unsatisfactory nature of the Peace from the

---

[70] For the attempted Megarian *coup* of 343 B.C., see Demosthenes *De Falsa Legatione* 204, 326 and 334, and *4th Philippic* 9. For a second in 341 B.C., see Plutarch *Phocion* 15.

Athenian point of view was demonstrated by the insistence of
Philip's opponents on its revision (ἐπανόρθωσις), on terms
more favourable to Athens. Among the terms proposed by the
Athenians, who sent Hegesippus to Pella in the spring of
343 B.C., were (a) the substitution of a clause that each
side should have what belonged to it (i.e. that Athens
should recover Amphipolis, Pydna, Methone and Potidaea) for
the clause in the original peace that each side should have
what it possessed at the time of ratification, (b) the restoration to Cersobleptes of Serrium and Doriscus, places
taken by Philip between the arrangement and the signing of
the peace treaty and (c) the return to Athens of Halonesus,
an insignificant island owned by the Athenians, which had
fallen into the hands of pirates. These pirates had been
expelled by Philip who had possessed himself of the island,
the return of which was now, at the instigation of Demosthenes and Hegesippus, demanded by Athens. Philip's initial
response had been to reject Hegesippus' proposals in their
entirety, but in the spring of 342 B.C. he sent a conciliatory embassy to Athens. He could not possibly hand back
Amphipolis and the other cities, since he had already bestowed their territories on his *hetairoi*, but he did agree to submit the question of the Thracian towns to arbitration, and
to 'give' Halonesus to Athens. Demosthenes and Hegesippus
persuaded the Athenians not to accept it as a gift of Philip,
since this would be tantamount to denying their own earlier
ownership and to accepting that Philip's seizure of the island was legal; instead they insisted that he must be prepared to 'return' it (ἀποδοῦναι as opposed to δοῦναι).[71]

Discouraged by the Athenian reaction to what he regarded
as a genuine concession, Philip proceeded to consolidate
his power in Thessaly, and from there went on to Thrace, where
he dethroned Cersobleptes and transformed the country into
what was virtually a Macedonian province (342-341 B.C.).
About this time, hostilities broke out in the Chersonese
where Diopeithes, the general sent to supervise a new Athenian *cleruchy*, came into conflict with the city of Cardia,
an ally of Philip since 352 B.C., and attacked and plundered
Thracian territory that was now under Macedonian rule.

---

[71] The speech *On Halonesus*, the seventh in the Demosthenic
corpus, probably the work of Hegesippus, was delivered
in reply to Philip's embassy. The temper of the Athenians is plainly exhibited by their acceptance of such a
verbal quibble (περὶ συλλαβῶν διαφέρομενος) says Aeschines
(*Against Ctesiphon* 83). Cf. the gibe of Antiphanes the
comic poet, as cited by Plutarch *Dem*. 9.5:
  - ὁ δεσπότης δὲ πάντα τὰ παρὰ τοῦ πατρὸς
  ἀπέλαβεν ὥσπερ ἔλαβεν. - ἠγάπησε γ' ἂν
  τὸ ῥῆμα τοῦτο παραλαβὼν Δημοσθένης.

Philip protested to Athens about Diopeithes' activities, and demanded his recall. A debate was held in the assembly in the spring of 341 B.C. to discuss the situation in the Chersonese, at which Demosthenes delivered the speech *On the Chersonese*. In this speech, he not only defends Diopeithes' actions, but attacks Philip on the grounds that Athens is now at war with him in practice, if not in name. 'He has broken the peace,' says the orator, 'and is the enemy and foe of the whole city, even of the ground on which it stands',[72] a view which found further expression in the *Third Philippic*, delivered the same summer, a speech marked out by the clarity and vigour of its thought and language as a masterpiece of political oratory. 'Philip', he insists, 'denies that he is making war; but so far am I from agreeing that, in these actions of his, he is keeping the peace he made with you, that I say that in making an attempt upon Megara, in seeking to set up tyrannies in Euboea, in advancing now upon Thrace, in plotting and scheming in the Peloponnese, he is breaking the peace and making war upon you; unless you mean to insist that those who are setting up engines of war against you are maintaining the peace until they have brought them actually up to your walls.'[73] This speech was rapidly followed by the *Fourth Philippic*, in which Demosthenes revises his attitude to the Theoric Fund,[74] possibly because it was now controlled by his own supporters, and makes an open proposal to seek assistance from Persia.[75]

The energetic appeals of Demosthenes had their effect. Diopeithes was retained in the Chersonese; embassies were sent out, even to Persia,[76] and an anti-Macedonian coali-

---

[72] *On the Chersonese* 39
[73] *3rd Philippic* 17
[74] *4th Philippic* 36-42. On the Theoric Fund, see Appendix B below.
[75] *4th Philippic* 31-41. The speech was long considered spurious, mainly because two long passages (chapters 11-17 and 55-70) occur with slight variations also in the speech *On the Chersonese* (chapters 38-45 and 52-67). Modern scholars tend to accept the authenticity of the speech by assuming that it was never published in his lifetime, but found among his papers after his death. It is also supposed that the oration *On the Chersonese* consisted originally only of chapters 1-37 with a brief conclusion, and that passages were incorporated from the *4th Philippic* to expand it for publication.
[76] The embassy to Persia, headed by Ephialtes, returned without the promise of assistance, but equipped with money; see [Plutarch] *Moralia* 847F.

tion was gradually built up by 340 B.C.[77] By this time Philip's activites in Thrace had excited great alarm in Perinthus and Byzantium, technically cities in his alliance. Demosthenes accordingly proceeded to the Hellespont and there gained their adherence. Against Perinthus Philip brought to bear in vain all the resources which skill in the conduct of sieges could suggest; and an attack on Byzantium proved equally unsuccessful. Two fleets were sent to its aid by the Athenians, who now openly declared war on Macedonia (340 B.C.), and Philip was forced to abandon his campaign. The Scythians were causing trouble in the north and he now turned his arms against them. After a successful expedition, he returned to Macedonia in the summer of 339 B.C. but was attacked *en route* by the Triballians and stripped of much of his booty. Thus the current of affairs seemed at last to have turned against him.

At Athens meanwhile, Demosthenes received from his grateful fellow-countrymen a golden crown at the Dionysia as a recognition of his services. With a view to the struggle which must sooner or later decide the issue between Athens and Macedon, he now applied himself to the carrying out of a reform in connection with the financing of the navy. Under Demosthenes' new scheme, the trierarchic symmories were abolished, 900 of the 1200 rich Athenians were released from their obligations, and the 300 wealthiest citizens were now obliged to pay in proportion to their means. These 300 were naturally among the most bitter opponents of the new scheme, since they presumably were now required to pay much more than they had done in the past. Nevertheless the majority of citizens considered the proposal fair, and hoped that the efficiency of the fleet would be greatly improved by the reform. Another scheme which Demosthenes at last saw realised was the application to military purposes of the Theoric monies, a reform which he had already suggested in the *Olynthiacs* and elsewhere.[78]

While Philip was engaged in Scythia, the concerns of the Amphictyons once more afforded him an opportunity of intervening in the affairs of Greece. When the Amphictyonic Council met at Delphi in the autumn of 340 B.C., a charge of cultivating land sacred to Apollo was brought by Aeschines against the inhabitants of the Locrian town of

---

[77] The members of this coalition were the Euboean League, Corinth and colonies, Megara, Achaea and Acarnania. See Demosthenes *On the Crown* 237, Plutarch *Dem.* 17.4 and *Moralia* 851B.

[78] For the Theoric Fund, see Appendix B below.

Amphissa.⁷⁹ An armed conflict took place between the
Amphissans and the Amphictyons, and subsequently an Amphictyonic War against Amphissa was declared at a special meeting of the Council. Some of the members, notably Athens
and Thebes, refrained from participating in the proceedings;
the Amphictyonic forces met with but little success and at
the next regular meeting of the Council in the autumn of
339 B.C. a proposal was made by Thessalian and other dele-
gates, possibly at Philip's instigation, that the Macedonian
king should be invited to conduct the war. The invitation
was given and promptly accepted: he now had the right to
come into central Greece legally, with Apollo's blessing.

In the late autumn of 339 B.C., Philip arrived in Phocis,
and fortified the town of Elatea, a strategic position
south of Thermopylae and commanding the road southward into Boeotia and Attica. The news of Philip's presence at
Elatea filled the Athenians with dismay.⁸⁰ If Thebes should
take the Macedonian side - and between Athens and Thebes
there was an old, bitter animosity - Attica lay open to
Philip's attack. In this crisis, Demosthenes' eloquence
served his country well. With nine others he went to Thebes
to plead for an alliance; an embassy from Philip was present
also but in the end the offers and arguments of Demosthenes
and his colleagues prevailed.⁸¹ When Philip after capturing Amphissa and Naupactus entered the north-west of Boeotia,
he was confronted at Chaeronea by the united forces of Thebes
and Athens (late summer 338 B.C.). Demosthenes himself served in the ranks of the hoplites, bearing a shield on which
were emblazoned the words ἀγαθῇ τύχῃ (with good fortune).
But the generalship of Philip and the superiority of his
troops gained a decisive victory, although the Thebans in
particular fought bravely and fell where they stood. Like
many of his compatriots, Demosthenes fled from the field

---

[79] According to Demosthenes (*On the Crown* 143ff.), the charge
was part of a plot to create an opportunity for Philip in
another 'Sacred' War. Aeschines on the contrary maintained
(*Against Ctesiphon* 115ff.) that the Amphissans intended to
make an accusation against Athens and that by anticipating
their charge he saved Athens from a conflict with the Amphictyons. Scholars have long debated, with differing conclusions, whether the Amphissan charge against Athens was inspired by Philip or by his ally Thebes.
[80] See the famous picture of the scene at Athens in Demosthenes
(*On the Crown* 169ff.).
[81] A lively description of this embassy is to be found in the
speech *On the Crown* (211ff.) Demosthenes himself puts the
achievement of this alliance in the forefront of his success, but note also the sneers of Aeschines (*Against Ctesiphon* 137ff. and 237).

when the extent of Philip's victory became clear,[82] but his prestige remained unimpaired. To him was assigned the honour of reciting the encomium over the bones of those who had fallen at Chaeronea, thus 'showing by the especial honour and esteem which they displayed towards their adviser that they did not repent of the acts which he had advised'.[83]

---

[82] The cowardice of Demosthenes was much exaggerated by his opponents, and is mentioned no less than six times by Aeschines in the course of his speech *Against Ctesiphon* (151, 159, 174-5, 181, 187 and 253); see also Plutarch *Dem.* 20.2. An improved version of the story is reported in [Plutarch] *Moralia* 845F, according to which a bramble bush caught Demosthenes' cloak as he was running away, whereupon he pleaded 'Take me alive'.

[83] Plutarch *Dem.* 21.2. An inferior speech, purporting to have been delivered by Demosthenes, is extant as the sixtieth oration in the extant corpus. One hopes, for the sake of his reputation, that the speech is spurious.

5 The Triumph of Macedon and the Final Effort

The battle of Chaeronea marked the beginning of a new era in Greece.[84] Thebes suffered the loss of her hegemony in Boeotia and a Macedonian garrison was established in the Cadmea. It had been expected that Philip would follow up his success in the field with an assault upon Athens. A body of commissioners, among whom was Demosthenes, had been appointed to strengthen the fortifications of the city (τειχοποιοί) but Philip, having in view the difficulty of attacking a strongly defended city that was still powerful at sea and impatient of the delay which a protracted siege would cause to his cherished plan of invading Asia, granted to the Athenians what Demosthenes himself admitted to be not illiberal terms: what remained of the Athenian Confederacy was to be dissolved and all claim to the Thracian Chersonese was to be abandoned; but no Macedonian troops were to be stationed in Attica and the *cleruchies* on Lemnos, Imbros, Scyros and Samos were to remain. Philip now had little difficulty in inducing the states of Greece generally, in assembly at Corinth, to participate in a new Common Peace guaranteed by Macedonian military supremacy and to furnish the contingents which, in his new role of *hegemon* of the League of Corinth, Philip intended to lead against Persia (337 B.C.). Only Sparta remained defiant and preferred to see her territory overrrun and stripped away rather than join the League.

In 336 B.C. Philip fell by the assassin's hand.[85] The moment seemed favourable for putting an end to Macedonian domination. Thessaly was disaffected and Thebes endeavoured to expel the garrison of Macedonians from her citadel. At Athens Demosthenes had received private intelligence of Philip's murder and presented himself in the Council with cheerful countenance, pretending to have had a dream which portended a great benefit for the city. When subsequently a public announcement of the event reached the city, the Athenians offered a sacrificial thanksgiving for the good tidings and voted a crown to the assassin. Although his daughter was newly dead, Demosthenes appeared in festive apparel with a garland on his head. But the joy was short-lived. Amid the dangers that beset him, the new monarch Alexander acted with a promptitude that disconcerted his

---

[84] Cf. Demosthenes *On the Crown* 214 κατακλυσμὸν γεγενῆσθαι τῶν πραγμάτων (a flood had swept over the world).
[85] The crime was generally believed to have been instigated by Philip's wife Olympias, who had been ousted in favour of Cleopatra the niece of his general Attalus, and by Alexander who feared for his position as heir-apparent. Officially, however, the murder was ascribed to Persian money and the personal grievances of the assassin, Pausanias.

adversaries. Re-establishing his authority in Thessaly, he proceeded to Thermopylae, where he won recognition from the Amphictyons as head of their league. Thebes submitted, Athens sent a conciliatory embassy, and at a general meeting of the League of Corinth, Alexander was acknowledged as *hegemon* in succession to his father.

In the following year (335 B.C.) Alexander turned his arms against the Thracians and the Illyrians. In his absence the cities of Greece began once more to plot against him, and Demosthenes did his utmost to provoke a war. He helped the Thebans to obtain arms with which they attacked the Macedonians in the Cadmea, and the Athenians made preparations to lend assistance. Demosthenes sought to rouse the satraps of the Great King to make war on Alexander, whom he described as 'a boy' and 'a jack-of-all-trades and master of none'.[86] But when Alexander appeared in Greece, the opposition to him collapsed. The Athenians sent an embassy to deprecate his wrath. Demosthenes was appointed one of the ambassadors but, fearing to face the angry king, turned back at Mount Cithaeron on the northern borders of Attica without having accomplished his mission. Deserted by Athens, Thebes nevertheless maintained a stout resistance but fell a victim in the end to the overwhelming strength of the Macedonians. To discourage subsequent revolt by other cities, Alexander ordered the city to be levelled to the ground. From Athens Alexander demanded the surrender of those chiefly responsible for the movement against him, amongst whom were the orators Demosthenes and Lycurgus, together with several anti-Macedonian generals.

When the demand was submitted to the Athenians, Demosthenes is said to have reminded them of the story of the sheep that surrendered the watch-dogs to the wolves: as a merchant sold not merely the sample of wheat displayed to his customer but the whole stock of which it formed but a part, so, he warned them, they would surrender not merely the individuals specified by Alexander but the whole community of Athens as well. Eventually Demades, whose sympathy with Macedon was well known, was induced[87] to ask Alexander to withdraw his demand and the king agreed to be content with the expulsion of the general Charidemus.[88]

---

[86] Plutarch *Dem*. 23.2. παῖδα καὶ Μαργίτην ἀποκαλῶν. Margites, the hero of a burlesque poem attributed by some Greeks to Homer, πόλλ' ἠπίστατο ἔργα, κακῶς δ' ἠπίστατο πάντα
[87] It is said that he received five talents from the persons threatened. (Plutarch *Dem*. 23.5).
[88] Other anti-Macedonians whose surrender had been originally demanded, including Ephialtes and Thrasybulus, felt their position to be untenable, and withdrew to Asia.

After Alexander's departure to the east, a fresh movement against Macedon was set afoot in Greece. Agis III, king of Sparta, with Persian subsidies, enlisted support from Achaea, Elis and most of the Arcadian cities, and made an attack on Megalopolis, now the centre of Macedonian influence in the Peloponnese (331 B.C.). Antipater, the Macedonian regent, marching quickly to the relief of the city, crushed the confederates in a battle in which Agis himself perished on the field. Athens, deeming it unsafe to become involved in so rash a venture, took no part in the struggle. It must now have seemed to an observer that the fortunes of Demosthenes were at a low ebb. Encouraged by this, Demosthenes' old adversary Aeschines now delivered an attack which he had threatened six years before. When in 336 B.C. the murder of Philip had filled the opponents of Macedon with new hope, a certain Ctesiphon had proposed in the Council that the services of Demosthenes to the state, particularly in regard to the restoration of the city's fortifications, should be recognised by the bestowal of a golden crown, that the presentation of the crown should take place in the theatre at the time of the Great Dionysia, and that the reason for its bestowal be proclaimed by the herald to the assembled multitude. Before the proposal could be brought before the Assembly, Aeschines laid against Ctesiphon an indictment for having put forward a motion which contravened the law (γραφὴ παρανόμων). The effect of Aeschines' actions was to render the bestowal of the crown impossible until the validity of his charge against Ctesiphon had been tested in the law courts. The illegality alleged was threefold: (a) the bestowal of a crown which had been decreed by the Council or Assembly could not legally be made in the place or on the occasion proposed; (b) no crown could legally be conferred upon one who had not passed the official audit (εὔθυνα) in connection with any office which he had held and Demosthenes, as a Commissioner of the Theoric Fund and Commissioner for the Repair of Fortifications (τειχοποιός), was still liable to such an audit (ὑπεύθυνος); (c) the services of Demosthenes did not merit such recognition. The first two objections were technical and Demosthenes deals but cursorily with them in the speech which he delivered on behalf of the defendant Ctesiphon.[89] All his eloquence is concentrated on the third item in Aeschines' indictment. His answer takes the form of a vindication of the policy to which he had devoted his life. 'It was due to my policy', he declares, 'which the prosecutor assails, that instead of joining Philip in an invasion of our land, as all men

---

[89] *On the Crown*, the eighteenth and most famous speech in the Demosthenic corpus.

thought they would,⁹⁰ the Thebans stood shoulder to shoulder
with us and barred his path; that instead of battle being
joined in Attica, it was joined ninety miles away from the
city on the frontier of Boeotia; that instead of privateers
from Euboea pillaging and ravaging us, no attack was made
upon Attica from the sea during the whole of the war; that
instead of Philip laying hands on Byzantium and having control of the Hellespont, the people of Byzantium fought with
us against him.'⁹¹ In the end, Demosthenes gained a signal
triumph. Failing to secure one-fifth of the votes of the
jury, Aeschines was obliged to pay the statutory fine of
1000 *drachmae*, and debarred from bringing any further actions. Being unable to pay the amount required, he withdrew to Rhodes, where, as teacher and lecturer, he lived
for the remainder of his days.

Yet, although active in the law-courts and successful in
obtaining a favourable verdict in the case against Ctesiphon,
politically Demosthenes remained throughout these years in a
subordinate position. The leading men in Athenian affairs
were Phocion, Demades, and especially Lycurgus, who although
(unlike the other two) he had been opposed to Macedon, retained the control of financial affairs.⁹² Relations between
Athens and Macedon remained, outwardly at least, amicable
enough until 324 B.C., when two events occurred which threatened once more to bring about a collision. Firstly, Alexander
had his celebrated Exiles' Decree announced at the Olympic
Games of that year, ordering the restoration of exiles to all
member states of the League of Corinth. This decree provoked
angry resistance at Athens, since its implementation would
have involved the abandonment of the *cleruchy* on Samos and
the restoration of the island to its exiled former inhabitants.
The Athenians lodged a strong protest with Alexander and had
still not complied with the decree at the time of his death
the following year. The second event which provoked the collision was the Harpalus affair. Harpalus, a Macedonian noble
left in charge of the royal treasury at Babylon, had misappro-
priated some of the monies committed to his trust, in the

---

⁹⁰ Demosthenes himself once shared this opinion. Cf. *1st
Olynthiac* 25-26 ἂν δ' ἐκεῖνα Φίλιππος λάβῃ, τίς αὐτὸν κωλύσει
δεῦρο βαδίζειν; Θηβαῖοι; μὴ λίαν πικρὸν εἰπεῖν ᾖ - καὶ
συνεισβαλοῦσιν ἑτοίμως.
⁹¹ *On the Crown* 229-30.
⁹² Lycurgus continued as head of the Exchequer (Ταμίας ἐπὶ
τῇ διοικήσει) for three four-year periods (336-324 B.C.).
Though he could not officially hold office for two consecutive four-year periods, the post was nominally held
by his friend Xenocles of Sphettus for the second of the
three periods.

belief that Alexander would never return from India alive. However when he learned that the king was now on his way back, fearing to face him, he fled with 6000 mercenaries and 5000 talents of the treasure to Greece. When he presented himself at Athens, where he had been made an honorary citizen, the city was disinclined to receive him. Thereupon he withdrew to Taenarum but, returning later without his mercenaries, he found refuge at Athens as a private citizen. His surrender was naturally demanded by Alexander and the Athenians, on the proposal of Demosthenes agreed to deliver him up if the king sent officers to receive him into custody. But they refused to hand the fugitive over to Antipater, the regent of Macedonia, or to Philoxenus, who had control in Asia Minor, and declared that they would retain such monies as Harpalus had in his possession with a view to restoring them to Alexander, from whom they had been stolen. The amount in question was said by Harpalus to be 700 talents. It was deposited on the Acropolis under the charge of commissioners, of whom Demosthenes was one, but no definite record was kept of the actual sum. Harpalus soon escaped, almost certainly with the connivance of those in whose custody he was being kept. It was then discovered that the money on the Acropolis was less by one half than had formerly been supposed. Rumour was active, and Demosthenes sought to counter it by proposing that the Council of the Areopagus be deputed to hold an enquiry into the affair. After a considerable interval that body reported that certain leading Athenians had been guilty of receiving bribes. One of these was Demosthenes himself; he had received, it was asserted, 20 talents. The orator was impeached in the law-courts[93] and condemned to pay a fine of 50 talents. Being unable to pay so heavy a penalty, he was imprisoned, and later escaped into exile spent for the most part in Aegina and Troezen.[94]

---

[93] Among the speeches written for the prosecution in the case were the first oration of Deinarchus and the fifth of Hyperides, partially extant in a fragmentary condition.

[94] The question of Demosthenes' guilt or innocence has been much canvassed. Though Harpalus need not have been telling the truth in asserting that 700 talents had been deposited on the Acropolis, and though we are ignorant both of the conditions under which the Areopagus drew up its report and of the evidence on which the report was based, it may well be that Demosthenes was guilty of appropriating some of the money. Probably he was intending to put it to good use in raising funds for a future war with Macedonia. At all levels his venality was taken for granted by Plutarch (*Dem.* 14.2 and 25.4; also cf. *Comparison of Demosthenes and Cicero* 3.5-6 and *Moralia* 846A). Cf. also the damning assertion of the contemporary comic poet Timophanes: Δημοσθένης τάλαντα πεντήκοντ' ἔχει'

In 323 B.C. Alexander died at Babylon in his thirty-third year. A rising in Greece against Macedon followed, usually termed the Lamian War, in which Athens, together with Aetolia and Thessaly, took an active part. The Greek coalition gathered a considerable number of mercenaries, and when Antipater marched southwards through Thessaly, he was outmanoeuvred near Thermopylae and compelled to shut himself up with his forces in Lamia. There he was besieged by his enemies, who were commanded by the Athenian Leosthenes, a professional soldier who had seen military service under Alexander himself. Meanwhile Athens was seeking aid from the Peloponnese. Embassies were despatched to the various cities and Demosthenes, although an exile, supported their pleadings to the utmost of his power. Antipater on his side did not lack advocates; in particular two exiles from Athens, Pytheas and Callimedon, opposed the efforts of the Athenian representatives to rally the Peloponnesians to their cause. Demosthenes' services were recognised by his recall from exile. A trireme was sent to bring him from Aegina, and the magistrates and entire population of the city welcomed him home. When he landed once more upon his native soil, he lifted his hands in thanks to the gods, declaring he had been vouchsafed a return more glorious than that of Alcibiades, since it was due to persuasion and not to force.

The siege of Lamia was pressed vigorously by Leosthenes but, while he was inspecting the blockading trenches, he was killed by a stone. Early in 322 B.C., Leonnatus, the governor of Hellespontine Phrygia, arrived in Thessaly with an army and compelled the Greeks to withdraw their forces from Lamia in order to give him battle. The Macedonians were defeated and Leonnatus fell. But Antipater, joining the survivors, retreated into Macedonia to wait the arrival of reinforcements. Craterus with an army of veterans was already on his way from the east; his troops united with those of Antipater and marched into Thessaly; at Crannon in the late summer they achieved a doubtful victory over Leosthenes' successor Antiphilus. Though far from decisive, the Macedonian victory discouraged the Greeks to such an extent that the resistance collapsed and the coalition broke up. When the victorious Macedonians arrived in Thebes, Athens made her submission. A property qualification for citizenship was imposed, Demosthenes, Hyperides and others of their party fled from the city and were condemned to death in absentia and a Macedonian garrison was established in Munychia. Demosthenes took sanctuary in the temple of Poseidon on Calauria, a small island off the coast of Argolis, where he was confronted by an emissary of Antipater, a certain Archias, who had formerly been an actor but from his subsequent activities earned the nickname of 'the exile-hunter' (ὁ φυγαδοθήρας). Archias sought to induce Demosthenes to leave his refuge by blandishments and fair words. 'Your acting never convinced me, Archias,' replied the orator, 'nor will your promises do so now.'

Retiring within the temple, he made as if to write, biting his pen as though in thought. Presently covering his head he lay down. Archias bade him rise and renewed his professions and promises. But Demosthenes had no thought of falling into his hands alive. He had taken the poison which he had long kept in readiness,[95] and now felt that he was near his end. He looked steadily at Archias and, with a last gibe at his old profession, told him now to play the part of Creon in the tragedy and refuse burial to his body.[96] With stumbling footsteps, supported by his captors, he went forth from the temple, lest by dying within it he should pollute Poseidon's holy place which Macedonian violence had profaned. As he passed the altar, which stood in front of the temple, he fell to the earth and with a groan breathed his last.

Demosthenes received no official recognition at Athens till 280 B.C., when a decree was passed on the proposal of his nephew Demochares, himself a politician of some distinction, granting to the oldest member of the family to which the orator belonged maintenance for life at public expense and a front seat at all spectacles. Demosthenes himself was honoured with the erection of a bronze statue in the Athenian agora, the work of the sculptor Polyeuctus (see cover illustration). On the base of the statue, the Athenians engraved what they considered to be a truly fitting epitaph:
εἴπερ ἴσην ῥώμην γνώμῃ, Δημόσθενες, εἶχες,
οὔποτ' ἂν Ἑλλήνων ἦρξεν Ἄρης Μακεδών.
(if only your strength had been equal to your spirit, Demosthenes, then never would Macedonian Ares have ruled over the Greeks).

---

[95] The poison was concealed, according to different stories, in the pen, in a ring, or in a piece of cloth.
[96] Creon refused burial to the body of Polynices in Sophocles' *Antigone* (198-206).

II

THE ORATORY OF DEMOSTHENES

1   *The Three Categories of Speech*

Ancient critics recognised three types of speech:-
- (a) The <u>political</u> or <u>deliberative</u> speech (λόγος συμβουλευτικός), spoken in an assembly, council or senate, in which the orator urges the audience to adopt or to decline to adopt some particular course of action, and concerned with establishing the expediency or harmfulness of that particular course.
- (b) The <u>legal</u> or <u>forensic</u> speech (λόγος δικανικός), spoken in a court of law, either for the prosecution or defence, and concerned to establish the justice or injustice of some action.
- (c) The <u>display</u> or <u>ceremonial</u> speech (λόγος ἐπιδεικτικός), spoken on a ceremonial occasion, spoken either in praise or censure and concerned to prove someone or something worthy of honour or the reverse. Examples of this type of speech are those delivered on the occasion of a great pan-Hellenic festival (e.g. the *Olympiacus* of Lysias, delivered at the Olympic Festival of 388 B.C., in which the orator urges the Greeks to unite and overthrow the tyranny of Dionysius of Syracuse), speeches devoted entirely to singing the praises of an individual, whether mythological (e.g. Isocarates' *Helen*) or historical (e.g. Isocrates' *Evagoras*), and the *epitaphios* or Funeral Speech, delivered on the occasion of a public funeral of Athenians who had died in battle, and devoted to a eulogy of Athens and of the dead (e.g. Lysias 2 and Hyperides 6).

2. *The Divisions of Ancient Speeches*

The traditional division of an ancient speech, as set out in the rhetorical handbooks (e.g. Cicero's *De Inventione*) is as follows:
- (a) <u>Introduction</u> (προοίμιον / *exordium*), devised with the aim of preparing the audience for the rest of the speech and of securing goodwill.
- (b) <u>Narrative</u> (διήγησις / *narratio*).
- (c) <u>Proof</u> (πίστις / *confirmatio*), the marshalling of arguments designed to support the case and make it credible to the audience. Two kinds of proof were recognised:
    - (i) Factual or direct proofs (ἄτεχνοι), e.g. the citation of laws or the texts of decrees, the evidence of witnesses.
    - (ii) Technical or indirect proofs (ἔντεχνοι), e.g. arguments based on probability, expediency, pre-

cedent and character (of both prosecutor and defendant).
(d) Conclusion (ἐπίλογος / peroratio), often subdivided into recapitulation (ἀνακεφαλαίωσις / enumeratio) and emotional appeal, including an address to the audience and to the gods.

Apart from a regular introduction and conclusion, Demosthenes makes no attempt to adhere to the standard pattern, and in the *Olynthiacs,* as in his other deliberative speeches, he fails to distinguish narrative from proof, which are inextricably linked. In the case of *pistis*, factual proofs have no place in deliberative speeches of this sort, while of the various types of indirect proof, Philip's character is singled out for attack, as if he were the regular defendant in a judicial trial and Demosthenes the prosecutor.

3 *Analysis of the Olynthiacs*

The main object of the following analysis of the speeches is to throw some light upon the plan upon which they have been composed.

In each speech a practical proposal constitutes the central nucleus (cf. 1.16-20; 2.11-13; 3.10-20). A prefatory notice of this proposal may appear at the opening of the speech - e.g. the expedition to Olynthus, suggested in 1.2, is fully expounded in 1.16-18; or towards the close some aspect of it may undergo further development - e.g. the application of the Theoric Fund (see Appendix B below) to the public service, suggested in 3.10-20, is elaborated in 3.33-35.

The portions of the speech on either side of this nucleus are designed to exhibit the position of affairs which has given rise to the proposal. The orator dwells on the situation in its brighter or its darker aspect according as he desires to appeal to his audience through their hopes or through their fears. In 1 encouragement and warning are intermingled; in 2 encouragement predominates, in 3 the tone is mainly one of grave admonition. In the latter part of his speech Demosthenes not infrequently returns to a point already insisted upon in the earlier part, reinforcing his previous argument by approaching the topic afresh from a different point of view - e.g. in 2 the weakness of Philip is shown, first (2.5-10), by a review of his relations with other powers, and, secondly (2.14-21), by a consideration of the condition of Macedonia and the character of the king's entourage.

Each speech commences with a formal introductory passage and ends with a conclusion designed to be of happy omen.

1st Olynthiac

1. Introduction. You would give much to learn the policy which is in your interest. Listen to your advisers' counsels, both meditated and spontaneous, and it will be easy to select the course which is to your advantage.
2-5. Philip's strength and weakness. Action is imperative. We must send a force to help Olynthus and ambassadors to watch events. Philip has advantages, but he had disadvantages too. He has an ill record in the past, and as a tyrant, is regarded with distrust.
6-9. Athens' opportunity. Action cannot be deferred. In Olynthus we have a stable ally. Had we used our past opportunities, we should have escaped our present difficulties which have made Philip great.
9-13. The danger of neglect. Heaven has been kind, though, like the spendthrift, we have not recognized our blessings. If Philip secures Olynthus, he will be invincible. Recall the energy and ambition which have marked his career.
14-15. The price of present ease. Philip is active, we are remiss. Like those who borrow at high interest we shall have to pay a heavy reckoning.
16-18. A plan of campaign. Although your anger at failure does not always fall upon those responsible, I will put before you my plan. Despatch *two* armies - one to succour Olynthus, one to attack Macedonia. Either alone will be ineffective.
19-20. A financial suggestion. Money you have in plenty - if you will use it for war instead of festivals. Otherwise a special tax must be levied.
21-24. Philip's difficulties; Athens' chance. Philip's expectations have not been fulfilled. His financial resources are in some degree threatened; his subjects are ready to revolt. Success has made him reckless. Seize the occassion; fight and summon others to the fray.
25-27. Invasion the penalty of inaction. War must come, if not now abroad, hereafter at home. Olynthus is the only bar to Philip's advance. An invasion of Attica would both ruin and disgrace us.
28. Conclusion. Let all combine to keep the war abroad - men of wealth, men of military age, men of affairs. The acts of these last you will estimate according to the fortune in which you find yourselves. Heaven grant that fortune be fair!

2nd Olynthiac

1-2. Introduction. In offering us such allies as the Olynthians Heaven itself has helped us. It is now for us to help ourselves.
3-4. Philip's glory; Athens' shame. I will not speak of Philip's power. It is a glory to him but a disgrace to us, for it is to some among us that he owes it. I will speak rather of what is to his discredit.

5-8. Philip's duplicity and its consequence. A review of his actions will exhibit his past treachery and prove that it can no longer serve him in the future. He rose through deceiving all with whom he dealt. Their eyes have now been opened and he will fall.
9-10. The insecurity of Philip's power. Force cannot keep what fraud has won. Power founded on wickedness and greed collapses of itself.
11-13. Demosthenes' plan. Send help to Olynthus and an embassy to Thessaly to foment opposition to Philip. Words - especially *our* words - without deeds are vain. Act, raise money, fight, and Philip's weakness will reveal itself.
14-21. Macedonia's unsound condition. United with another power Macedonia may have been of some account; alone she is weak. Her people are distressed by ceaseless campaigning and loss of trade. Philip has surrounded himself with inefficiency and profligacy. As in the physical body, so in the body politic, latent evil will, under stress, make its presence apparent.
22-26. Athens' inaction. Fortune is not kinder to Philip than to us, but *he* acts while *we* are idle. It is not strange that he wins, but that we, with our past record, now fail to act. Our present case is due to mutual recrimination and hoping that others will act. Persistence in what has ruined us cannot lead to improvement.
27-30. Evils to be reformed. We must change our policy and play our part. At present your generals have to employ their troops where they can obtain pay for them. Your politics are dominated by factions. Be your own masters. If all the burdens are thrown upon one section alone, that section will fail you.
31. Conclusion. In a word - All must bear their fair share of taxation and military service. All must have equal right to be heard. Advice must be accepted, not because of its author, but on its merits. So will your whole position change for the better.

3rd Olynthiac

1-2. Introduction. We have to consider, not retaliation upon Philip, but the safety of ourselves and our allies.
3. The need of frankness. It is difficult to address you. You lack will, not knowledge. Honest speech may improve your position; speech designed only to please has ruined it.
4-5. Athens' remissness in the past. Two or three years ago an ambitious scheme was followed by inadequate action. Philip's illness gave you your chance. Instead of seizing it you abandoned your effort.
6-9. Athens' present opportunity. Now the Olynthians are at war with Philip. Lend prompt and vigorous aid. To fail to do so will involve, not disgrace alone, but peril. There is no other power to stand between us and Philip.

10-13. **Legal reforms the first step.** At present certain laws are a bar to salutary proposals. Compel those who introduced those laws to secure their repeal.
14-15. **Action the supreme necessity.** Decrees alone are useless. Otherwise your position would be a far different one. Action alone is wanting to ensure success.
16-18. **The call is to every man.** We have every reason to oppose Philip. It is we who have made him powerful, though, like fugitives in a rout, we shall blame any one but ourselves. Cease recrimination and unite in discovering the best policy. If that policy involves burdens, that is not the fault of its advocate.
19-20. **The deceitfulness of wishes.** We cannot spend the same money on festivals and on war. Let us disregard wishes and face facts. It would be shameful to suffer lack of means to prevent us from opposing Philip.
21-26. **The story of the Past.** I seek, not personal popularity as do modern statesmen, but the city's safety as did the statesmen of old. Consider their achievements - supremacy in Greece, wealth, power abroad, triumphs on land and sea. Their private fortunes remained humble; their object was the city's wealth, not their own; their means good faith, religion and equity.
27-29. **The contrast of the Present.** Under our modern statesmen, with a clear field, we have lost territory and allies; have spent treasure in vain; and have raised up against ourselves a powerful enemy. While the state's fortunes have declined, those of her statesmen have prospered.
30-32. **The Reason.** The change is due to your lack of control over your leaders. You are their servants and cringe to them. How then can you have the lofty spirit of old? A man's *morale* is determined by his habits. You do not like to hear the truth; I am surprised you have suffered it from me.
33-36. **The Remedy.** Reform your ways. Serve, act, put your monies to a proper use. At present these do you no real good. Service in some capacity should be the condition of receiving payment from the state. Thus both the state and the individual are benfited. Do not talk about your *mercenaries'* successes, but serve *yourselves*. Stand firm in the post of honour which your forefathers won and bequeathed to you.
36. **Conclusion.** I have stated roughly what I think of advantage. God grant you choose what is best for the state and for us all!

4 *Demosthenes' Use of Rhetorical Devices*

The effectiveness of the *Olynthiacs* is greatly enhanced by Demosthenes' mastery of rhetorical devices, which are used to impress the audience and to retain its attention. Above all, he is anxious to ensure as much variety as possible, in tone, rhythm and length of period, in order to avoid monotony and to create the impression that he is speaking *ex tempore*.

Among the devices employed to achieve these results may be mentioned the following:

(a) Variation in the person of the verb: Demosthenes skilfully rings the changes in the person of the verb, passing easily from the first person, in which he offers his own opinion and advice, to the second person, in which the activities of his audience are expressed, and from the second person to the third, to record the exploits of Philip or of the Olynthians. In particular he varies his address to the audience between the first and second person, referring to them sometimes as 'we' and at other times 'you', to remind them of their personal involvement and thus ensure that their attention does not wander.

(b) Variation between statement, command and question: Though most of the content of the *Olynthiacs* is naturally cast in the form of statements, Demosthenes is well aware that statements alone are not enough to keep his audience fully stimulated. He is therefore careful to cast portions in the form of questions or commands, as he in turn exhorts, orders and interrogates his audience. A sustained passage in the imperative mood is 3.10-13 - μὴ θαυμάσητε ... νομοθέτας καθίστατε ... μὴ θῆσθε νόμον ... τοὺς εἰς τὸ παρὸν βλάπτοντας ὑμᾶς λύσατε ... ζητεῖτε ... μὴ σκοπεῖτε ... μηδαμῶς ἀξιοῦτε. Even more frequent is the introduction of questions, which keep the audience attentive in a way that mere statements do not. Particularly common is the *rhetorical question*, which is asked not for information but for effect, in that the orator knows the answer already. Sometimes the answer is so obvious that he does not feel any need to provide it, at other times he supplies it himself. In either case, the device rouses attention and expresses a point much more vividly, more emotionally and more memorably than a simple statement. Examples of rhetorical question *without* an answer may be found at 1.15, 24 and 27 and 3.15; rhetorical questions *with* answer provided occur at 1.15 and 25, 2.26 and 28, and 3.27 and 30. Particularly vivid are passages such as 1.25-26 and 3.16, where statements are replaced entirely by a whole series of questions.

(c) Challenges addressed to the audience: As an alternative to firing question, Demosthenes will issue a challenge to the audience, inviting its participation in the argument. Examples are 1.12 - εἰ δὲ προησόμεθα ... τούτους τοὺς ἀνθρώπους εἶτ' Ὄλυνθον ἐκεῖνος καταστρέψεται, φρασάτω τις ἐμοί τί τὸ κωλῦον ἔτ' αὐτὸν ἔσται βαδίζειν ὅποι βούλεται; and 3.28 - ἢ φρασάτω τις ἐμοί παρελθών, πόθεν ἄλλοθεν ἰσχυρὸς γέγονεν ἢ παρ' ἡμῶν αὐτῶν Φίλιππος. Like a question, an invitation to speak couched in this way helps to create the impression that the orator is not simply haranguing his audience, but involving it in the discussion, thus retaining its attention.

(d) Introduction of an element of conversation: Since nothing appears less monotonous than the introduction of a conversational element into a speech, Demosthenes is fond of adopting the device of conjuring up an imaginary objector to raise a difficulty (προκατάληψις / anteoccupatio), to which he provides an immediate answer (ὑποφορά / subiectio). Usually, though not invariably, this objection is cast in the form of a question (e.g. 1.14, 19 and 26; 3.10, 19 and 29). Also noteworthy is Demosthenes' attack on some contemporary orators who are concerned more with courting popularity than with giving salutary advice (3.22). In the passage he cites three typical questions that are always in the mouths of such men (τί βούλεσθε; τί γράψω; τί ὑμῖν χαρίσωμαι;), and doubtless departed from his normal tone of delivery at this point in order to give an impersonation of one of the orators he had in mind (προσωποποιία / conformatio). Cf. Quintilian 11.1.29 - *utimur fictione personarum et velut ore alieno loquimur, dandique sunt iis, quibus vocem accomodamus, sui mores.*

(e) Various other devices are used to suggest spontaneity of composition:

    (i) Parenthesis: a deliberate breaking off of the argument by a temporary interruption of the sentence structure, in order to insert a new statement; the original construction is then eventually resumed. Examples are 1.3 - ἀξιόπιστος δ' ἂν εἰκότως φαίνοιτο; 2.18 - πρὸς γὰρ αὖ τοῖς ἄλλοις καὶ τὴν φιλοτιμίαν ἀνυπέρβλητον εἶναι; 2.28 - Ἀμφίπολίς γ' ἂν ληφθῇ, παραχρῆμ' ὑμεῖς κομιεῖσθε; and 3.10 - εἰσὶ γὰρ ὑμῖν ἱκανοί.

    (ii) Anacoluthon: a deliberate breaking off of the sentence structure by the insertion of some new statement; unlike parenthesis, the original construction is not resumed, but the thought is followed up in a different construction. Two examples may be cited from the *Olynthiacs*:

(a) 1.24 - λογιζόμενος εἰ Φίλιππος λάβοι καθ' ἡμῶν τοιοῦτον καῖρον καὶ πόλεμος γένοιτο πρὸς τῇ χώρᾳ, πῶς ἂν αὐτὸν οἴεσθ' ἑτοίμως ἐφ' ὑμᾶς ἐλθεῖν; εἶτ' οὐκ αἰσχύνεσθ, εἰ μηδ' ἃ πάθοιτ' ἄν, εἰ δύναιτ' ἐκεῖνος, ταῦτα ποιῆσαι καιρὸν ἔχοντες οὐ τολμήσετε; (Considering that if Philip were to obtain so great an opportunity against us and war were to come against our land, how readily do you suppose he would march against you? Then are you not ashamed that even if what he would have had done to you if he had the power - would you not venture to do this when you have the opportunity?). Here there is anacoluthon in both sentences; in the first λογιζόμενος is picked up by a question, instead of a statement, then the construction of the clause beginning αἰσχυνεσθ' εἰ is broken off after εἰ δύναιτ' ἐκεῖνος, and the orator instead proceeds to ask an energetic question. We even have a change of negative from μή (in εἰ μηδ') to οὐ.

(b) 3.27 - νυνὶ δὲ πῶς ἡμῖν ὑπὸ τῶν χρηστῶν τῶν νῦν τὰ πράγματ' ἔχει; οἷς - τὰ μὲν ἄλλα σιωπῶ, πόλλ' ἂν ἔχων εἰπεῖν, ἀλλ' ὅσης ἅπαντες ὁρᾶτ' ἐρημίας ἐπειλημμένοι (But how do our affairs stand to-day, thanks to these worthy fellows? Why, we - I omit much of what I could mention - but you all see what a clear field we had obtained.) Here the pronoun οἷς is left with no conceivable construction, because of the insertion of the parenthesis that immediately follows it, and the sentence then resumes as if the word had never been used in the first place.

(iii) <u>Paraleipsis</u> / *praeteritio*: a claim to be suppressing information which in fact is mentioned. By claiming not to mention material, the orator creates the impression that he does not need it, that he can afford to ignore it, that his case is satisfactory even without it, that he does not consider it to be important, when in fact he is bringing it to the attention of his audience even more effectively than if he had not resorted to the device. An example may be cited from 1.13 - τὰς δ' ἐπ' Ἰλλυριοὺς καὶ Παίονας αὐτοῦ καὶ πρὸς Ἀρύββαν καὶ ὅποι τις ἂν εἴποι παραλείπω στρατείας.

(iv) <u>Parasiopesis</u> / *reticentia*: a claim to be supressing information which is *not* mentioned; a useful device employed by an orator when he wishes to conceal his lack of information on a subject. Examples are 1.9 - καὶ πάλιν ἡνίκα Πύδνα, Ποτείδαια, Μεθώνη, Παγασαί, τἆλλα, ἵνα μὴ καθ' ἕκαστα λέγων διατρίβω, πολιορκούμεν' ἀπηγγέλλετο; and 3.27 - οἷς - τὰ μὲν ἄλλα σιωπῶ, πόλλ' ἂν ἔχων εἰπεῖν, ἀλλ' ὅσης ἅπαντες ὁρᾶτ' ἐρημίας ἐπειλημμένοι.

(f) **Figures of Speech** frequently occur in the *Olynthiacs* as follows:

   (i) **Metaphor**: Demosthenes uses metaphor sparingly, boldly and effectively to illustrate the argument more clearly rather than for purposes of literary embellishment. In the *Olynthiacs*, the following passages are worthy of mention; of which only the sixth example (3.27-28) is at all elaborate:

   1.2 - the present crisis calls on the Athenians, almost crying out loud (μόνον οὐχὶ λέγει φωνὴν ἀφιείς);

   2.10 - injustice, perjury and falsehood are fed upon hopes and blossom, only to be detected and wither away (ἤνθησεν ἐπὶ ταῖς ἐλπίσιν ... χρόνῳ δὲ φωρᾶται καὶ περὶ αὐτὰ καταρρεῖ);

   2.21 - war grapples with a city on its frontiers (ἐπειδὰν δ' ὅμορος πόλεμος συμπλακῇ - a metaphor from wrestling);

   3.3 - most of our interests have slipped through our hands (τὰ πλείω τῶν πραγμάτων ἡμᾶς ἐκπεφευγέναι - a hunting metaphor);

   3.7 - a great city lying in wait for opportunities when they are offered (πόλιν μεγάλην ἐφορμεῖν τοῖς ἑαυτοῦ καιροῖς - a nautical metaphor of a blockading vessel);

   3.27-28 - we had a clear field (ἐρημίας ἐπειλημμένοι) ... there is no city worthy of competing against us for supremacy (περὶ τῶν πρωτείων ἡμῖν ἀντιτάξασθαι) ... we could have been umpires of the claims of others (τὰ τῶν ἄλλων δίκαια βραβεύειν) ... we have trained Philip (ἠσκήκαμεν) to be powerful - an elaborate and prolonged metaphor derived from the Public Games;

   3.31 - the Athenians were emasculated, with their sinews cut (ἐκνενευρισμένοι);

   3.36 - the Athenians must not abandon their position (μὴ παραχωρεῖν τῆς τάξεως - a military metaphor).

   (ii) **Simile**: Demosthenes' similes are memorable for their vividness, clarity and originality. In the *Olynthiacs*, the following examples occur:

   1.11 - simile from money making: we are failing either to make the best use of our opportunities or to recognise our blessings, in the manner of a spendthrift whose sense of gratitude is lost along with his gains;

1.15 - simile from money lending: we are in danger of having to pay a heavy price for our indolence, just as men who borrow money recklessly at high rates of interest enjoy a temporary accommodation only to forfeit their estates in the end;

2.10 - simile from building: the state must be founded on truth and justice if it is not to collapse, just as a ship or a house is strong only if it rests on a solid foundation;

2.21 - simile derived from the human body: the weaknesses of a city fighting on foreign soil are hidden, only to be revealed when the fighting occurs on its own frontier, just as the weaknesses of the human body are latent while it is in good physical condition, but are shown up under the effects of illness;

2.29 - simile derived from tax-paying: the Athenians are riven by faction and conduct their politics just as they used to pay the property tax (*eisphora*) by board or syndicate (*symmory*) and each faction has its own orator, general and supporters, who correspond respectively to the *hegemon*, deputy *hegemon* and taxpayers in the *symmories*;

3.33 - simile derived from medicine: the state payments received by the Athenians neither bring lasting benefit nor encourage them to abandon them in favour of a new alternative, but leave them in a state of inaction, in the same manner as a diet prescribed by a doctor, which neither restores the patient's strength nor weakens him to the point of death.

(iii) <u>Antithesis</u>: the contrast of words, phrases, sentences or ideas that are opposed to one another. Examples of this figure are too numerous to cite, but particularly noteworthy are the elaborate contrast between the Athenians of the past and those of the present (3.21-29), and the double contrast of words at 2.26 - δι' ὧν ἐκ <u>χρηστῶν</u> φαῦλα τὰ πράγματα τῆς πόλεως γέγονεν, διὰ τούτων ἐλπίζετε τῶν αὐτῶν πράξεων ἐκ φαύλων αὐτὰ χρηστὰ γενήσεσθαι

(iv) <u>Chiasmus</u>: the repetition of a pair of words or ideas arranged in such a way that the order in which they are mentioned in the first phrase is inverted in the second. Examples of this device include 2.24 - τὰ ὑμέτερ' αὐτῶν ἀνηλίσκετ' <u>εἰσφέροντες</u> καὶ προύκινδυνεύετε <u>στρατευόμενοι</u>,

νυνὶ δ' ὀκνεῖτ' ἐξιέναι καὶ μάλιστ' εἰσφέρειν ὑπὲρ
τῶν ὑμετέρων αὐτῶν κτημάτων; and 3.30 - τί δὴ ποθ'
ἅπαντ' εἶχε καλῶς τότε, καὶ νῦν οὐκ ὀρθῶς;

(v) <u>Asyndeton</u>: the omission of conjunctions or connectives, in order to speed up the flow of the orator's
language. Examples are 1.12 - (omission of conjunctions) τὸ πρῶτον Ἀμφίπολιν λαβών, μετὰ ταῦτα Πύδναν,
πάλιν Ποτείδαιαν, Μεθώνην αὖθις, εἶτα Θετταλίας ἐπέβη
μετὰ ταῦτα Φεράς, Παγασάς, Μαγνησίαν, πάνθ' ὃν ἐβούλετ'
εὐτρεπίσας τρόπον ᾤχετ' εἰς Θρᾴκην; and 3.6-7 - (omission of connectives) 1) θεάσασθ' ὃν τρόπον ὑμεῖς ἐστρατηγηκότες πάντ' ἔσεσθ' ὑπὲρ Φιλίππου. 2) ὑπῆρχον
Ὀλύνθιοι δύναμίν τινα κεκτημένοι, καὶ διέκειθ' οὕτω
τὰ πράγματα. 3) οὔτε Φίλιππος ἐθάρρει τούτους οὔθ'
οὗτοι Φίλιππον. ἐπραξάμεν ἡμεῖς κἀκεῖνοι πρὸς ἡμᾶς
εἰρήνην ... 4) ἦν τοῦθ' ὥσπερ ἐμπόδισμά τι Φιλίππῳ ...
5) ἐκπολεμῶσαι δεῖν ᾠόμεθα τοὺς ἀνθρώπους ἐκ παντὸς
τρόπου ... In the second passage there is no connective at the beginning of sentences (2) (3) (4) and (5).
Syntactically sentence (2) serves as an explanation
for the state of affairs set forth in sentence (1),
while (3) (4) and (5) in turn are given as explanations of the situation set forth in the second part
of sentence (2) ('asyndetic explanations'). The omission of connectives makes for vividness, as the
orator creates the impression that he is speaking *ex
tempore*, cataloguing the explanations one by one as
he recites them (cf. also 3.34, with note in Commentary
below).

(vi) <u>Polysyndeton</u>: the reverse of the previous figure, consisting of the repetition of conjunctions in a series
of coordinate words or phrases, e.g. 1.4 - τὸ γὰρ εἶναι
πάντων ἐκεῖνον ἕν' ὄντα κύριον <u>καὶ</u> ῥητῶν <u>καὶ</u> ἀπορρήτων
<u>καὶ</u> ἅμα στρατηγὸν <u>καὶ</u> δεσπότην <u>καὶ</u> τάμιαν <u>καὶ</u> πανταχοῦ
αὐτὸν παρεῖναι τῷ στρατεύματι ... By repeating καί,
Demosthenes strives to create the impression that his
list of Philip's advantages is more impressive than it
is in fact, and to bring home to his audience more effectively the menace posed by Philip to the Athenians.

(vii) <u>Oxymoron</u>: the juxtaposition of words that appear to be
mutually contradictory, as at 2.6 - τὸ θρυλούμενον ποτ'
ἀπόρρητον (the state secret that was on everyone's lips).

(viii) <u>Irony</u>: the use of a word in a sense diametrically opposed to its real meaning, as at 3.27 - ὑπὸ τῶν χρηστῶν
τῶν νῦν (by our current worthy politicians), where the
meaning is intended to be pejorative; and 3.31 καὶ τὸ
πάντων ἀνδρειότατον, τῶν ὑμετέρων αὐτῶν χάριν προσοφείλετε (the most manly thing of all, you thank them for
what you own).

(ix) Antistrophe / *conversio*: the repetition of a word at the end of two or more successive clauses or sentences. Examples include 1.4 - πρὸς μὲν τὸ τὰ τοῦ πολέμου ταχὺ καὶ κατὰ καιρὸν πράττεσθαι πολλῷ <u>προέχει</u>, πρὸς δὲ τὰς καταλλαγὰς ... ἐναντίως <u>ἔχει</u>; and 1.11 - ἂν μὲν γάρ, ὅσ' ἂν τις λάβῃ καὶ σώσῃ, μεγάλην ἔχει τῇ τύχῃ <u>τὴν χάριν</u>, ἂν δ' ἀναλώσας λάθῃ, συνανήλωσε καὶ τὸ μεμνῆσθαι <u>τὴν χάριν</u>.

(x) Aporia or Diaporesis / *dubitatio*: an expression of feigned doubt about how or whether to make some point, for the sake of appearing spontaneous, as 3.3 - ἐγὼ δ' οὐχ ὅτι χρὴ περὶ τῶν παρόντων συμβουλεῦσαι χαλεπώτατον ἡγοῦμαι, ἀλλ' ἐκεῖν' ἀπορῶ, τίνα χρὴ τρόπον ... πρὸς ὑμᾶς περὶ αὐτῶν εἰπεῖν.

(xi) Anadiplosis / *duplicatio*: the repetition of the same word or words within a clause, in order to give them emphasis (cf. Quintilian 9.1.32 - *geminatio verborum habet interdum vim, leporem alias*). Examples are 2.10 - οὐ γὰρ ἔστιν, οὐκ ἔστιν, ὦ ἄνδρες Ἀθηναῖοι, ἀδικοῦντα καὶ ἐπιορκοῦντα καὶ ψευδόμενον δύναμιν βεβαίαν κτήσασθαι; and 3.33 - ἐὰν οὖν ἀλλὰ νῦν ... ἐθελήσετε στρατεύεσθαί τε καὶ πράττειν ἀξίως ὑμῶν αὐτῶν ... ἴσως ἄν, ἴσως, ὦ ἄνδρες Ἀθηναῖοι, τέλειόν τι καὶ μέγα κτήσαισθ' ἀγαθόν.

(xii) Pleonasm / *amplificatio*: the use of two synonymous or near synonymous words, usually nouns, verbs or adjectives, alongside one another. This is one of the most common devices in Demosthenes, which he employs as a highly effective means of bringing home some important point to the audience. Examples are numerous, and the following selection, in no way intended to be comprehensive, well illustrates the wide-spread use to which the orator puts the figure:

Nouns

2.10 τὰς ἀρχὰς καὶ τὰς ὑποθέσεις
2.13 πολλὴν δὴ τὴν μετάστασιν καὶ μεγάλην δεικτέον τὴν μεταβολήν
2.14 ἡ Μακεδονικὴ δύναμις καὶ ἀρχή
2.15 τοῖς πολέμοις καὶ ταῖς στρατείαις
2.18 ἔμπειρος πολέμου καὶ ἀγώνων
3.3 ὁ μὲν οὖν παρὼν καιρός, εἴπερ ποτέ, πολλῆς φροντίδος καὶ βουλῆς δεῖται

Verbs

1.12 ἆρα λογίζεταί τις ὑμῶν καὶ θεωρεῖ
1.18 προσκαθεδεῖται καὶ προσεδρεύσει τοῖς πράγμασι
1.21 ταράττει καὶ πολλὴν ἀθυμίαν αὐτῷ παρέχει

2.6 θεωρῶν καὶ σκοπῶν εὑρίσκω
2.9 ἅπαντ' ἀνεχαίτισε καὶ διέλυσεν
2.14 Θετταλοῖς στασιάζουσι καὶ τεταραγμένοις
2.16 λυποῦνται καὶ συνεχῶς ταλαιπωροῦσι

Adjectives

2.18 εἰ δέ τις σώφρων ἢ δίκαιος
3.32 ἔστι δ' οὐδέποτ', οἶμαι, μέγα καὶ νεανικὸν φρόνημα λαβεῖν μικρὰ καὶ φαῦλα πράττοντας

(xiii) <u>Hyperbaton</u>: the separation of words that naturally belong together in order to give them greater emphasis. Examples are 1.2 - <u>τῶν</u> <u>πραγμάτων</u> ὑμῖν <u>ἐκείνων</u> αὐτοῖς ἀντιληπτέον ἐστι and 1.21 - ἄξιον δ' ἐνθυμηθῆναι ... <u>τὰ</u> <u>πράγματ'</u> ἐν ᾧ καθέστηκε νυνὶ <u>τὰ</u> <u>Φιλίππου</u>

(xiv) <u>Parataxis</u>: the juxtaposition of two independent clauses, of which the former is logically subordinate to the latter. This device is usually accompanied by the omission of connectives (*asyndeton*). An example is 3.34 - ἔξεστιν ἄγειν ἡσυχίαν· οἴκοι μένων βελτίων ... συμβαίνει τι τοιοῦτον οἷον καὶ τὰ νῦν· στρατιώτης αὐτὸς ὑπάρχων ἀπὸ τῶν αὑτῶν τούτων λημμάτων ... ἔστι τις ἔξω τῆς ἡλικίας ἡμῶν· ὅσ' αὑτὸς ... νῦν λαμβάνων οὐκ ὠφελεῖ, ταῦτα ... λαμβάνων παντ' ἐφορῶν καὶ διοικῶν ἃ χρὴ πράττεσθαι (if it were possible to keep the peace, he is better off staying at home. Suppose some sort of condition like the present were to arise, he would be better off serving in person as a soldier in payment of those same contributions. Or supposing that one of you were outside military age, he would be better supervising and managing everything that needs to be done, in receipt of what he now receives without in any way serving the state).

III

THE SOURCES OF THE TEXT

The MSS. of Demosthenes exceed 150 in number. The tradition which they represent is derived from the recension of the text made by the scholars of Alexandria in the third century B.C., but the oldest of the existing MSS. was not written earlier than the tenth century A.D. There have been found in Egypt small portions of the Demosthenic writings, which were inscribed upon papyrus prior to the Christian era. Two such fragments contain parts of *2nd Olynthiac* 10 and 15 but exhibit no reading unknown to the MSS.

The most important MS., usually denominated by the letter S (formerly belonging to a Sosandrian monastery), is in the Bibliotheque Nationale, Paris. It is written on parchment in minuscule letters, and is ascribed to the early part of the tenth century A.D. It has been corrected, not only by the original scribe but by several later hands as well, and contains in the margin a large number of alternative readings and notes. As compared with other MSS. it presents, generally speaking, a terser and more vigorous text, being comparatively free from interpolation and the admixture of glosses. Such mistakes as occur are almost without exception clerical errors which can be readily corrected.

Apart from this Paris MS. chief authority is generally ascribed to a MS. written on parchment probably in the eleventh century A.D. and denominated A (i.e. Augustanus, formerly in Augsburg = Augusta Vindelicorum), and now in Munich. This MS has suffered from mutilation, one result of which is that it now lacks a considerable portion of the text of the Olynthiac speeches. There exist, however, some sheets, evidently of a later date, which contain the whole of the missing portions with the exception of the earlier part of *1st Olynthiac*.

Another MS. which is of considerable value in the establishment of the text is M (i.e. Marcianus, in the Library of St. Mark, Venice). It is an eleventh century MS. written on parchment and containing a large number of notes in the margin as well as frequent corrections by various hands in the text.

The speeches of Demosthenes were well known to, and freely quoted by, later writers. Such quotations however, while they may occasionally serve to confirm a reading, cannot fairly be employed to set aside the evidence of the MSS. If made from memory the quotation may be inaccurate; if made from the written words, we have no means of estimating the value of the text from which it was drawn. Indeed Dionysius of Halicarnassus (first century B.C.), who quotes the opening of Demosthenes *3rd Philippic* four times, presents us with *three* varieties of text. Still less trustworthy as sources of

information concerning the text are those echoes of
Demosthenes' writings to be found in rhetoricians, like
Libanius (fourth century A.D.), and parodists, like Lucian
(second century A.D.). In such compositions it is clearly
impossible to disentangle with confidence the original words
of Demosthenes from the accretions and alterations due to
the writer of a later age.

APPENDIX

A   THE ORDER OF THE OLYNTHIAC SPEECHES

The traditional order of the *Olynthiacs* was first challenged by Dionysius of Halicarnassus,[1] who may have connected the three speeches with the three appeals for assistance made by the Chalcidians to Athens. However, as the subject of Olynthus must have been raised in the Athenian assembly on various occasions, it is unnecessary to relate the delivery of each *Olynthiac* to a specific debate that resulted in the despatch of a relief force.

Though there is no conclusive evidence, internal or external, in favour of any particular order, it is possible to reach some conclusion about the approximate date of the delivery of the speeches as a whole. In the first two speeches, Demosthenes argues for the despatch of assistance without in any way suggesting that any previous expeditions have been sent out[2] and, while the danger to Olynthus is emphasised more in the first than in the second speech, in neither is there any indication that the city is under siege. Indeed at 1.17, Demosthenes even argues that his projected expedition should save the Chalcidian cities, many of which had already fallen to Philip by the end of the first campaigning season. Again, though both speeches mention dissatisfaction in Thessaly,[3] neither refers to the outbreak of hostilities in that country which obliged Philip to intervene in the winter of 349/8 B.C.[4] These considerations point to a date for the two speeches fairly early in the course of the Olynthian war, not long after the outbreak of the fighting, and to a connection with the first Chalcidian appeal to Athens. They may thus be dated somewhere in the summer of 349 B.C.

It is difficult, if not impossible, to reach any definite conclusions on the relative order of the two speeches. It is undoubtedly the case that in the first speech Demosthenes lays greater emphasis on the danger facing Olynthus, and in the second on the need to revive Athenian morale. If therefore the orator believed that the danger to Olynthus was increasing by the hour, the second speech ought to be the earlier, but it can equally well be seen as a supplementary

---

[1] Dion. Hal. *1st Letter to Ammaeus* 1.4
[2] 1.2 - ψηφίσασθαι μὲν ἤδη τὴν βοήθειαν; 2.11 φημὶ δὴ δεῖν ἡμᾶς τοῖς 'Ολυνθίοις βοηθεῖν.
[3] 1.22; 2.11.
[4] Diodorus 16.52.9.

speech, delivered in response to some particular mood of
despondency affecting his audience. Our ignorance of the
detailed circumstances in which the second speech was delivered makes any definite decision on the order impossible.

The *3rd Olynthiac*, however, can reasonably be regarded
as the latest of the three. Not only is it by far the
gravest in tone, but the explicit advice about reforming the
Theoric Fund (see B below) made at 3.10ff. should be interpreted as an elaboration of the hint already made at 1.19-
20. The reference to the lateness of the hour (3.33)[5] has
been taken to mean that the siege of Olynthus must by now
have begun, but the orator may perhaps be thinking not of
the Olynthian War in particular but rather of the strategy
employed by Athens in fighting Philip in general: after a
whole series of unsuccessful campaigns against him based on
inadequate funding and the use of mercenaries, it is still
not too late to look for success at Olynthus or indeed any-
where else, if only the Athenians will change their attitude. The allusion at 3.35 to the victory of an Athenian
mercenary force[6] may perhaps be an indication that at least
one relief force has already been despatched, though the
passage may have a general rather than a specific reference.

More helpful in establishing an approximate date for the
speech is the absence of any reference to the trouble which
broke out in Euboea in the winter of 349 B.C. and undermined
Athenian influence in the strategically important island.[7]
As Demosthenes might reasonably be thought likely to mention,
if only to rebut, the difficulties of fighting in Chalcidice
and Euboea simultaneously, his silence suggests that the
Euboean revolt had not yet broken out when the speech was
delivered, and that it should therefore be dated before the
winter of 349/8 B.C. Again, if the orator is at all accurate
at 3.4 in claiming that two or three years have elapsed since
Philip's siege of Heraeum Teichos in Thrace in the month of
Maemacterion (i.e. roughly November, 352 B.C.),[8] he should
be speaking not later than Pyanepsion (roughly October),
349 B.C. Moreover, his proposal at 3.10 to establish a
board of *nomothetai* to consider legislative changes makes
sense only if the speech was delivered at the time of, or
shortly before, the first *prytany* of the year (corresponding

---

[5] ἐὰν οὖν ἀλλὰ νῦν γ' ἔτι ... ἐθελήσητε στρατεύεσθαι
[6] ὅτι δ' οἱ τοῦ δεῖνος νικῶσι ξένοι ταῦτα πυνθάνεσθαι.
[7] Aeschines 3.86-88; Plutarch *Phocion* 12-13.
[8] μέμνησθ' ὅτι ἀπηγγέλθη Φίλιππος ὑμῖν ἐν Θρᾴκῃ τρίτον
ἢ τέταρτον ἔτος τουτί, Ἡραῖον τεῖχος πολιορκῶν. τότε
τοίνυν μὴν ἦν Μαιμακτηριών.

approximately to Hecatombaeon or July), since only at this
time could the cumbersome machinery for the adoption of
new or for the repeal of existing legislation be set in
motion. These arguments together do suggest that the
third oration is not far removed in time from the other two,
and that all three speeches depict the situation as it existed during the first of the two campaigning seasons into
which the Olynthian War may be divided, i.e. the campaigning season of 349 B.C.

* * * * * *

B   THE THEORIC FUND

The Theoric Fund (τὸ θεωρικόν), mentioned in the *Olynthiacs* at 1.19.20 and 3.10-11, 19 and 13 was a fund established to provide for the distribution of state payments
to the poor to enable them to attend the major religious
festivals of Athens. Theoric payments are first recorded in the mid-fifth century as the work of Pericles[9]
and are subsequently ascribed to some of the demagogues who
succeeded him.[10] Such distributions, if indeed they were
made in the way Plutarch asserts, can have been held only
sporadically, on special occasions and for certain specific
purposes, and not on a regular basis.

The real creation of the Theoric Fund, and the beginning
of regular state payments from it, were the work of demagogue
Agyrrhius.[11] The date is uncertain, but as the Athenians are
unlikely to have considered the establishment of such a fund
in the immediate aftermath of their defeat in the Peloponnesian War and the civil war of 404/3 B.C., its creation may

---

[9] Plutarch *Pericles* 9.1-2 - ἄλλοι δὲ πολλοὶ πρῶτον ὑπ' ἐκείνου
(sc. τοῦ Περικλέους) φασὶ τὸν δῆμον ἐπὶ κληρουχίας καὶ
θεωρικὰ καὶ μισθῶν διανομὰς προαχθῆναι ... καὶ ταχὺ θεωρικοῖς καὶ δικαστικοῖς λήμμασι ἄλλαις τε μισθοφοραῖς καὶ
χορηγίαις συνδεκάσας τὸ πλῆθος.
[10] Plutarch *Aristides* 24.3 - Περικλέους δ' ἀποθανόντος ...
οἱ δημαγωγοί ... ὡς τὸν δῆμον εἰς διανομὰς καὶ θεωρικὰ
καὶ κατασκευὰς ἀγαλμάτων καὶ ἱερῶν προσαγαγόντες.
[11] Harpocration *s.v.* θεωρικά· θεωρικὰ ἦν τινὰ ἐν κοινῷ
χρήματα ἀπὸ τῶν τῆς πόλεως προσόδων συναγόμενα ... ὧν
πρῶτος ἤρξατο Ἀγύρριος ὁ δημαγωγός.

well be connected with the receipt of the Persian subsidy
in 395/4: certainly the fund is first clearly attested in
this year.[12]

At the same time in the decade 360-50, perhaps in 352
B.C., the Theoric Fund was greatly expanded as the result
of the enactment by the financier Eubulus of a law author-
ising the transfer to it of the entire surplus of income
over expenditure from each of the city's treasuries. A new
board of Theoric Commissioners (οἱ ἐπὶ τὸ θεωρικόν), chosen
by election, not sortition (an indication of the importance
of the newly enlarged fund) was created to administer the
fund, which was now used not only for theoric purposes, but
to defray the cost of any other operations which the Commissioners might from time to time approve. These came collectively to exercise supervision over all the financial trans-
actions of the Athenian state. A description of the Theoric
Fund as it functioned subsequent to Eubulus' law is given
by Aeschines.[13]

The motive for Eubulus' reform of the Theoric Fund was
partly to increase administrative efficiency and partly to
discourage rash declarations of war in a time of financial
difficulty. For the war fund (τὰ στρατιωτικά), first attested in 349/8 B.C.[14] but probably in existence for some
time before,[15] though it may, prior to the passage of Eubulus'
reform, have been financed from the surpluses of the various

---

[12] Zenobius 3.27 - ἐπὶ Διοφάντου (i.e. 395/4 B.C.) τὸ
θεωρικὸν ἐγένετο δραχμή.
[13] Aeschines 3.25 - πρότερον μὲν τοίνυν ... ἀντιγραφεὺς ἦν
χειροτονητὸς τῇ πόλει, ὃς καθ' ἑκάστην πρυτανείαν ἀπελογί-
ζετο τὰς προσόδους τῷ δήμῳ. διὰ δὲ τὴν πρὸς Εὔβουλον γενο-
μένην πίστιν ὑμῖν οἱ ἐπὶ τὸ θεωρικὸν κεχειροτονημένοι ἦρχον
μὲν ... τὴν τοῦ ἀντιγραφέως ἀρχήν, ἦρχον δὲ τὴν τῶν ἀποδεκ-
τῶν καὶ νεωρίων ἦρχον, καὶ σκευοθήκην ᾠκοδόμουν, ἦσαν δὲ
καὶ ὁδοποιοί, καὶ σχεδὸν τὴν ὅλην διοίκησιν εἶχον τῆς
πόλεως.
[14] IG 11² 207b line 11.
[15] See G. A. Cawkwell, 'Demosthenes and the Stratiotic Fund',
Mnemosyne Series 4, n.15 (1962) 377-83, where it is argued
that the Stratiotic Fund must date from the formation of
the Second Athenian Confederacy in 378/7 B.C. at latest.

treasuries,[16] was certainly financed from 352 onwards entirely from the levying of property tax (*eisphora*) and from the contributions (*syntaxis*) paid by the members of the Second Athenian Confederacy. Since the sums raised from these sources proved totally inadequate to cover military expenses on anything like the scale favoured by Demosthenes, he could obtain the money he wanted only by advocating the use of the Theoric Fund for military purposes, both in the *Olynthiacs* and in other deliberative speeches of the 350s and 340s B.C.[17]

Playing upon the reluctance of the Athenians to forego their theoric payments in time of war, as would undoubtedly have happened had the surpluses been diverted to the Stratiotic Fund, Eubulus skilfully developed the Theoric Fund to safeguard the maintenance of peace. Demosthenes likewise was aware of the risk of incurring unpopularity by openly proposing the repeal of Eubulus' law, and contented himself with hints and expressions of opinion only.[18] It seems

---

[16] This assertion is made by the author of the pseudo-Demosthenic speech *Against Neaera* (59.4) for periods when Athens was at war: κελευόντων μὲν τῶν νόμων, ὅταν πόλεμος ᾖ, τὰ περιόντα χρήματα τῆς διοικήσεως στρατιωτικὰ εἶναι. The statement is manifestly untrue for the period 352-339; for, as Athens was at war with Philip throughout the decade 356-46 and again from 340 B.C., there would have been no need for Demosthenes to hint at and for Apollodorus actually to propose the transfer of surpluses from the Theoric to the Stratiotic Fund in 349; still less could Apollodorus have been condemned for proposing an illegal measure. The claim may be no more than special pleading on the part of the speaker, but a passage in Libanius' *Hypothesis to the First Olynthiac* (§5) suggests that it may well have been true at an earlier period, prior to the passage of Eubulus' law: νόμον ἔθεντο περὶ τοῦ θεωρικοῦ τούτων χρημάτων θάνατον ἀπειλοῦντα τῷ γράψαντι μετατεθῆναί τε ταῦτ' εἰς τὴν ἀρχαίαν τάξιν καὶ γενέσθαι στρατιωτικά.

[17] In addition to the two passages in the *Olynthiacs*, this opinion is expressed at 13.2 and 9ff. (*On Organisation*, dated ca. 350 B.C., if genuine), at 4.35 (*First Philippic*, 351 B.C.), and at 8.26ff. (*On the Chersonese*, 342/1 B.C.). For the contrary view, see 10.36ff. (*Fourth Philippic*, 341 B.C.).

[18] See especially 1.19-20, where he is at great pains to prove that he is not actually proposing the repeal of Eubulus' law. A similar coyness is displayed at 4.35 and 8.26ff. Only at 3.10-11 does he openly advocate the law's repeal, but even so he was content to leave the introduction of fresh legislation to others.

unlikely that Eubulus introduced a law imposing the death penalty on anyone seeking to annul his Theoric Law, as is alleged by Libanius,[19] since a measure of this sort would have been quite superfluous.

Eventually however an impetuous young politician by the name of Apollodorus, in the same year as the delivery of the *Olynthiacs* - though whether before or after their delivery is unknown - did venture to risk opprobrium by making such a proposal, only to be prosecuted by his enemy Stephanus for proposing an illegal measure (γραφὴ παρανόμων). His condemnation and the fifteen talent fine, though later reduced to one talent, discouraged any further attempts to repeal the Theoric Law for some time. Instead, Eubulus' opponents sought to reduce the amount spent on state payments by instituting in 346/5 a revision of the citizen lists,[20] and the Theoric Law was not finally repealed till 339/8 B.C., some time after the end of his political career, and perhaps even after his death, the date of which is unknown,[21] at a time of crisis when war with Philip had again broken out and the culmination of the struggle was imminent. The proposal that surpluses should be transferred from the Theoric to the Stratiotic Fund was successfully moved by Demosthenes.[22]

The amount of money spent by the Athenians on theoric distributions has been variously assessed. The actual sum paid on a *per capita* basis was 1 drachma (6 obols) in 395/4 B.C.,[23] but, as we know neither the frequency of payments

---

[19] Libanius *Hypothesis to First Olynthiac* (§5). Such a law most certainly did not exist in 349 B.C., when Apollodorus ventured to propose the repeal of the Theoric Law: he was merely fined 15 talents, subsequently reduced still further to 1 talent (59.6-8).
[20] The Decree of Demophilus, for which see Aeschines 1.77-86. The fifty-seventh speech of Demosthenes in the extant corpus was probably written on the occasion of an appeal by his client who had lost his citizenship as a result of this decree.
[21] He is last attested in 343 B.C., when he appeared in court as a witness on behalf of Aeschines, who was being prosecuted by Demosthenes for corruption and treason.
[22] Philochorus fgt. 56A - Λυσιμαχίδης ᾿Αχαρνεύς. ἐπὶ τούτου ... τὰ χρήματα ἐψηφίσαντο πάντ' εἶναι στρατιωτικά, Δημοσθένους γράψαντος.
[23] Philochorus fgt. 33; Zenobius 3.27.

nor the number of recipients and as we have no figures
for the amount paid in the time of Demosthenes, it is
impossible to obtain anything like an accurate estimate
of the extent to which the Stratiotic Fund would have
gained had Demosthenes' wish for the transfer of the theoric
monies been implemented in 349 B.C.[24]

---

[24] For a convenient discussion of the problem, see A. H. M.
Jones, *Athenian Democracy* (Oxford, 1957) 33-5; 'in the
middle of the fourth century, the *theorica* must have been
financially very small beer, and Demosthenes was rather
foolish to make himself and his policy unpopular by trying to transfer it to the war fund.' For a criticism of
this and other views, see J. J. Buchanan, *Theorika: A
study of Monetary Distributions to the Athenian Citizenry
during the Fifth and Fourth Centuries B.C.* (New York,
1962) 83-88, who concludes, 'with the range of from 25
to 90 talents I see no cause to quarrel.'

SELECT BIBLIOGRAPHY

1. **TRANSLATIONS OF THE OLYNTHIACS**

   A. W. Pickard - Cambridge, in *Demosthenes' Public Orations* (London, 1906, reprinted in Everyman Library, London and New York, 1963).

   J. H. Vince, in *Demosthenes*, Vol. I (Loeb Classical Library, London and Harvard, 1930).

   A. N. W. Saunders, in *Greek Political Oratory* (Penguin Classics, Harmondsworth, 1970).

   J. R. Ellis and
   R. D. Milns, in *The Spectre of Philip: Demosthenes' First Philippic, Olynthiacs and Speech on the Peace* (Sydney, 1970).

2. **DEMOSTHENES AND GREEK ORATORY**

   G. Kennedy: *The Art of Persuasion in Greece* (Princeton and London, 1963).

   L. Pearson: 'The Development of Demosthenes as a Political Orator' in *Phoenix* 18 (1964) 95-109.

   J. R. Ellis: 'The Order of the Olynthiacs' in *Historia 16 (1967) 108-112*.

   L. Pearson: *The Art of Demosthenes* (Beitrage zur Klassischen Philologie, Heft 68, Meisenheim am Glan, 1976).

   H. Montgomery: *The Way to Chaeronea* (Oslo, 1983).

3. **DEMOSTHENES AND ATHENS**

   A. W. Pickard - Cambridge: *Demosthenes and the Last Days of Greek Freedom* (Putnam's Heroes of the Nations, London and New York, 1914).

   H. A. Dunkel: 'Was Demosthenes a Panhellenist? in *Classical Philology* 33 (1938) 291-305.

   A. H. M. Jones: *Athenian Democracy* (Oxford, 1957).

G. L. Cawkwell: 'The Defence of Olynthus' in *Classical Quarterly* 12 (1962) 122-140.

W. Jaegar: *Demosthenes: the Origin and Growth of his Policy* (Berkeley, 1938, reprinted New York, 1963).

J. M. Carter: 'Athens, Euboea and Olynthus' in *Historia* 20 (1971) 418-429.

4. *OLYNTHUS AND CHALCIDICE*

A. B. West: *The History of the Chalcidic League* (Madison, Wisconsin, 1918).

M. Gude: *A History of Olynthus* (Baltimore, 1933).

J. A. O. Larsen: *Greek Federal States* (Oxford, 1968) esp. pp. 58-77.

5. *PHILIP AND MACEDONIA*

J. R. Ellis: *Phillip II and Macedonian Imperialism* (London, 1976).

G. L. Cawkwell: *Philip of Macedon* (London and Boston, 1978).

N. G. L. Hammond and
G. T. Griffith: *A History of Macedonia*, Vol. II 550-336 B.C. (Oxford, 1979).

M. B. Hatzopoulos and
L. D. Loukopoulos: *Philip of Macedon* (London, 1981).

ΟΛΥΝΘΙΑΚΟΣ Α

Ἀντὶ πολλῶν ἄν, ὦ ἄνδρες Ἀθηναῖοι, χρημάτων 1 ὑμᾶς ἑλέσθαι νομίζω, εἰ φανερὸν γένοιτο τὸ μέλλον συνοίσειν τῇ πόλει περὶ ὧν νυνὶ σκοπεῖτε. ὅτε τοίνυν τοῦθ᾽ οὕτως ἔχει, προσήκει προθύμως ἐθέλειν ἀκούειν τῶν βουλομένων συμβουλεύειν· οὐ γὰρ μόνον εἴ τι χρήσιμον ἐσκεμμένος ἥκει τις, τοῦτ᾽ ἂν ἀκούσαντες λάβοιτε, ἀλλὰ καὶ τῆς ὑμετέρας τύχης ὑπολαμβάνω πολλὰ τῶν δεόντων ἐκ τοῦ παραχρῆμ᾽ ἐνίοις ἂν ἐπελθεῖν εἰπεῖν, ὥστ᾽ ἐξ ἁπάντων ῥᾳδίαν τὴν τοῦ συμφέροντος ὑμῖν αἵρεσιν γενέσθαι.

Ὁ μὲν οὖν παρὼν καιρός, ὦ ἄνδρες Ἀθηναῖοι, 2 μόνον οὐχὶ λέγει φωνὴν ἀφιεὶς ὅτι τῶν πραγμάτων ὑμῖν ἐκείνων αὐτοῖς ἀντιληπτέον ἐστίν, εἴπερ ὑπὲρ σωτηρίας αὐτῶν φροντίζετε· ἡμεῖς δ᾽ οὐκ οἶδ᾽ ὅντινά μοι δοκοῦμεν ἔχειν τρόπον πρὸς αὐτά. ἔστι δὴ τά γ᾽ ἐμοὶ δοκοῦντα, ψηφίσασθαι μὲν ἤδη τὴν βοήθειαν καὶ παρασκευάσασθαι τὴν ταχίστην, ὅπως ἐνθένδε βοηθήσητε καὶ μὴ πάθητε ταὐτὸν ὅπερ καὶ πρότερον, πρεσβείαν δὲ πέμπειν, ἥτις ταῦτ᾽ ἐρεῖ καὶ παρέσται τοῖς πράγμασιν. ὡς ἔστι μάλιστα τοῦτο δέος, μὴ 3 πανοῦργος ὢν καὶ δεινὸς ἄνθρωπος πράγμασι χρῆσθαι, τὰ μὲν εἴκων, ἡνίκ᾽ ἂν τύχῃ, τὰ δ᾽ ἀπειλῶν (ἀξιόπιστος δ᾽ ἂν εἰκότως φαίνοιτο), τὰ δ᾽ ἡμᾶς διαβάλλων καὶ τὴν ἀπουσίαν τὴν ἡμετέραν, τρέψηται καὶ παρασπάσηταί τι τῶν ὅλων πραγμάτων. οὐ μὴν 4 ἀλλ᾽ ἐπιεικῶς, ὦ ἄνδρες Ἀθηναῖοι, τοῦθ᾽ ὃ δυσμαχώ-

ΔΗΜΟΣΘΕΝΟΥΣ

τατόν ἐστι τῶν Φιλίππου πραγμάτων, καὶ βέλτιστον ὑμῖν· τὸ γὰρ εἶναι πάντων ἐκεῖνον ἕν᾽ ὄντα κύριον καὶ ῥητῶν καὶ ἀπορρήτων, καὶ ἅμα στρατηγὸν καὶ δεσπότην καὶ ταμίαν, καὶ πανταχοῦ αὐτὸν παρεῖναι τῷ στρατεύματι, πρὸς μὲν τὸ τὰ τοῦ πολέμου ταχὺ καὶ κατὰ καιρὸν πράττεσθαι πολλῷ προέχει, πρὸς δὲ τὰς καταλλαγάς, ἃς ἂν ἐκεῖνος ποιήσαιθ᾽ ἄσμενος
5 πρὸς Ὀλυνθίους, ἐναντίως ἔχει. δῆλον γάρ ἐστι τοῖς Ὀλυνθίοις ὅτι νῦν οὐ περὶ δόξης οὐδ᾽ ὑπὲρ μέρους χώρας κινδυνεύουσιν, ἀλλ᾽ ἀναστάσεως καὶ ἀνδραποδισμοῦ τῆς πατρίδος, καὶ ἴσασιν ἅ τ᾽ Ἀμφιπολιτῶν ἐποίησε τοὺς παραδόντας αὐτῷ τὴν πόλιν καὶ Πυδναίων τοὺς ὑποδεξαμένους· καὶ ὅλως ἄπιστον, οἶμαι, ταῖς πολιτείαις ἡ τυραννίς, ἄλλως τε κἂν ὅμορον χώραν ἔχωσι.
6 Ταῦτ᾽ οὖν ἐγνωκότας ὑμᾶς, ὦ ἄνδρες Ἀθηναῖοι, καὶ τἄλλ᾽ ἃ προσήκει πάντ᾽ ἐνθυμουμένους φημὶ δεῖν ἐθελῆσαι καὶ παροξυνθῆναι καὶ τῷ πολέμῳ προσέχειν εἴπερ ποτὲ καὶ νῦν, χρήματ᾽ εἰσφέροντας προθύμως καὶ αὐτοὺς ἐξιόντας καὶ μηδὲν ἐλλείποντας. οὐδὲ γὰρ λόγος οὐδὲ σκῆψις ἔθ᾽ ὑμῖν τοῦ μὴ
7 τὰ δέοντα ποιεῖν ἐθέλειν ὑπολείπεται. νυνὶ γὰρ ὃ πάντες ἐθρυλεῖτε, ὡς Ὀλυνθίους ἐκπολεμῶσαι δεῖ Φιλίππῳ, γέγονεν αὐτόματον, καὶ ταῦθ᾽ ὡς ἂν ὑμῖν μάλιστα συμφέροι. εἰ μὲν γὰρ ὑφ᾽ ὑμῶν πεισθέντες ἀνείλοντο τὸν πόλεμον, σφαλεροὶ σύμμαχοι καὶ μέχρι του ταῦτ᾽ ἂν ἐγνωκότες ἦσαν ἴσως· ἐπειδὴ δ᾽ ἐκ τῶν πρὸς αὐτοὺς ἐγκλημάτων μισοῦσιν, βεβαίαν εἰκὸς τὴν ἔχθραν αὐτοὺς ὑπὲρ ὧν φοβοῦνται καὶ πεπόνθα-
8 σιν ἔχειν. οὐ δεῖ δὴ τοιοῦτον, ὦ ἄνδρες Ἀθηναῖοι, παραπεπτωκότα καιρὸν ἀφεῖναι, οὐδὲ παθεῖν ταὐτὸν

ΟΛΥΝΘΙΑΚΟΣ Α

ὅπερ ἤδη πολλάκις πρότερον πεπόνθατε. εἰ γὰρ ὅθ᾽ ἥκομεν Εὐβοεῦσιν βεβοηθηκότες καὶ παρῆσαν Ἀμφιπολιτῶν Ἱέραξ καὶ Στρατοκλῆς ἐπὶ τουτὶ τὸ βῆμα κελεύοντες ἡμᾶς πλεῖν καὶ παραλαμβάνειν τὴν πόλιν, τὴν αὐτὴν παρειχόμεθ᾽ ἡμεῖς ὑπὲρ ἡμῶν αὐτῶν προθυμίαν ἥνπερ ὑπὲρ τῆς Εὐβοέων σωτηρίας, εἴχετ᾽ ἂν Ἀμφίπολιν τότε καὶ πάντων τῶν μετὰ ταῦτ᾽ ἂν ἦτ᾽ ἀπηλλαγμένοι πραγμάτων. καὶ πάλιν ἡνίκα Πύδνα, 9 Ποτείδαια, Μεθώνη, Παγασαί, τἄλλ᾽, ἵνα μὴ καθ᾽ ἕκαστα λέγων διατρίβω, πολιορκούμεν᾽ ἀπηγγέλλετο, εἰ τότε τούτων ἑνὶ τῷ πρώτῳ προθύμως καὶ ὡς προσῆκεν ἐβοηθήσαμεν αὐτοί, ῥᾴονι καὶ πολὺ ταπεινοτέρῳ νῦν ἂν ἐχρώμεθα τῷ Φιλίππῳ. νῦν δὲ τὸ μὲν παρὸν ἀεὶ προϊέμενοι, τὰ δὲ μέλλοντ᾽ αὐτόματ᾽ οἰόμενοι σχήσειν καλῶς, ηὐξήσαμεν, ὦ ἄνδρες Ἀθηναῖοι, Φίλιππον ἡμεῖς καὶ κατεστήσαμεν τηλικοῦτον, ἡλίκος οὐδείς πω βασιλεὺς γέγονε Μακεδονίας.

Νυνὶ δὴ καιρὸς ἥκει τις, οὗτος ὁ τῶν Ὀλυνθίων, αὐτόματος τῇ πόλει, ὃς οὐδενός ἐστιν ἐλάττων τῶν προτέρων ἐκείνων. καὶ ἔμοιγε δοκεῖ τις ἄν, ὦ ἄνδρες 10 Ἀθηναῖοι, δίκαιος λογιστὴς τῶν παρὰ τῶν θεῶν ἡμῖν ὑπηργμένων καταστάς, καίπερ οὐκ ἐχόντων ὡς δεῖ πολλῶν, ὅμως μεγάλην ἂν ἔχειν αὐτοῖς χάριν, εἰκότως· τὸ μὲν γὰρ πόλλ᾽ ἀπολωλεκέναι κατὰ τὸν πόλεμον τῆς ἡμετέρας ἀμελείας ἄν τις θείη δικαίως, τὸ δὲ μήτε πάλαι τοῦτο πεπονθέναι πεφηνέναι τέ τιν᾽ ἡμῖν συμμαχίαν τούτων ἀντίρροπον, ἂν βουλώμεθα χρῆσθαι, τῆς παρ᾽ ἐκείνων εὐνοίας εὐεργέτημ᾽ ἂν ἔγωγε θείην. ἀλλ᾽, οἶμαι, παρόμοιόν ἐστιν ὅπερ καὶ 11 περὶ τῆς τῶν χρημάτων κτήσεως· ἂν μὲν γάρ, ὅσ᾽ ἄν τις λάβῃ, καὶ σώσῃ, μεγάλην ἔχει τῇ τύχῃ τὴν χάριν, ἂν δ' ἀναλώσας λάθῃ, συνανήλωσε καὶ τὸ μεμνῆσθαι [τὴν χάριν]. καὶ περὶ τῶν πραγμάτων οὕτως· οἱ μὴ χρησάμενοι τοῖς καιροῖς ὀρθῶς, οὐδ' εἰ συνέβη τι παρὰ τῶν θεῶν χρηστόν, μνημονεύουσι· πρὸς γὰρ τὸ τελευταῖον ἐκβὰν ἕκαστον τῶν πρὶν ὑπαρξάντων κρίνεται. διὸ καὶ σφόδρα δεῖ τῶν λοιπῶν ὑμᾶς, ὦ ἄνδρες Ἀθηναῖοι, φροντίσαι, ἵνα ταῦτ' ἐπανορθωσάμενοι τὴν ἐπὶ τοῖς πεπραγμένοις ἀδοξίαν

12 ἀποτριψώμεθα. εἰ δὲ προησόμεθ', ὦ ἄνδρες Ἀθηναῖοι, καὶ τούτους τοὺς ἀνθρώπους, εἶτ' Ὄλυνθον ἐκεῖνος καταστρέψεται, φρασάτω τις ἐμοὶ τί τὸ κωλῦον ἔτ' αὐτὸν ἔσται βαδίζειν ὅποι βούλεται. ἆρα λογίζεταί τις ὑμῶν, ὦ ἄνδρες Ἀθηναῖοι, καὶ θεωρεῖ τὸν τρόπον δι' ὃν μέγας γέγονεν ἀσθενὴς ὢν τὸ κατ' ἀρχὰς Φίλιππος; τὸ πρῶτον Ἀμφίπολιν λαβών, μετὰ ταῦτα Πύδναν, πάλιν Ποτείδαιαν, Μεθώνην

13 αὖθις, εἶτα Θετταλίας ἐπέβη· μετὰ ταῦτα Φεράς, Παγασάς, Μαγνησίαν, πάνθ' ὃν ἐβούλετ' εὐτρεπίσας τρόπον ᾤχετ' εἰς Θρᾴκην· εἶτ' ἐκεῖ τοὺς μὲν ἐκβαλών, τοὺς δὲ καταστήσας τῶν βασιλέων, ἠσθένησεν· πάλιν ῥάσας οὐκ ἐπὶ τὸ ῥᾳθυμεῖν ἀπέκλινεν, ἀλλ' εὐθὺς Ὀλυνθίοις ἐπεχείρησεν. τὰς δ' ἐπ' Ἰλλυριοὺς καὶ Παίονας αὐτοῦ καὶ πρὸς Ἀρύββαν καὶ ὅποι τις ἂν εἴποι παραλείπω στρατείας.

14 Τί οὖν, ἄν τις εἴποι, ταῦτα λέγεις ἡμῖν νῦν; ἵνα γνῶτ', ὦ ἄνδρες Ἀθηναῖοι, καὶ αἴσθησθ' ἀμφότερα, καὶ τὸ προΐεσθαι καθ' ἕκαστον ἀεί τι τῶν πραγμάτων ὡς ἀλυσιτελές, καὶ τὴν φιλοπραγμοσύνην ᾗ χρῆται καὶ συζῇ Φίλιππος, ὑφ' ἧς οὐκ ἔστιν ὅπως ἀγαπήσας τοῖς πεπραγμένοις ἡσυχίαν σχήσει. εἰ δ' ὁ μὲν ὡς ἀεί τι μεῖζον τῶν ὑπαρχόντων δεῖ πράττειν

ΟΛΥΝΘΙΑΚΟΣ Α

ἐγνωκὼς ἔσται, ἡμεῖς δ' ὡς οὐδενὸς ἀντιληπτέον ἐρρωμένως τῶν πραγμάτων, σκοπεῖσθ' εἰς τί ποτ' ἐλπὶς ταῦτα τελευτῆσαι. πρὸς θεῶν, τίς οὕτως 15 εὐήθης ἐστὶν ὑμῶν ὅστις ἀγνοεῖ τὸν ἐκεῖθεν πόλεμον δεῦρ' ἥξοντα, ἂν ἀμελήσωμεν; ἀλλὰ μήν, εἰ τοῦτο γενήσεται, δέδοικ', ὦ ἄνδρες Ἀθηναῖοι, μὴ τὸν αὐτὸν τρόπον ὥσπερ οἱ δανειζόμενοι ῥᾳδίως ἐπὶ τοῖς μεγάλοις [τόκοις] μικρὸν εὐπορήσαντες χρόνον ὕστερον καὶ τῶν ἀρχαίων ἀπέστησαν, οὕτως καὶ ἡμεῖς [ἂν] ἐπὶ πολλῷ φανῶμεν ἐρραθυμηκότες, καὶ ἅπαντα πρὸς ἡδονὴν ζητοῦντες πολλὰ καὶ χαλεπὰ ὧν οὐκ ἐβουλόμεθ' ὕστερον εἰς ἀνάγκην ἔλθωμεν ποιεῖν, καὶ κινδυνεύσωμεν περὶ τῶν ἐν αὐτῇ τῇ χώρᾳ.

Τὸ μὲν οὖν ἐπιτιμᾶν ἴσως φήσαι τις ἂν ῥᾴδιον 16 καὶ παντὸς εἶναι, τὸ δ' ὑπὲρ τῶν παρόντων ὅ τι δεῖ πράττειν ἀποφαίνεσθαι, τοῦτ' εἶναι συμβούλου. ἐγὼ δ' οὐκ ἀγνοῶ μέν, ὦ ἄνδρες Ἀθηναῖοι, τοῦθ', ὅτι πολλάκις ὑμεῖς οὐ τοὺς αἰτίους ἀλλὰ τοὺς ὑστάτους περὶ τῶν πραγμάτων εἰπόντας ἐν ὀργῇ ποιεῖσθε, ἄν τι μὴ κατὰ γνώμην ἐκβῇ· οὐ μὴν οἶμαι δεῖν τὴν ἰδίαν ἀσφάλειαν σκοποῦνθ' ὑποστείλασθαι περὶ ὧν ὑμῖν συμφέρειν ἡγοῦμαι. φημὶ δὴ διχῇ βοηθητέον εἶναι 17 τοῖς πράγμασιν ὑμῖν, τῷ τε τὰς πόλεις τοῖς Ὀλυνθίοις σῴζειν καὶ τοὺς τοῦτο ποιήσοντας στρατιώτας ἐκπέμπειν, καὶ τῷ τὴν ἐκείνου χώραν κακῶς ποιεῖν καὶ τριήρεσι καὶ στρατιώταις ἑτέροις· εἰ δὲ θατέρου τούτων ὀλιγωρήσετε, ὀκνῶ μὴ μάταιος ἡμῖν ἡ στρατεία γένηται. εἴτε γὰρ ὑμῶν τὴν ἐκείνου κακῶς 18 ποιούντων, ὑπομείνας τοῦτ' Ὄλυνθον παραστήσεται, ῥᾳδίως ἐπὶ τὴν οἰκείαν ἐλθὼν ἀμυνεῖται· εἴτε βοηθησάντων μόνον ὑμῶν εἰς Ὄλυνθον, ἀκινδύνως ὁρῶν ἔχοντα τὰ οἴκοι προσκαθεδεῖται καὶ προσεδρεύσει τοῖς πράγμασι, περιέσται τῷ χρόνῳ τῶν πολιορκουμένων. δεῖ δὴ πολλὴν καὶ διχῇ τὴν βοήθειαν εἶναι.

19 Καὶ περὶ μὲν τῆς βοηθείας ταῦτα γιγνώσκω· περὶ δὲ χρημάτων πόρου. ἔστιν, ὦ ἄνδρες Ἀθηναῖοι, χρήμαθ᾽ ὑμῖν, ἔστιν ὅσ᾽ οὐδενὶ τῶν ἄλλων ἀνθρώπων στρατιωτικά· ταῦτα δ᾽ ὑμεῖς οὕτως ὡς βούλεσθε λαμβάνετε. εἰ μὲν οὖν ταῦτα τοῖς στρατευομένοις ἀποδώσετε, οὐδενὸς ὑμῖν προσδεῖ πόρου, εἰ δὲ μή, προσδεῖ, μᾶλλον δ᾽ ἅπαντος ἐνδεῖ τοῦ πόρου. τί οὖν; ἄν τις εἴποι, σὺ γράφεις ταῦτ᾽ εἶναι στρατιω-
20 τικά; μὰ Δί᾽ οὐκ ἔγωγε. ἐγὼ μὲν γὰρ ἡγοῦμαι στρατιώτας δεῖν κατασκευασθῆναι καὶ ταῦτ᾽ εἶναι στρατιωτικὰ καὶ μίαν σύνταξιν εἶναι τὴν αὐτὴν τοῦ τε λαμβάνειν καὶ τοῦ ποιεῖν τὰ δέοντα, ὑμεῖς δ᾽ οὕτω πως ἄνευ πραγμάτων λαμβάνειν εἰς τὰς ἑορτάς. ἔστι δὴ λοιπόν, οἶμαι, πάντας εἰσφέρειν, ἂν πολλῶν δέῃ, πολλά, ἂν ὀλίγων, ὀλίγα. δεῖ δὲ χρημάτων, καὶ ἄνευ τούτων οὐδὲν ἔστι γενέσθαι τῶν δεόντων. λέγουσι δὲ καὶ ἄλλους τινὰς ἄλλοι πόρους, ὧν ἕλεσθ᾽ ὅστις ὑμῖν συμφέρειν δοκεῖ· καὶ ἕως ἐστὶ καιρός, ἀντιλάβεσθε τῶν πραγμάτων.

21 Ἄξιον δ᾽ ἐνθυμηθῆναι καὶ λογίσασθαι τὰ πράγματ᾽ ἐν ᾧ καθέστηκε νυνὶ τὰ Φιλίππου. οὔτε γάρ, ὡς δοκεῖ καὶ φήσειέ τις ἂν μὴ σκοπῶν ἀκριβῶς, εὐτρεπῶς οὐδ᾽ ὡς ἂν κάλλιστ᾽ αὐτῷ τὰ παρόντ᾽ ἔχει, οὔτ᾽ ἂν ἐξήνεγκε τὸν πόλεμόν ποτε τοῦτον ἐκεῖνος, εἰ πολεμεῖν ᾠήθη δεήσειν αὐτόν, ἀλλ᾽ ὡς ἐπιὼν ἅπαντα τότ᾽ ἤλπιζε τὰ πράγματ᾽ ἀναιρήσεσθαι, κᾆτα διέψευσται. τοῦτο δὴ πρῶτον αὐτὸν ταράττει παρὰ γνώμην γεγονὸς καὶ πολλὴν ἀθυμίαν αὐτῷ παρέχει,

ΟΛΥΝΘΙΑΚΟΣ Α

εἶτα τὰ τῶν Θετταλῶν· ταῦτα γὰρ ἄπιστα μὲν ἦν 22
δήπου φύσει καὶ ἀεὶ πᾶσιν ἀνθρώποις, κομιδῇ δ᾽,
ὥσπερ ἦν, καὶ ἔστι νῦν τούτῳ. καὶ γὰρ Παγασὰς
ἀπαιτεῖν αὐτόν εἰσιν ἐψηφισμένοι, καὶ Μαγνησίαν
κεκωλύκασι τειχίζειν. ἤκουον δ᾽ ἔγωγέ τινων ὡς
οὐδὲ τοὺς λιμένας καὶ τὰς ἀγορὰς ἔτι δώσοιεν αὐτῷ
καρποῦσθαι· τὰ γὰρ κοινὰ τὰ Θετταλῶν ἀπὸ τούτων
δέοι διοικεῖν, οὐ Φίλιππον λαμβάνειν. εἰ δὲ τούτων
ἀποστερήσεται τῶν χρημάτων, εἰς στενὸν κομιδῇ τὰ
τῆς τροφῆς τοῖς ξένοις αὐτῷ καταστήσεται. ἀλλὰ 23
μὴν τόν γε Παίονα καὶ τὸν Ἰλλυριὸν καὶ ἁπλῶς
τούτους ἅπαντας ἡγεῖσθαι χρὴ αὐτονόμους ἥδιον ἂν
καὶ ἐλευθέρους ἢ δούλους εἶναι· καὶ γὰρ ἀήθεις τοῦ
κατακούειν τινός εἰσι, καὶ ἄνθρωπος ὑβριστής, ὥς
φασιν. καὶ μὰ Δί᾽ οὐδὲν ἄπιστον ἴσως· τὸ γὰρ εὖ
πράττειν παρὰ τὴν ἀξίαν ἀφορμὴ τοῦ κακῶς φρονεῖν
τοῖς ἀνοήτοις γίγνεται, διόπερ πολλάκις δοκεῖ τὸ
φυλάξαι τἀγαθὰ τοῦ κτήσασθαι χαλεπώτερον εἶναι.
δεῖ τοίνυν ὑμᾶς, ὦ ἄνδρες Ἀθηναῖοι, τὴν ἀκαιρίαν 24
τὴν ἐκείνου καιρὸν ὑμέτερον νομίσαντας ἑτοίμως
συνάρασθαι τὰ πράγματα, καὶ πρεσβευομένους ἐφ᾽
ἃ δεῖ καὶ στρατευομένους αὐτοὺς καὶ παροξύνοντας
τοὺς ἄλλους ἅπαντας, λογιζομένους, εἰ Φίλιππος
λάβοι καθ᾽ ἡμῶν τοιοῦτον καιρὸν καὶ πόλεμος γένοιτο πρὸς τῇ χώρᾳ, πῶς ἂν αὐτὸν οἴεσθ᾽ ἑτοίμως ἐφ᾽
ὑμᾶς ἐλθεῖν; εἶτ᾽ οὐκ αἰσχύνεσθε, εἰ μηδ᾽ ἃ πάθοιτ᾽
ἄν, εἰ δύναιτ᾽ ἐκεῖνος, ταῦτα ποιῆσαι καιρὸν ἔχοντες
οὐ τολμήσετε;

Ἔτι τοίνυν, ὦ ἄνδρες Ἀθηναῖοι, μηδὲ τοῦθ᾽ ὑμᾶς 25
λανθανέτω, ὅτι νῦν αἵρεσίς ἐστιν ὑμῖν πότερ᾽ ὑμᾶς
ἐκεῖ χρὴ πολεμεῖν ἢ παρ᾽ ὑμῖν ἐκεῖνον. ἐὰν μὲν γὰρ
ἀντέχῃ τὰ τῶν Ὀλυνθίων, ὑμεῖς ἐκεῖ πολεμήσετε καὶ

ΔΗΜΟΣΘΕΝΟΥΣ ΟΛΥΝΘΙΑΚΟΣ Α

τὴν ἐκείνου κακῶς ποιήσετε, τὴν ὑπάρχουσαν καὶ τὴν οἰκείαν ταύτην ἀδεῶς καρπούμενοι· ἂν δ' ἐκεῖνα Φίλιππος λάβῃ, τίς αὐτὸν κωλύσει δεῦρο βαδίζειν; 26 Θηβαῖοι; μὴ λίαν πικρὸν εἰπεῖν ᾖ—καὶ συνεισβαλοῦσιν ἑτοίμως. ἀλλὰ Φωκεῖς; οἱ τὴν οἰκείαν οὐχ οἷοί τ' ὄντες φυλάττειν, ἐὰν μὴ βοηθήσηθ' ὑμεῖς ἢ ἄλλος τις. ἀλλ', ὦταν, οὐχὶ βουλήσεται. τῶν ἀτοπωτάτων μεντἂν εἴη, εἰ ἃ νῦν ἄνοιαν ὀφλισκάνων 27 ὅμως ἐκλαλεῖ, ταῦτα δυνηθεὶς μὴ πράξει. ἀλλὰ μὴν ἡλίκα γ' ἐστὶν τὰ διάφορ' ἐνθάδ' ἢ ἐκεῖ πολεμεῖν οὐδὲ λόγου προσδεῖν ἡγοῦμαι. εἰ γὰρ ὑμᾶς δεήσειεν αὐτοὺς τριάκονθ' ἡμέρας μόνας ἔξω γενέσθαι καὶ ὅσ' ἀνάγκη στρατοπέδῳ χρωμένους τῶν ἐκ τῆς χώρας λαμβάνειν, μηδενὸς ὄντος ἐν αὐτῇ πολεμίου λέγω, πλέον ἂν οἶμαι ζημιωθῆναι τοὺς γεωργοῦντας ὑμῶν ἢ ὅσ' εἰς ἅπαντα τὸν πρὸ τοῦ πόλεμον δεδαπάνησθε. εἰ δὲ δὴ πόλεμός τις ἥξει, πόσα χρὴ νομίσαι ζημιώσεσθαι; καὶ πρόσεσθ' ἡ ὕβρις καὶ ἔθ' ἡ τῶν πραγμάτων αἰσχύνη, οὐδεμιᾶς ἐλάττων ζημία τοῖς γε σώφροσιν.

28 Πάντα δὴ ταῦτα δεῖ συνιδόντας ἅπαντας βοηθεῖν καὶ ἀπωθεῖν ἐκεῖσε τὸν πόλεμον, τοὺς μὲν εὐπόρους, ἵν' ὑπὲρ τῶν πολλῶν ὧν καλῶς ποιοῦντες ἔχουσι μίκρ' ἀναλίσκοντες τὰ λοιπὰ καρπῶνται ἀδεῶς, τοὺς δ' ἐν ἡλικίᾳ, ἵνα τὴν τοῦ πολεμεῖν ἐμπειρίαν ἐν τῇ Φιλίππου χώρᾳ κτησάμενοι φοβεροὶ φύλακες τῆς οἰκείας ἀκεραίου γένωνται, τοὺς δὲ λέγοντας, ἵν' αἱ τῶν πεπολιτευμένων αὐτοῖς εὔθυναι ῥᾴδιαι γένωνται, ὡς ὁποῖ' ἄττ' ἂν ὑμᾶς περιστῇ τὰ πράγματα, τοιοῦτοι κριταὶ καὶ τῶν πεπραγμένων αὐτοῖς ἔσεσθε. χρηστὰ δ' εἴη παντὸς εἵνεκα.

ΟΛΥΝΘΙΑΚΟΣ Β

ΥΠΟΘΕΣΙΣ

Προσήκαντο μὲν τὴν πρεσβείαν τῶν Ὀλυνθίων οἱ Ἀθηναῖοι καὶ βοηθεῖν αὐτοῖς κεκρίκασι· μέλλουσι δὲ περὶ τὴν ἔξοδον καὶ δεδιόσιν ὡς δυσπολεμήτου τοῦ Φιλίππου παρελθὼν ὁ Δημοσθένης πειρᾶται θαρσύνειν τὸν δῆμον, ἐπιδεικνὺς ὡς ἀσθενῆ τὰ τοῦ Μακεδόνος πράγματα. καὶ γὰρ τοῖς συμμάχοις ὕποπτον αὐτὸν εἶναί φησι καὶ κατὰ τὴν ἰδίαν δύναμιν οὐκ ἰσχυρόν· τοὺς γὰρ Μακεδόνας ἀσθενεῖς εἶναι καθ' ἑαυτούς.

Ἐπὶ πολλῶν μὲν ἄν τις ἰδεῖν, ὦ ἄνδρες Ἀθηναῖοι, δοκεῖ μοι τὴν παρὰ τῶν θεῶν εὔνοιαν φανερὰν γιγνομένην τῇ πόλει, οὐχ ἥκιστα δ' ἐν τοῖς παροῦσι πράγμασι· τὸ γὰρ τοὺς πολεμήσοντας Φιλίππῳ γεγενῆσθαι καὶ χώραν ὅμορον καὶ δύναμίν τινα κεκτημένους, καὶ τὸ μέγιστον ἁπάντων, τὴν ὑπὲρ τοῦ πολέμου γνώμην τοιαύτην ἔχοντας, ὥστε τὰς πρὸς ἐκεῖνον διαλλαγὰς πρῶτον μὲν ἀπίστους, εἶτα τῆς ἑαυτῶν πατρίδος νομίζειν ἀνάστασιν, δαιμονίᾳ τινὶ καὶ θείᾳ παντάπασιν ἔοικεν εὐεργεσίᾳ. δεῖ 2 τοίνυν, ὦ ἄνδρες Ἀθηναῖοι, τοῦτ' ἤδη σκοπεῖν αὐτούς, ὅπως μὴ χείρους περὶ ἡμᾶς αὐτοὺς εἶναι δόξομεν τῶν ὑπαρχόντων, ὡς ἔστι τῶν αἰσχρῶν, μᾶλλον δὲ τῶν αἰσχίστων, μὴ μόνον πόλεων καὶ τόπων ὧν ἦμέν ποτε κύριοι φαίνεσθαι προϊεμένους, ἀλλὰ καὶ τῶν ὑπὸ τῆς τύχης παρασκευασθέντων συμμάχων καὶ καιρῶν.

3 Τὸ μὲν οὖν, ὦ ἄνδρες Ἀθηναῖοι, τὴν Φιλίππου ῥώμην διεξιέναι καὶ διὰ τούτων τῶν λόγων προτρέπειν τὰ δέοντα ποιεῖν ὑμᾶς, οὐχὶ καλῶς ἔχειν ἡγοῦμαι. διὰ τί; ὅτι μοι δοκεῖ πάνθ᾿ ὅσ᾿ ἂν εἴποι τις ὑπὲρ τούτων, ἐκείνῳ μὲν ἔχειν φιλοτιμίαν, ἡμῖν δ᾿ οὐχὶ καλῶς πεπρᾶχθαι ὁ μὲν γὰρ ὅσῳ πλεῖον᾿ ὑπὲρ τὴν ἀξίαν πεποίηκε τὴν αὐτοῦ, τοσούτῳ θαυμαστότερος παρὰ πᾶσι νομίζεται· ὑμεῖς δ᾿ ὅσῳ χεῖρον ἢ προσῆκε κέχρησθε τοῖς πράγμασιν, τοσούτῳ 4 πλεῖον᾿ αἰσχύνην ὠφλήκατε. ταῦτα μὲν οὖν παραλείψω. καὶ γὰρ εἰ μετ᾿ ἀληθείας τις, ὦ ἄνδρες Ἀθηναῖοι, σκοποῖτο, ἐνθένδ᾿ ἂν αὐτὸν ἴδοι μέγαν γεγενημένον, οὐχὶ παρ᾿ αὐτοῦ. ὧν οὖν ἐκεῖνος μὲν ὀφείλει τοῖς ὑπὲρ αὐτοῦ πεπολιτευμένοις χάριν, ὑμῖν δὲ δίκην προσήκει λαβεῖν, οὐχὶ νῦν ὁρῶ τὸν καιρὸν τοῦ λέγειν· ἃ δὲ καὶ χωρὶς τούτων ἔνι, καὶ βέλτιόν ἐστιν ἀκηκοέναι πάντας ὑμᾶς, καὶ μεγάλ᾿, ὦ ἄνδρες Ἀθηναῖοι, κατ᾿ ἐκείνου φαίνοιτ᾿ ἂν ὀνείδη βουλομένοις ὀρθῶς δοκιμάζειν, ταῦτ᾿ εἰπεῖν πειράσομαι.

5 Τὸ μὲν οὖν ἐπίορκον κἄπιστον καλεῖν ἄνευ τοῦ τὰ πεπραγμένα δεικνύναι, λοιδορίαν εἶναί τις ἂν φήσειεν κενὴν δικαίως· τὸ δὲ πάνθ᾿ ὅσα πώποτ᾿ ἔπραξε διεξιόντ᾿ ἐφ᾿ ἅπασι τούτοις ἐλέγχειν, καὶ βραχέος λόγου συμβαίνει δεῖσθαι, καὶ δυοῖν ἕνεχ᾿ ἡγοῦμαι συμφέρειν εἰρῆσθαι, τοῦ τ᾿ ἐκεῖνον, ὅπερ καὶ ἀληθὲς ὑπάρχει, φαῦλον φαίνεσθαι, καὶ τοὺς ὑπερεκπεπληγμένους ὡς ἄμαχόν τινα τὸν Φίλιππον ἰδεῖν

ΟΛΥΝΘΙΑΚΟΣ Β

ὅτι πάντα διεξελήλυθεν οἷς πρότερον παρακρουόμενος μέγας ηὐξήθη, καὶ πρὸς αὐτὴν ἥκει τὴν τελευτὴν τὰ πράγματ' αὐτοῦ. ἐγὼ γάρ, ὦ ἄνδρες Ἀθηναῖοι, 6 σφόδρ' ἂν ἡγούμην καὶ αὐτὸς φοβερὸν τὸν Φίλιππον καὶ θαυμαστόν, εἰ τὰ δίκαια πράττονθ' ἑώρων ηὐξημένον· νῦν δὲ θεωρῶν καὶ σκοπῶν εὑρίσκω τὴν μὲν ἡμετέραν εὐήθειαν τὸ κατ' ἀρχάς, ὅτ' Ὀλυνθίους ἀπήλαυνόν τινες ἐνθένδε βουλομένους ὑμῖν διαλεχθῆναι, τῷ τὴν Ἀμφίπολιν φάσκειν παραδώσειν καὶ τὸ θρυλούμενόν ποτ' ἀπόρρητον ἐκεῖνο κατασκευάσαι, τούτῳ προσαγαγόμενον, τὴν δ' Ὀλυνθίων φιλίαν μετὰ 7 ταῦτα τῷ Ποτείδαιαν οὖσαν ὑμετέραν ἐξελεῖν καὶ τοὺς μὲν πρότερον συμμάχους [ὑμᾶς] ἀδικῆσαι, παραδοῦναι δ' ἐκείνοις, Θετταλοὺς δὲ νῦν τὰ τελευταῖα τῷ Μαγνησίαν παραδώσειν ὑποσχέσθαι καὶ τὸν Φωκικὸν πόλεμον πολεμήσειν ὑπὲρ αὐτῶν ἀναδέξασθαι. ὅλως δ' οὐδείς ἐστιν ὅντιν' οὐ πεφενάκικ' ἐκεῖνος τῶν αὐτῷ χρησαμένων· τὴν γὰρ ἑκάστων ἄνοιαν ἀεὶ τῶν ἀγνοούντων αὐτὸν ἐξαπατῶν καὶ προσλαμβάνων οὕτως ηὐξήθη. ὥσπερ οὖν διὰ τούτ- 8 ων ἤρθη μέγας, ἡνίχ' ἕκαστοι συμφέρον αὐτὸν ἑαυτοῖς ᾤοντό τι πράξειν, οὕτως ὀφείλει διὰ τῶν αὐτῶν τούτων καὶ καθαιρεθῆναι πάλιν, ἐπειδὴ πάνθ' ἕνεχ' ἑαυτοῦ ποιῶν ἐξελήλεγκται. καιροῦ μὲν δή, ὦ ἄνδρες Ἀθηναῖοι, πρὸς τοῦτο πάρεστι Φιλίππῳ τὰ πράγματα· ἢ παρελθών τις ἐμοί, μᾶλλον δ' ὑμῖν δειξάτω, ὡς οὐκ ἀληθῆ ταῦτ' ἐγὼ λέγω, ἢ ὡς οἱ τὰ πρῶτ' ἐξηπατημένοι τὰ λοιπὰ πιστεύσουσιν. ἢ ὡς οἱ παρὰ τὴν αὐτῶν ἀξίαν δεδουλωμένοι [Θετταλοὶ] νῦν οὐκ ἂν ἐλεύθεροι γένοινθ' ἄσμενοι.

Καὶ μὴν εἴ τις ὑμῶν ταῦτα μὲν οὕτως ἔχειν 9

ἡγεῖται, οἴεται δὲ βίᾳ καθέξειν αὐτὸν τὰ πράγματα
τῷ τὰ χωρία καὶ λιμένας καὶ τὰ τοιαῦτα προειληφέναι, οὐκ ὀρθῶς οἴεται ὅταν μὲν γὰρ ὑπ' εὐνοίας
τὰ πράγματα συστῇ καὶ πᾶσι ταὐτὰ συμφέρῃ τοῖς
μετέχουσι τοῦ πολέμου, καὶ συμπονεῖν καὶ φέρειν
τὰς συμφορὰς καὶ μένειν ἐθέλουσιν ἄνθρωποι· ὅταν
δ' ἐκ πλεονεξίας καὶ πονηρίας τις ὥσπερ οὗτος
ἰσχύσῃ, ἡ πρώτη πρόφασις καὶ μικρὸν πταῖσμ'
10 ἅπαντ' ἀνεχαίτισε καὶ διέλυσεν. οὐ γὰρ ἔστιν, οὐκ
ἔστιν, ὦ ἄνδρες Ἀθηναῖοι, ἀδικοῦντα κἀπιορκοῦντα
καὶ ψευδόμενον δύναμιν βεβαίαν κτήσασθαι, ἀλλὰ
τὰ τοιαῦτ' εἰς μὲν ἅπαξ καὶ βραχὺν χρόνον ἀντέχει,
καὶ σφόδρα γ' ἤνθησεν ἐπὶ ταῖς ἐλπίσιν, ἂν τύχῃ, τῷ
χρόνῳ δὲ φωρᾶται καὶ περὶ αὐτὰ καταρρεῖ. ὥσπερ
γὰρ οἰκίας, οἶμαι, καὶ πλοίου καὶ τῶν ἄλλων τῶν
τοιούτων τὰ κάτωθεν ἰσχυρότατ' εἶναι δεῖ, οὕτω καὶ
τῶν πράξεων τὰς ἀρχὰς καὶ τὰς ὑποθέσεις ἀληθεῖς
καὶ δικαίας εἶναι προσήκει. τοῦτο δ' οὐκ ἔνι νῦν ἐν
τοῖς πεπραγμένοις Φιλίππῳ.

11 Φημὶ δὴ δεῖν ἡμᾶς τοῖς μὲν Ὀλυνθίοις βοηθεῖν,
καὶ ὅπως τις λέγει κάλλιστα καὶ τάχιστα, οὕτως
ἀρέσκει μοι. πρὸς δὲ Θετταλοὺς πρεσβείαν πέμπειν,
ἣ τοὺς μὲν διδάξει ταῦτα, τοὺς δὲ παροξυνεῖ· καὶ γὰρ
νῦν εἰσιν ἐψηφισμένοι Παγασὰς ἀπαιτεῖν καὶ περὶ
12 Μαγνησίας λόγους ποιεῖσθαι. σκοπεῖσθε μέντοι
τοῦτ', ὦ ἄνδρες Ἀθηναῖοι, ὅπως μὴ λόγους ἐροῦσιν
μόνον οἱ παρ' ἡμῶν πρέσβεις, ἀλλὰ καὶ ἔργον τι
δεικνύειν ἕξουσιν, ἐξεληλυθότων ὑμῶν ἀξίως τῆς
πόλεως καὶ ὄντων ἐπὶ τοῖς πράγμασιν· ὡς ἅπας μὲν
λόγος, ἂν ἀπῇ τὰ πράγματα, μάταιόν τι φαίνεται
καὶ κενόν, μάλιστα δ' ὁ παρὰ τῆς ἡμετέρας πόλεως·

ΟΛΥΝΘΙΑΚΟΣ Β

ὅσῳ γὰρ ἑτοιμότατ' αὐτῷ δοκοῦμεν χρῆσθαι, τοσούτῳ μᾶλλον ἀπιστοῦσι πάντες αὐτῷ. πολλὴν δὴ τὴν 13 μετάστασιν καὶ μεγάλην δεικτέον τὴν μεταβολήν, εἰσφέροντας, ἐξιόντας, ἅπαντα ποιοῦντας ἑτοίμως, εἴπερ τις ὑμῖν προσέξει τὸν νοῦν. κἂν ταῦτ' ἐθελήσηθ' ὡς προσήκει καὶ δεῖ περαίνειν, οὐ μόνον, ὦ ἄνδρες Ἀθηναῖοι, τὰ συμμαχικὰ ἀσθενῶς καὶ ἀπίστως ἔχοντα φανήσεται Φιλίππῳ, ἀλλὰ καὶ τὰ τῆς οἰκείας ἀρχῆς καὶ δυνάμεως κακῶς ἔχοντ' ἐξελεγχθήσεται.

Ὅλως μὲν γὰρ ἡ Μακεδονικὴ δύναμις καὶ ἀρχὴ 14 ἐν μὲν προσθήκῃ μερίς ἐστίν τις οὐ μικρά, οἷον ὑπῆρξέν ποθ' ὑμῖν ἐπὶ Τιμοθέου πρὸς Ὀλυνθίους· πάλιν αὖ πρὸς Ποτείδαιαν Ὀλυνθίοις ἐφάνη τι τοῦτο συναμφότερον· νυνὶ δὲ Θετταλοῖς στασιάζουσι καὶ τεταραγμένοις ἐπὶ τὴν τυραννικὴν οἰκίαν ἐβοήθησεν· καὶ ὅποι τις ἂν, οἶμαι, προσθῇ κἂν μικρὰν δύναμιν, πάντ' ὠφελεῖ· αὐτὴ δὲ καθ' αὑτὴν ἀσθενὴς καὶ πολλῶν κακῶν ἐστι μεστή. καὶ γὰρ οὗτος 15 ἅπασι τούτοις, οἷς ἄν τις μέγαν αὐτὸν ἡγήσαιτο, τοῖς πολέμοις καὶ ταῖς στρατείαις, ἔτ' ἐπισφαλεστέραν ἢ ὑπῆρχε φύσει κατεσκεύακεν αὐτῷ. μὴ γὰρ οἴεσθ', ὦ ἄνδρες Ἀθηναῖοι, τοῖς αὐτοῖς Φίλιππόν τε χαίρειν καὶ τοὺς ἀρχομένους, ἀλλ' ὁ μὲν δόξης ἐπιθυμεῖ καὶ τοῦτ' ἐζήλωκε καὶ προῄρηται πράττων καὶ κινδυνεύων, ἂν συμβῇ τι, παθεῖν, τὴν τοῦ διαπράξασθαι ταῦθ' ἃ μηδεὶς πώποτ' ἄλλος Μακεδόνων βασιλεὺς δόξαν ἀντὶ τοῦ ζῆν ἀσφαλῶς ᾑρημένος· τοῖς δὲ τῆς μὲν φιλοτιμίας τῆς ἀπὸ τούτων οὐ μέτ- 16 εστι, κοπτόμενοι δ' ἀεὶ ταῖς στρατείαις ταύταις ταῖς ἄνω κάτω λυποῦνται καὶ συνεχῶς ταλαιπωροῦσιν,

ΔΗΜΟΣΘΕΝΟΥΣ

οὔτ' ἐπὶ τοῖς ἔργοις οὔτ' ἐπὶ τοῖς αὐτῶν ἰδίοις ἐώμενοι διατρίβειν, οὔθ' ὅσ' ἂν ποιήσωσιν οὕτως ὅπως ἂν δύνωνται, ταῦτ' ἔχοντες διαθέσθαι, κεκλειμένων τῶν 17 ἐμπορίων τῶν ἐν τῇ χώρᾳ διὰ τὸν πόλεμον. οἱ μὲν οὖν πολλοὶ Μακεδόνων πῶς ἔχουσι Φιλίππῳ, ἐκ τούτων ἄν τις σκέψαιτ' οὐ χαλεπῶς· οἱ δὲ δὴ περὶ αὐτὸν ὄντες ξένοι καὶ πεζέταιροι δόξαν μὲν ἔχουσιν ὡς εἰσὶ θαυμαστοὶ καὶ συγκεκροτημένοι τὰ τοῦ πολέμου, ὡς δ' ἐγὼ τῶν ἐν αὐτῇ τῇ χώρᾳ γεγενημένων τινὸς ἤκουον, ἀνδρὸς οὐδαμῶς οἵου τε ψεύδεσθαι, 18 οὐδένων εἰσὶν βελτίους. εἰ μὲν γάρ τις ἀνήρ ἐστιν ἐν αὐτοῖς οἷος ἔμπειρος πολέμου καὶ ἀγώνων, τούτους μὲν φιλοτιμίᾳ πάντας ἀπωθεῖν αὐτὸν ἔφη, βουλόμενον πάνθ' αὐτοῦ δοκεῖν εἶναι τὰ ἔργα· πρὸς γὰρ αὖ τοῖς ἄλλοις καὶ τὴν φιλοτιμίαν ἀνυπέρβλητον εἶναι· εἰ δέ τις σώφρων ἢ δίκαιος ἄλλως, τὴν καθ' ἡμέραν ἀκρασίαν τοῦ βίου καὶ μέθην καὶ κορδακισμοὺς οὐ δυνάμενος φέρειν, παρεῶσθαι καὶ ἐν 19 οὐδενὸς εἶναι μέρει τὸν τοιοῦτον. λοιποὺς δὴ περὶ αὐτὸν εἶναι λῃστὰς καὶ κόλακας καὶ τοιούτους ἀνθρώπους, οἵους μεθυσθέντας ὀρχεῖσθαι τοιαῦθ' οἷ' ἐγὼ νῦν ὀκνῶ πρὸς ὑμᾶς ὀνομάσαι. δῆλον δ' ὅτι ταῦτ' ἐστὶν ἀληθῆ· καὶ γὰρ οὓς ἐνθένδε πάντες ἀπήλαυνον ὡς πολὺ τῶν θαυματοποιῶν ἀσελγεστέρους ὄντας, Καλλίαν ἐκεῖνον τὸν δημόσιον καὶ τοιούτους ἀνθρώπους, μίμους γελοίων καὶ ποιητὰς αἰσχρῶν ᾀσμάτων, ὧν εἰς τοὺς συνόντας ποιοῦσιν ἕνεκα τοῦ γελασθῆναι, 20 τούτους ἀγαπᾷ καὶ περὶ αὐτὸν ἔχει. καίτοι ταῦτα, καὶ εἰ μικρά τις ἡγεῖται, μεγάλ', ὦ ἄνδρες Ἀθηναῖοι, δείγματα τῆς ἐκείνου γνώμης καὶ κακοδαιμονίας ἐστὶν τοῖς εὖ φρονοῦσιν. ἀλλ', οἶμαι, νῦν μὲν ἐπισκοτεῖ

ΟΛΥΝΘΙΑΚΟΣ Β

τούτοις τὸ κατορθοῦν· αἱ γὰρ εὐπραξίαι δειναὶ συγκρύψαι τὰ τοιαῦτ' ὀνείδη εἰ δέ τι πταίσει, τότ' ἀκριβῶς αὐτοῦ ταῦτ' ἐξετασθήσεται. δοκεῖ δ' ἔμοιγ'. ὦ ἄνδρες Ἀθηναῖοι, δείξειν οὐκ εἰς μακράν, ἂν οἵ τε θεοὶ θέλωσι καὶ ὑμεῖς βούλησθε. ὥσπερ γὰρ ἐν τοῖς 21 σώμασιν, τέως μὲν ἂν ἐρρωμένος ᾖ τις, οὐδὲν ἐπαισθάνεται, ἐπὰν δ' ἀρρώστημά τι συμβῇ, πάντα κινεῖται, κἂν ῥῆγμα κἂν στρέμμα κἂν ἄλλο τι τῶν ὑπαρχόντων σαθρὸν ᾖ, οὕτω καὶ τῶν πόλεων καὶ τῶν τυράννων, ἕως μὲν ἂν ἔξω πολεμῶσιν, ἀφανῆ τὰ κακὰ τοῖς πολλοῖς ἐστιν, ἐπειδὰν δ' ὅμορος πόλεμος συμπλακῇ, πάντ' ἐποίησεν ἔκδηλα.

Εἰ δέ τις ὑμῶν, ὦ ἄνδρες Ἀθηναῖοι, τὸν Φίλιππον 22 εὐτυχοῦνθ' ὁρῶν ταύτῃ φοβερὸν προσπολεμῆσαι νομίζει, σώφρονος μὲν ἀνθρώπου λογισμῷ χρῆται· μεγάλη γὰρ ῥοπή, μᾶλλον δὲ τὸ ὅλον ἡ τύχη παρὰ πάντ' ἐστὶ τὰ τῶν ἀνθρώπων πράγματα· οὐ μὴν ἀλλ' ἔγωγ', εἴ τις αἵρεσίν μοι δοίη, τὴν τῆς ἡμετέρας πόλεως τύχην ἂν ἑλοίμην, ἐθελόντων ἃ προσήκει ποιεῖν ὑμῶν αὐτῶν καὶ κατὰ μικρόν, ἢ τὴν ἐκείνου· πολὺ γὰρ πλείους ἀφορμὰς εἰς τὸ τὴν παρὰ τῶν θεῶν εὔνοιαν ἔχειν ὁρῶ ὑμῖν ἐνούσας ἢ 'κείνῳ. ἀλλ', 23 οἶμαι, καθήμεθ' οὐδὲν ποιοῦντες· οὐκ ἔνι δ' αὐτὸν ἀργοῦντ' οὐδὲ τοῖς φίλοις ἐπιτάττειν ὑπὲρ αὐτοῦ τι ποιεῖν, μή τί γε δὴ τοῖς θεοῖς. οὐ δὴ θαυμαστόν ἐστιν, εἰ στρατευόμενος καὶ πονῶν ἐκεῖνος αὐτὸς καὶ παρὼν ἐφ' ἅπασι καὶ μήτε καιρὸν μήθ' ὥραν παραλείπων ἡμῶν μελλόντων καὶ ψηφιζομένων καὶ πυνθανομένων περιγίγνεται οὐδὲ θαυμάζω τοῦτ' ἐγώ· τοὐναντίον γὰρ ἂν ἦν θαυμαστόν, εἰ μηδὲν ποιοῦντες ἡμεῖς ὧν τοῖς πολεμοῦσι προσήκει τοῦ

ΔΗΜΟΣΘΕΝΟΥΣ

24 πάντα ποιοῦντος περιῆμεν. ἀλλ' ἐκεῖνο θαυμάζω, εἰ Λακεδαιμονίοις μέν ποτ', ὦ ἄνδρες Ἀθηναῖοι, ὑπὲρ τῶν Ἑλληνικῶν δικαίων ἀντήρατε, καὶ πόλλ' ἰδίᾳ πλεονεκτῆσαι πολλάκις ὑμῖν ἐξὸν οὐκ ἠθελήσατε, ἀλλ' ἵν' οἱ ἄλλοι τύχωσι τῶν δικαίων, τὰ ὑμέτερ' αὐτῶν ἀνηλίσκετ' εἰσφέροντες καὶ προὐκινδυνεύετε στρατευόμενοι, νυνὶ δ' ὀκνεῖτ' ἐξιέναι καὶ μέλλετ' εἰσφέρειν ὑπὲρ τῶν ὑμετέρων αὐτῶν κτημάτων, καὶ τοὺς μὲν ἄλλους σεσώκατε πολλάκις πάντας καὶ καθ' ἕν' αὐτῶν ἐν μέρει, τὰ δ' ὑμέτερ' αὐτῶν ἀπολ-
25 ωλεκότες κάθησθε. ταῦτα θαυμάζω, κἄτι πρὸς τούτοις, εἰ μηδεὶς ὑμῶν, ὦ ἄνδρες Ἀθηναῖοι, δύναται λογίσασθαι, πόσον πολεμεῖτε χρόνον Φιλίππῳ καὶ τί ποιούντων ὑμῶν ὁ χρόνος διελήλυθεν οὗτος. ἴστε γὰρ δήπου τοῦθ', ὅτι μελλόντων αὐτῶν, ἑτέρους τινὰς ἐλπιζόντων πράξειν, αἰτιωμένων ἀλλήλους, κρινόντων, πάλιν ἐλπιζόντων, σχεδὸν ταῦθ' ἅπερ νυνὶ
26 ποιούντων, ἅπας ὁ χρόνος διελήλυθεν. εἶθ' οὕτως ἀγνωμόνως ἔχετ', ὦ ἄνδρες Ἀθηναῖοι, ὥστε δι' ὧν ἐκ χρηστῶν φαῦλα τὰ πράγματα τῆς πόλεως γέγονεν, διὰ τούτων ἐλπίζετε τῶν αὐτῶν πράξεων ἐκ φαύλων αὐτὰ χρηστὰ γενήσεσθαι; ἀλλ' οὔτ' εὔλογον οὔτ' ἔχον ἐστὶ φύσιν τοῦτό γε· πολὺ γὰρ ῥᾷον ἔχοντας φυλάττειν ἢ κτήσασθαι πάντα πέφυκεν. νῦν δ' ὅ τι μὲν φυλάξομεν, οὐδέν ἐστιν ὑπὸ τοῦ πολέμου λοιπὸν τῶν πρότερον, κτήσασθαι δὲ δεῖ. αὐτῶν οὖν ἡμῶν ἔργον τοῦτ' ἤδη.
27 Φημὶ δὴ δεῖν εἰσφέρειν χρήματα, αὐτοὺς ἐξιέναι προθύμως, μηδέν' αἰτιᾶσθαι πρὶν ἂν τῶν πραγμάτων κρατήσητε, τηνικαῦτα δ' ἀπ' αὐτῶν τῶν ἔργων κρίναντας τοὺς μὲν ἀξίους ἐπαίνου τιμᾶν, τοὺς δ' ἀδι-

κοῦντας κολάζειν, τὰς προφάσεις δ' ἀφελεῖν καὶ τὰ καθ' ὑμᾶς ἐλλείμματα· οὐ γάρ ἐστι πικρῶς ἐξετάσαι τί πέπρακται τοῖς ἄλλοις, ἂν μὴ παρ' ὑμῶν αὐτῶν πρῶτον ὑπάρξῃ τὰ δέοντα. τίνος γὰρ ἕνεκ', ὦ ἄνδρες 28 Ἀθηναῖοι, νομίζετε τοῦτον μὲν φεύγειν τὸν πόλεμον πάντας ὅσους ἂν ἐκπέμψητε στρατηγούς, ἰδίους δ' εὑρίσκειν πολέμους, εἰ δεῖ τι τῶν ὄντων καὶ περὶ τῶν στρατηγῶν εἰπεῖν; ὅτι ἐνταῦθα μέν ἐστι τὰ ἆθλ' ὑπὲρ ὧν ἐστιν ὁ πόλεμος ὑμέτερα [Ἀμφίπολις] κἂν ληφθῇ παραχρῆμ' ὑμεῖς κομιεῖσθε, οἱ δὲ κίνδυνοι τῶν ἐφεστηκότων ἴδιοι, μισθὸς δ' οὐκ ἔστιν· ἐκεῖ δὲ κίνδυνοι μὲν ἐλάττους, τὰ δὲ λήμματα τῶν ἐφεστηκότων καὶ τῶν στρατιωτῶν, Λάμψακος, Σίγειον, τὰ πλοῖ' ἃ συλῶσιν. ἐπ' οὖν τὸ λυσιτελοῦν αὐτοῖς ἕκαστοι χωροῦσιν. ὑμεῖς δ' ὅταν μὲν εἰς τὰ πράγ- 29 ματ' ἀποβλέψητε φαύλως ἔχοντα, τοὺς ἐφεστηκότας κρίνετε, ὅταν δὲ δόντες λόγον τὰς ἀνάγκας ἀκούσητε ταύτας, ἀφίετε. περίεστιν τοίνυν ὑμῖν ἀλλήλοις ἐρίζειν καὶ διεστάναι, τοῖς μὲν ταῦτα πεπεισμένοις, τοῖς δὲ ταῦτα, τὰ κοινὰ δ' ἔχειν φαύλως. πρότερον μὲν γάρ, ὦ ἄνδρες Ἀθηναῖοι, εἰσεφέρετε κατὰ συμμορίας, νυνὶ δὲ πολιτεύεσθε κατὰ συμμορίας. ῥήτωρ ἡγεμὼν ἑκατέρων καὶ στρατηγὸς ὑπὸ τούτῳ καὶ οἱ βοησόμενοι τριακόσιοι· οἱ δ' ἄλλοι προσνενέμησθε, οἱ μὲν ὡς τούτους, οἱ δ' ὡς ἐκείνους. δεῖ δὴ ταῦτ' 30 ἐπανέντας καὶ ὑμῶν αὐτῶν ἔτι καὶ νῦν γενομένους κοινὸν καὶ τὸ βουλεύεσθαι καὶ τὸ λέγειν καὶ τὸ πράττειν ποιῆσαι. εἰ δὲ τοῖς μὲν ὥσπερ ἐκ τυραννίδος ὑμῶν ἐπιτάττειν ἀποδώσετε, τοῖς δ' ἀναγκάζεσθαι τριηραρχεῖν, εἰσφέρειν, στρατεύεσθαι, τοῖς δὲ ψηφίζεσθαι κατὰ τούτων μόνον, ἄλλο δὲ μηδ' ὁτιοῦν συμπονεῖν, οὐχὶ γενήσεται τῶν δεόντων ὑμῖν οὐδὲν ἐν καιρῷ· τὸ γὰρ ἠδικημένον ἀεὶ μέρος ἐλλείψει, εἶθ᾽ ὑμῖν τούτους κολάζειν ἀντὶ τῶν ἐχθρῶν ἐξέσται.

31 Λέγω δὴ κεφάλαιον, πάντας εἰσφέρειν ἀφ᾽ ὅσων ἕκαστος ἔχει τὸ ἴσον· πάντας ἐξιέναι κατὰ μέρος, ἕως ἂν ἅπαντες στρατεύσησθε· πᾶσι τοῖς παριοῦσι λόγον διδόναι, καὶ τὰ βέλτισθ᾽ ὧν ἂν ἀκούσηθ᾽ αἱρεῖσθαι, μὴ ἂν ὁ δεῖν᾽ ἢ ὁ δεῖν᾽ εἴπῃ. κἂν ταῦτα ποιῆτε, οὐ τὸν εἰπόντα μόνον παραχρῆμ᾽ ἐπαινέσεσθε, ἀλλὰ καὶ ὑμᾶς αὐτοὺς ὕστερον, βέλτιον τῶν ὅλων πραγμάτων ὑμῖν ἐχόντων.

ΟΛΥΝΘΙΑΚΟΣ Γ

ΥΠΟΘΕΣΙΣ

Ἔπεμψαν βοήθειαν τοῖς Ὀλυνθίοις οἱ Ἀθηναῖοι, καί τι κατορθοῦν ἔδοξαν δι' αὐτῆς· καὶ ταῦτ' αὐτοῖς ἀπηγγέλλετο. ὁ δὲ δῆμος περιχαρής, οἵ τε ῥήτορες παρακαλοῦντες ἐπὶ τιμωρίαν Φιλίππου. ὁ δὲ Δημοσθένης δεδοικὼς μὴ θαρσήσαντες, ὡς τὰ πάντα νενικηκότες καὶ ἱκανὴν βοήθειαν πεποιημένοι τοῖς Ὀλυνθίοις, τῶν λοιπῶν ὀλιγωρήσωσι, διὰ τοῦτο παρελθὼν ἐπικόπτει τὴν ἀλαζονείαν αὐτῶν καὶ πρὸς εὐλάβειαν σώφρονα τὴν γνώμην μεθίστησι, λέγων οὐ περὶ τῆς Φιλίππου τιμωρίας νῦν αὐτοῖς εἶναι τὸν λόγον, ἀλλὰ περὶ τῆς τῶν συμμάχων σωτηρίας. οἶδεν γὰρ ὅτι καὶ Ἀθηναῖοι καὶ ἄλλοι πού τινες τοῦ μὲν μὴ τὰ οἰκεῖα προέσθαι ποιοῦνται φροντίδα, περὶ δὲ τὸ τιμωρήσασθαι τοὺς ἐναντίους ἧττον σπουδάζουσιν. ἐν 2 δὲ τούτῳ τῷ λόγῳ καὶ τῆς περὶ τῶν θεωρικῶν χρημάτων συμβουλῆς φανερώτερον ἅπτεται, καὶ ἀξιοῖ λυθῆναι τοὺς νόμους τοὺς ἐπιτιθέντας ζημίαν τοῖς γράψασιν αὐτὰ γενέσθαι στρατιωτικά, ἵν' ἀδεὲς ᾖ τὸ συμβουλεύειν τὰ βέλτιστα. παραινεῖ δὲ καὶ ὅλως πρὸς τὸν τῶν προγόνων ζῆλον ἀναστῆναι καὶ στρατεύεσθαι σώμασιν οἰκείοις, καὶ ἐπιτιμήσει πολλῇ κέχρηται κατὰ τοῦ δήμου θ' ὡς ἐκλελυμένου καὶ τῶν δημαγωγῶν ὡς οὐκ ὀρθῶς προϊσταμένων τῆς πόλεως.

Οὐχὶ ταὐτὰ παρίσταταί μοι γιγνώσκειν, ὦ ἄνδρες Ἀθηναῖοι, ὅταν τ' εἰς τὰ πράγματ' ἀποβλέψω καὶ ὅταν πρὸς τοὺς λόγους οὓς ἀκούω· τοὺς μὲν γὰρ λόγους περὶ τοῦ τιμωρήσασθαι Φίλιππον ὁρῶ γιγνομένους, τὰ δὲ πράγματ' εἰς τοῦτο προήκοντα, ὥσθ' ὅπως μὴ πεισόμεθ' αὐτοὶ πρότερον κακῶς σκέψασθαι δέον. οὐδὲν οὖν ἄλλο μοι δοκοῦσιν οἱ τὰ τοιαῦτα λέγοντες ἢ τὴν ὑπόθεσιν, περὶ ἧς βουλεύεσθε, οὐχὶ

2 τὴν οὖσαν παριστάντες ὑμῖν ἁμαρτάνειν. ἐγὼ δ' ὅτι μέν ποτ' ἐξῆν τῇ πόλει καὶ τὰ αὑτῆς ἔχειν ἀσφαλῶς καὶ Φίλιππον τιμωρήσασθαι, καὶ μάλ' ἀκριβῶς οἶδα· ἐπ' ἐμοῦ γάρ, οὐ πάλαι, γέγονε ταῦτ' ἀμφότερα· νῦν μέντοι πέπεισμαι τοῦθ' ἱκανὸν προλαβεῖν ἡμῖν εἶναι τὴν πρώτην, ὅπως τοὺς συμμάχους σώσομεν. ἐὰν γὰρ τοῦτο βεβαίως ὑπάρξῃ, τότε καὶ περὶ τοῦ τίνα τιμωρήσεταί τις καὶ ὃν τρόπον ἐξέσται σκοπεῖν· πρὶν δὲ τὴν ἀρχὴν ὀρθῶς ὑποθέσθαι μάταιον ἡγοῦμαι περὶ τῆς τελευτῆς ὁντινοῦν ποιεῖσθαι λόγον.

3 Ὁ μὲν οὖν παρὼν καιρός, εἴπερ ποτέ, πολλῆς φροντίδος καὶ βουλῆς δεῖται· ἐγὼ δ' οὐχ ὅ τι χρὴ περὶ τῶν παρόντων συμβουλεῦσαι χαλεπώτατον ἡγοῦμαι, ἀλλ' ἐκεῖν' ἀπορῶ, τίνα χρὴ τρόπον, ὦ ἄνδρες Ἀθηναῖοι, πρὸς ὑμᾶς περὶ αὐτῶν εἰπεῖν. πέπεισμαι γὰρ ἐξ ὧν παρὼν καὶ ἀκούων σύνοιδα, τὰ πλείω τῶν πραγμάτων ἡμᾶς ἐκπεφευγέναι τῷ μὴ βούλεσθαι τὰ δέοντα ποιεῖν ἢ τῷ μὴ συνιέναι. ἀξιῶ δ' ὑμᾶς, ἂν μετὰ παρρησίας ποιῶμαι τοὺς λόγους, ὑπομένειν, τοῦτο θεωροῦντας, εἰ τἀληθῆ λέγω. καὶ διὰ τοῦτο, ἵνα τὰ λοιπὰ βελτίω γένηται· ὁρᾶτε γὰρ ὡς ἐκ τοῦ πρὸς χάριν δημηγορεῖν ἐνίους εἰς πᾶν προελήλυθε μοχθηρίας τὰ παρόντα.

4 Ἀναγκαῖον δ' ὑπολαμβάνω μικρὰ τῶν γεγενη-

ΟΛΥΝΘΙΑΚΟΣ Γ

μένων πρῶτον ὑμᾶς ὑπομνῆσαι. μέμνησθ', ὦ ἄνδρες Ἀθηναῖοι, ὅτ' ἀπηγγέλθη Φίλιππος ὑμῖν ἐν Θρᾴκῃ τρίτον ἢ τέταρτον ἔτος τουτὶ Ἡραῖον τεῖχος πολιορκῶν. τότε τοίνυν μὴν μὲν ἦν μαιμακτηριών, πολλῶν δὲ λόγων καὶ θορύβου γιγνομένου παρ' ὑμῖν ἐψηφίσασθε τετταράκοντα τριήρεις καθέλκειν καὶ τοὺς μέχρι πέντε καὶ τετταράκοντ' ἐτῶν αὐτοὺς ἐμβαίνειν καὶ τάλανθ' ἑξήκοντ' εἰσφέρειν. καὶ μετὰ ταῦτα 5 διελθόντος τοῦ ἐνιαυτοῦ τούτου, ἑκατομβαιών, μεταγειτνιών, βοηδρομιών—τούτου τοῦ μηνὸς μόγις μετὰ τὰ μυστήρια δέκα ναῦς ἀπεστείλατ' ἔχοντα κενὰς Χαρίδημον καὶ πέντε τάλαντ' ἀργυρίου. ὡς γὰρ ἠγγέλθη Φίλιππος ἀσθενῶν ἢ τεθνεώς (ἦλθε γὰρ ἀμφότερα), οὐκέτι καιρὸν οὐδένα τοῦ βοηθεῖν νομίσαντες ἀφεῖτ', ὦ ἄνδρες Ἀθηναῖοι, τὸν ἀπόστολον. ἦν δ' οὗτος ὁ καιρὸς αὐτός· εἰ γὰρ τότ' ἐκεῖσ' ἐβοηθήσαμεν, ὥσπερ ἐψηφισάμεθα, προθύμως, οὐκ ἂν ἠνώχλει νῦν ἡμῖν ὁ Φίλιππος σωθείς.

Τὰ μὲν δὴ τότε πραχθέντ' οὐκ ἂν ἄλλως ἔχοι. 6 νῦν δ' ἑτέρου πολέμου καιρὸς ἥκει τις, δι' ὃν καὶ περὶ τούτων ἐμνήσθην, ἵνα μὴ ταὐτὰ πάθητε. τί δὴ χρησόμεθ', ὦ ἄνδρες Ἀθηναῖοι, τούτῳ; εἰ γὰρ μὴ βοηθήσετε παντὶ σθένει κατὰ τὸ δυνατόν, θεάσασθ' ὃν τρόπον ὑμεῖς ἐστρατηγηκότες πάντ' ἔσεσθ' ὑπὲρ Φιλίππου. ὑπῆρχον Ὀλύνθιοι δύναμίν τινα κεκτη- 7 μένοι καὶ διέκειθ' οὕτω τὰ πράγματα· οὔτε Φίλιππος ἐθάρρει τούτους οὔθ' οὗτοι Φίλιππον. ἐπράξαμεν ἡμεῖς κἀκεῖνοι πρὸς ἡμᾶς εἰρήνην· ἦν τοῦθ' ὥσπερ ἐμπόδισμά τι τῷ Φιλίππῳ καὶ δυσχερές, πόλιν μεγάλην ἐφορμεῖν τοῖς ἑαυτοῦ καιροῖς διηλλαγμένην πρὸς ἡμᾶς. ἐκπολεμῶσαι δεῖν ᾠόμεθα τοὺς ἀνθρώ-

πους ἐκ παντὸς τρόπου, καὶ ὃ ἅπαντες ἐθρύλουν,
8 πέπρακται νυνὶ τοῦθ' ὁπωσδήποτε. τί οὖν ὑπόλοιπον, ὦ ἄνδρες Ἀθηναῖοι, πλὴν βοηθεῖν ἐρρωμένως καὶ προθύμως; ἐγὼ μὲν οὐχ ὁρῶ· χωρὶς γὰρ τῆς περιστάσης ἂν ἡμᾶς αἰσχύνης, εἰ καθυφείμεθά τι τῶν πραγμάτων, οὐδὲ τὸι φόβον, ὦ ἄνδρες Ἀθηναῖοι, μικρὸν ὁρῶ τὸν τῶν μετὰ ταῦτα, ἐχόντων μὲν ὡς ἔχουσι Θηβαίων ἡμῖν, ἀπειρηκότων δὲ χρήμασι Φωκέων, μηδενὸς δ' ἐμποδὼν ὄντος Φιλίππῳ τὰ παρόντα καταστρεψαμένῳ πρὸς ταῦτ' ἐπικλῖναι τὰ
9 πράγματα. ἀλλὰ μὴν εἴ τις ὑμῶν εἰς τοῦτ' ἀναβάλλεται ποιήσειν τὰ δέοντα, ἰδεῖν ἐγγύθεν βούλεται τὰ δεινά, ἐξὸν ἀκούειν ἄλλοθι γιγνόμενα, καὶ βοηθοὺς ἑαυτῷ ζητεῖν, ἐξὸν νῦν ἑτέροις αὐτὸν βοηθεῖν· ὅτι γὰρ εἰς τοῦτο περιστήσεται τὰ πράγματα, ἐὰν τὰ παρόντα προώμεθα, σχεδὸν ἴσμεν ἅπαντες δήπου.
10 Ἀλλ' ὅτι μὲν δὴ δεῖ βοηθεῖν, εἴποι τις ἄν, πάντες ἐγνώκαμεν, καὶ βοηθήσομεν· τὸ δ' ὅπως, τοῦτο λέγε. μὴ τοίνυν, ὦ ἄνδρες Ἀθηναῖοι, θαυμάσητε, ἂν παράδοξον εἴπω τι τοῖς πολλοῖς. νομοθέτας καθίσατε. ἐν δὲ τούτοις τοῖς νομοθέταις μὴ θῆσθε νόμον μηδένα (εἰσὶ γὰρ ὑμῖν ἱκανοί), ἀλλὰ τοὺς εἰς τὸ
11 παρὸν βλάπτοντας ὑμᾶς λύσατε. λέγω τοὺς περὶ τῶν θεωρικῶν, σαφῶς οὑτωσί, καὶ τοὺς περὶ τῶν στρατευομένων ἐνίους, ὧν οἱ μὲν τὰ στρατιωτικὰ τοῖς οἴκοι μένουσι διανέμουσι θεωρικά, οἱ δὲ τοὺς ἀτακτοῦντας ἀθῴους καθιστᾶσιν, εἶτα καὶ τοὺς τὰ δέοντα ποιεῖν βουλομένους ἀθυμοτέρους ποιοῦσιν. ἐπειδὰν δὲ ταῦτα λύσητε καὶ τὴν τοῦ τὰ βέλτιστα λέγειν ὁδὸν παράσχητ' ἀσφαλῆ, τηνικαῦτα τὸν γράψονθ' ἃ πάντες ἴσθ' ὅτι συμφέρει ζητεῖτε.

ΟΛΥΝΘΙΑΚΟΣ Γ

πρὶν δὲ ταῦτα πρᾶξαι μὴ σκοπεῖτε τίς εἰπὼν τὰ 12
βέλτισθ' ὑπὲρ ὑμῶν ὑφ' ὑμῶν ἀπολέσθαι βουλή-
σεται· οὐ γὰρ εὑρήσετε, ἄλλως τε καὶ τούτου μόνου
περιγίγνεσθαι μέλλοντος, παθεῖν ἀδίκως τι κακὸν
τὸν ταῦτ' εἰπόντα καὶ γράψαντα, μηδὲν δ' ὠφελῆσαι
τὰ πράγματα, ἀλλὰ καὶ εἰς τὸ λοιπὸν μᾶλλον ἔτ'
ἢ νῦν τὸ τὰ βέλτιστα λέγειν φοβερώτερον ποιῆσαι.
καὶ λύειν γ', ὦ ἄνδρες Ἀθηναῖοι, τοὺς νόμους δεῖ
τούτους τοὺς αὐτοὺς ἀξιοῦν οἵπερ καὶ τεθήκασιν· οὐ 13
γάρ ἐστι δίκαιον, τὴν μὲν χάριν, ἣ πᾶσαν ἔβλαπτε
τὴν πόλιν, τοῖς τότε θεῖσιν ὑπάρχειν, τὴν δ' ἀπέχθειαν, δι' ἧς ἂν ἅπαντες ἄμεινον πράξαιμεν, τῷ νῦν
τὰ βέλτιστ' εἰπόντι ζημίαν γενέσθαι. πρὶν δὲ ταῦτ'
εὐτρεπίσαι μηδαμῶς, ὦ ἄνδρες Ἀθηναῖοι, μηδέν'
ἀξιοῦτε τηλικοῦτον εἶναι παρ' ὑμῖν, ὥστε τοὺς νόμους
τούτους παραβάντα μὴ δοῦναι δίκην, μηδ' οὕτως
ἀνόητον, ὥστ' εἰς προῦπτον κακὸν αὑτὸν ἐμβαλεῖν.

Οὐ μὴν οὐδ' ἐκεῖνό γ' ὑμᾶς ἀγνοεῖν δεῖ, ὦ ἄνδρες 14
Ἀθηναῖοι, ὅτι ψήφισμ' οὐδενὸς ἄξιόν ἐστιν, ἂν μὴ
προσγένηται τὸ ποιεῖν ἐθέλειν τά γε δόξαντα προθύμως ὑμᾶς. εἰ γὰρ αὐτάρκη τὰ ψηφίσματ' ἦν ἢ
ὑμᾶς ἀναγκάζειν ἃ προσήκει πράττειν ἢ περὶ ὧν
γραφείη διαπράξασθαι, οὔτ' ἂν ὑμεῖς πολλὰ ψηφιζόμενοι μικρά, μᾶλλον δ' οὐδὲν ἐπράττετε τούτων, οὔτε
Φίλιππος τοσοῦτον ὑβρίκει χρόνον· πάλαι γὰρ ἂν
ἕνεκά γε ψηφισμάτων ἐδεδώκει δίκην. ἀλλ' οὐχ 15
οὕτω ταῦτ' ἔχει· τὸ γὰρ πράττειν τοῦ λέγειν καὶ
χειροτονεῖν ὕστερον ὂν τῇ τάξει πρότερον τῇ δυνάμει
καὶ κρεῖττόν ἐστιν. τοῦτ' οὖν δεῖ προσεῖναι, τὰ δ'
ἄλλ' ὑπάρχει. καὶ γὰρ εἰπεῖν τὰ δέοντα παρ' ὑμῖν
εἰσιν, ὦ ἄνδρες Ἀθηναῖοι, δυνάμενοι, καὶ γνῶναι

πάντων ὑμεῖς ὀξύτατοι τὰ ῥηθέντα· καὶ πρᾶξαι δὲ δυνήσεσθε νῦν, ἐὰν ὀρθῶς ποιῆτε.

16 Τίνα γὰρ χρόνον ἢ τίνα καιρόν, ὦ ἄνδρες Ἀθηναῖοι, τοῦ παρόντος βελτίω ζητεῖτε; ἢ πόθ' ἃ δεῖ πράξετ', εἰ μὴ νῦν; οὐχ ἅπαντα μὲν ἡμῶν προείληφε τὰ χωρί' ἄνθρωπος, εἰ δὲ καὶ ταύτης κύριος τῆς χώρας γενήσεται, πάντων αἴσχιστα πεισόμεθα; οὐχ οὕς, εἰ πολεμήσαιεν, ἑτοίμως σώσειν ὑπισχνούμεθα, οὗτοι νῦν πολεμοῦσιν; οὐκ ἐχθρός; οὐκ ἔχων τὰ ἡμέτερα; οὐ βάρβαρος; οὐχ ὅ τι ἂν εἴποι τις;

17 ἀλλὰ πρὸς θεῶν πάντ' ἐάσαντες καὶ μόνον οὐχὶ συγκατασκευάσαντες αὐτῷ τότε τοὺς αἰτίους οἵτινες τούτων ζητήσομεν; οὐ γὰρ αὐτοί γ' αἴτιοι φήσομεν εἶναι, σαφῶς οἶδα τοῦτ' ἐγώ. οὐδὲ γὰρ ἐν τοῖς τοῦ πολέμου κινδύνοις τῶν φυγόντων οὐδεὶς ἑαυτοῦ κατηγορεῖ, ἀλλὰ τοῦ στρατηγοῦ καὶ τῶν πλησίον καὶ πάντων μᾶλλον, ἥττηνται δ' ὅμως διὰ πάντας τοὺς φυγόντας δήπου· μένειν γὰρ ἐξῆν τῷ κατηγοροῦντι τῶν ἄλλων, εἰ δ' ἐποίει τοῦθ' ἕκαστος, ἐνίκων ἄν.

18 καὶ νῦν, οὐ λέγει τις τὰ βέλτιστα· ἀναστὰς ἄλλος εἰπάτω, μὴ τοῦτον αἰτιάσθω. ἕτερος λέγει τις βελτίω· ταῦτα ποιεῖτ' ἀγαθῇ τύχῃ. ἀλλ' οὐχ ἡδέα ταῦτα· οὐκέτι τοῦθ' ὁ λέγων ἀδικεῖ, πλὴν εἰ δέον εὔξασθαι παραλείπει. εὔξασθαι μὲν γάρ, ὦ ἄνδρες Ἀθηναῖοι, ῥᾴδιον εἰς ταὐτὸ πάνθ' ὅσα βούλεταί τις ἀθροίσαντ' ἐν ὀλίγῳ, ἑλέσθαι δ' ὅταν περὶ πραγμάτων προτεθῇ σκοπεῖν, οὐκέθ' ὁμοίως εὔπορον, ἀλλὰ δεῖ τὰ βέλτιστ' ἀντὶ τῶν ἡδέων, ἂν μὴ συναμφότερ' ἐξῇ, λαμβάνειν.

19 Εἰ δέ τις ἡμῖν ἔχει καὶ τὰ θεωρικὰ ἐᾶν καὶ πόρους ἑτέρους λέγειν στρατιωτικούς, οὐχ οὗτος κρείττων; εἴποι τις ἄν. φήμ' ἔγωγε, εἴπερ ἔστιν,

ΟΛΥΝΘΙΑΚΟΣ Γ

ὦ ἄνδρες Ἀθηναῖοι· ἀλλὰ θαυμάζω, εἴ τῴ ποτ' ἀνθρώπων ἢ γέγονεν ἢ γενήσεται, ἂν τὰ παρόντ' ἀναλώσῃ πρὸς ἃ μὴ δεῖ, τῶν ἀπόντων εὐπορῆσαι πρὸς ἃ δεῖ. ἀλλ', οἶμαι, μέγα τοῖς τοιούτοις ὑπάρχει λόγοις ἡ παρ' ἑκάστου βούλησις, διόπερ ῥᾷστον ἁπάντων ἐστὶν αὑτὸν ἐξαπατῆσαι· ὃ γὰρ βούλεται, τοῦθ' ἕκαστος καὶ οἴεται, τὰ δὲ πράγματα πολλάκις οὐχ οὕτω πέφυκεν. ὁρᾶτ' οὖν, ὦ ἄνδρες Ἀθηναῖοι, 20 ταῦθ' οὕτως, ὅπως καὶ τὰ πράγματ' ἐνδέχεται καὶ δυνήσεσθ' ἐξιέναι καὶ μισθὸν ἕξετε. οὔ τοι σωφρόνων οὐδὲ γενναίων ἐστὶν ἀνθρώπων ἐλλείποντάς τι δι' ἔνδειαν χρημάτων τῶν τοῦ πολέμου εὐχερῶς τὰ τοιαῦτ' ὀνείδη φέρειν, οὐδ' ἐπὶ μὲν Κορινθίους καὶ Μεγαρέας ἁρπάσαντας τὰ ὅπλα πορεύεσθαι, Φίλιππον δ' ἐᾶν πόλεις Ἑλληνίδας ἀνδραποδίζεσθαι δι' ἀπορίαν ἐφοδίων τοῖς στρατευομένοις.

Καὶ ταῦτ' οὐχ ἵν' ἀπέχθωμαί τισιν ὑμῶν, τὴν 21 ἄλλως προῄρημαι λέγειν· οὐ γὰρ οὕτως ἄφρων οὐδ' ἀτυχής εἰμ' ἐγώ, ὥστ' ἀπεχθάνεσθαι βούλεσθαι μηδὲν ὠφελεῖν νομίζων· ἀλλὰ δικαίου πολίτου κρίνω τὴν τῶν πραγμάτων σωτηρίαν ἀντὶ τῆς ἐν τῷ λέγειν χάριτος αἱρεῖσθαι, καὶ τοὺς ἐπὶ τῶν προγόνων ἡμῶν λέγοντας ἀκούω, ὥσπερ ἴσως καὶ ὑμεῖς, οὓς ἐπαινοῦσι μὲν οἱ παριόντες ἅπαντες, μιμοῦνται δ' οὐ πάνυ, τούτῳ τῷ ἔθει καὶ τῷ τρόπῳ τῆς πολιτείας χρῆσθαι, τὸν Ἀριστείδην ἐκεῖνον, τὸν Νικίαν, τὸν ὁμώνυμον ἐμαυτῷ, τὸν Περικλέα. ἐξ οὗ δ' οἱ 22 διερωτῶντες ὑμᾶς οὗτοι πεφήνασι ῥήτορες, τί βούλεσθε; τί γράψω; τί ὑμῖν χαρίσωμαι; προπέποται τῆς παραυτίχ' ἡδονῆς καὶ χάριτος τὰ τῆς πόλεως πράγματα, καὶ τοιαυτὶ συμβαίνει, καὶ τὰ μὲν τούτων

ΔΗΜΟΣΘΕΝΟΥΣ

23 πάντα καλῶς ἔχει, τὰ δ' ὑμέτερ' αἰσχρῶς. καίτοι σκέψασθ' ὦ ἄνδρες Ἀθηναῖοι, ἅ τις ἂν κεφάλαι' εἰπεῖν ἔχοι τῶν τ' ἐπὶ τῶν προγόνων ἔργων καὶ τῶν ἐφ' ὑμῶν. ἔσται δὲ βραχὺς καὶ γνώριμος ὑμῖν ὁ λόγος· οὐ γὰρ ἀλλοτρίοις ὑμῖν χρωμένοις παραδείγμασιν ἀλλ' οἰκείοις, ὦ ἄνδρες Ἀθηναῖοι, εὐδαίμοσιν 24 ἔξεστι γενέσθαι. ἐκεῖνοι τοίνυν, οἷς οὐκ ἐχαρίζονθ' οἱ λέγοντες οὐδ' ἐφίλουν αὐτοὺς ὥσπερ ὑμᾶς οὗτοι νῦν, πέντε μὲν καὶ τετταράκοντ' ἔτη τῶν Ἑλλήνων ἦρξαν ἑκόντων, πλείω δ' ἢ μύρια τάλαντ' εἰς τὴν ἀκρόπολιν ἀνήγαγον. ὑπήκουε δ' ὁ ταύτην τὴν χώραν ἔχων αὐτοῖς βασιλεύς, ὥσπερ ἐστὶ προσῆκον βάρβαρον Ἕλλησι, πολλὰ δὲ καὶ καλὰ καὶ πεζῇ καὶ ναυμαχοῦντες ἔστησαν τρόπαι' αὐτοὶ στρατευόμενοι, μόνοι δ' ἀνθρώπων κρείττω τὴν ἐπὶ τοῖς ἔργοις δόξαν 25 τῶν φθονούντων κατέλιπον. ἐπὶ μὲν δὴ τῶν Ἑλληνικῶν ἦσαν τοιοῦτοι. ἐν δὲ τοῖς κατὰ τὴν πόλιν αὐτὴν θεάσασθ' ὁποῖοι, ἔν τε τοῖς κοινοῖς καὶ ἐν τοῖς ἰδίοις. δημοσίᾳ μὲν τοίνυν οἰκοδομήματα καὶ κάλλη τοιαῦτα καὶ τοσαῦτα κατεσκεύασαν ἡμῖν ἱερῶν καὶ τῶν ἐν τούτοις ἀναθημάτων, ὥστε μηδενὶ τῶν ἐπιγιγνομένων ὑπερβολὴν λελεῖφθαι· ἰδίᾳ δ' οὕτω σώφρονες ἦσαν καὶ σφόδρ' ἐν τῷ τῆς πολιτείας ἤθει 26 μένοντες, ὥστε τὴν Ἀριστείδου καὶ τὴν Μιλτιάδου καὶ τῶν τότε λαμπρῶν οἰκίαν εἴ τις ἄρ' οἶδεν ὑμῶν ὁποία ποτ' ἐστίν, ὁρᾷ τῆς τοῦ γείτονος οὐδὲν σεμνοτέραν οὖσαν· οὐ γὰρ εἰς περιουσίαν ἐπράττετ' αὐτοῖς τὰ τῆς πόλεως, ἀλλὰ τὸ κοινὸν αὔξειν ἕκαστος ᾤετο δεῖν. ἐκ δὲ τοῦ τὰ μὲν Ἑλληνικὰ πιστῶς, τὰ δὲ πρὸς τοὺς θεοὺς εὐσεβῶς, τὰ δ' ἐν αὑτοῖς ἴσως διοικεῖν μεγάλην εἰκότως ἐκτήσαντ' εὐδαιμονίαν.

ΟΛΥΝΘΙΑΚΟΣ Γ

Τότε μὲν δὴ τοῦτον τὸν τρόπον εἶχε τὰ πράγματ' 27 ἐκείνοις, χρωμένοις οἷς εἶπον προστάταις. νυνὶ δὲ πῶς ἡμῖν ὑπὸ τῶν χρηστῶν τῶν νῦν τὰ πράγματ' ἔχει; ἆρά γ' ὁμοίως καὶ παραπλησίως; οἷς—τὰ μὲν ἄλλα σιωπῶ πόλλ' ἂν ἔχων εἰπεῖν, ἀλλ' ὅσης ἅπαντες ὁρᾶτ' ἐρημίας ἐπειλημμένοι, καὶ Λακεδαιμονίων μὲν ἀπολωλότων, Θηβαίων δ' ἀσχόλων ὄντων, τῶν δ' ἄλλων οὐδενὸς ὄντος ἀξιόχρεω περὶ τῶν πρωτείων ἡμῖν ἀντιτάξασθαι, ἐξὸν δ' ἡμῖν καὶ τὰ ἡμέτερ' αὐτῶν ἀσφαλῶς ἔχειν καὶ τὰ τῶν ἄλλων δίκαια βραβεύειν, ἀπεστερήμεθα μὲν χώρας οἰκείας, 28 πλείω δ' ἢ χίλια καὶ πεντακόσια τάλαντ' ἀνηλώκαμεν εἰς οὐδὲν δέον, οὓς δ' ἐν τῷ πολέμῳ συμμάχους ἐκτησάμεθα, εἰρήνης οὔσης ἀπολωλέκασιν οὗτοι, ἐχθρὸν δ' ἐφ' ἡμᾶς αὐτοὺς τηλικοῦτον ἠσκήκαμεν. ἢ φρασάτω τις ἐμοὶ παρελθών, πόθεν ἄλλοθεν ἰσχυρὸς γέγονεν ἢ παρ' ἡμῶν αὐτῶν Φίλιππος. ἀλλ', 29 ὦταν, εἰ ταῦτα φαύλως, τά γ' ἐν αὐτῇ τῇ πόλει νῦν ἄμεινον ἔχει. καὶ τί ἂν εἰπεῖν τις ἔχοι; τὰς ἐπάλξεις ἃς κονιῶμεν, καὶ τὰς ὁδοὺς ἃς ἐπισκευάζομεν, καὶ κρήνας, καὶ λήρους; ἀποβλέψατε δὴ πρὸς τοὺς ταῦτα πολιτευομένους, ὧν οἱ μὲν ἐκ πτωχῶν πλούσιοι γεγόνασιν, οἱ δ' ἐξ ἀδόξων ἔντιμοι, ἔνιοι δὲ τὰς ἰδίας οἰκίας τῶν δημοσίων οἰκοδομημάτων σεμνοτέρας εἰσὶ κατεσκευασμένοι· ὅσῳ δὲ τὰ τῆς πόλεως ἐλάττω γέγονεν, τοσούτῳ τὰ τούτων ηὔξηται.

Τί δὴ τὸ πάντων αἴτιον τούτων, καὶ τί δή ποθ' 30 ἅπαντ' εἶχε καλῶς τότε, καὶ νῦν οὐκ ὀρθῶς; ὅτι τότε μὲν πράττειν καὶ στρατεύεσθαι τολμῶν αὐτὸς ὁ δῆμος δεσπότης τῶν πολιτευομένων ἦν καὶ κύριος αὐτὸς ἁπάντων τῶν ἀγαθῶν, καὶ ἀγαπητὸν ἦν παρὰ

ΔΗΜΟΣΘΕΝΟΥΣ

τοῦ δήμου τῶν ἄλλων ἑκάστῳ καὶ τιμῆς καὶ ἀρχῆς
31 καὶ ἀγαθοῦ τινος μεταλαβεῖν· νῦν δὲ τοὐναντίον
κύριοι μὲν οἱ πολιτευόμενοι τῶν ἀγαθῶν καὶ διὰ
τούτων ἅπαντα πράττεται, ὑμεῖς δ᾽ ὁ δῆμος ἐκνενευρισμένοι καὶ περιῃρημένοι χρήματα, συμμάχους, ἐν
ὑπηρέτου καὶ προσθήκης μέρει γεγένησθε, ἀγαπῶντες
ἐὰν μεταδιδῶσι θεωρικῶν ὑμῖν ἢ Βοηδρόμια πέμψωσιν οὗτοι, καὶ τὸ πάντων ἀνδρειότατον, τῶν ὑμετέρων
αὐτῶν χάριν προσοφείλετε. οἱ δ᾽ ἐν αὐτῇ τῇ πόλει
καθείρξαντες ὑμᾶς ἐπάγουσιν ἐπὶ ταῦτα καὶ τιθα-
32 σεύουσι χειροήθεις αὑτοῖς ποιοῦντες. ἔστι δ᾽ οὐδέποτ᾽,
οἶμαι, μέγα καὶ νεανικὸν φρόνημα λαβεῖν μικρὰ καὶ
φαῦλα πράττοντας· ὁποῖ᾽ ἄττα γὰρ ἂν τὰ ἐπιτηδεύματα τῶν ἀνθρώπων ᾖ, τοιοῦτον ἀνάγκη καὶ τὸ
φρόνημ᾽ ἔχειν. ταῦτα μὰ τὴν Δήμητρ᾽ οὐκ ἂν θαυ-
μάσαιμ᾽ εἰ μείζων εἰπόντι ἐμοὶ γένοιτο παρ᾽ ὑμῶν
βλάβη τῶν πεποιηκότων αὐτὰ γενέσθαι· οὐδὲ γὰρ
παρρησία περὶ πάντων ἀεὶ παρ᾽ ἡμῖν ἐστιν, ἀλλ᾽
ἔγωγ᾽ ὅτι καὶ νῦν γέγονε θαυμάζω.

33 Ἐὰν οὖν ἀλλὰ νῦν γ᾽ ἔτ᾽ ἀπαλλαγέντες τούτων
τῶν ἐθῶν ἐθελήσητε στρατεύεσθαί τε καὶ πράττειν
ἀξίως ὑμῶν αὐτῶν, καὶ ταῖς περιουσίαις ταῖς οἴκοι
ταύταις ἀφορμαῖς ἐπὶ τὰ ἔξω τῶν ἀγαθῶν χρήσησθε,
ἴσως ἄν, ἴσως, ὦ ἄνδρες Ἀθηναῖοι, τέλειόν τι καὶ
μέγα κτήσαισθ᾽ ἀγαθὸν καὶ τῶν τοιούτων λημμάτων
ἀπαλλαγείητε, ἃ τοῖς ἀσθενοῦσι παρὰ τῶν ἰατρῶν
σιτίοις διδομένοις ἔοικε. καὶ γὰρ ἐκεῖν᾽ οὔτ᾽ ἰσχὺν
ἐντίθησιν οὔτ᾽ ἀποθνῄσκειν ἐᾷ· καὶ ταῦθ᾽ ἃ νέμεσθε
νῦν ὑμεῖς, οὔτε τοσαῦτ᾽ ἐστίν, ὥστ᾽ ὠφέλειαν ἔχειν
τινὰ διαρκῆ, οὔτ᾽ ἀπογνόντας ἄλλο τι πράττειν ἐᾷ,
ἀλλ᾽ ἔστι ταῦτα τὴν ἑκάστου ῥᾳθυμίαν ἡμῶν ἐπαυξάν-

ΟΛΥΝΘΙΑΚΟΣ Γ

οντα. οὐκοῦν σὺ μισθοφορὰν λέγεις; φήσει τις. 34
καὶ παραχρῆμά γε τὴν αὐτὴν σύνταξιν ἁπάντων,
ὦ ἄνδρες Ἀθηναῖοι, ἵνα τῶν κοινῶν ἕκαστος τὸ μέρος
λαμβάνων, ὅτου δέοιθ' ἡ πόλις, τοῦθ' ὑπάρχοι.
ἔξεστιν ἄγειν ἡσυχίαν· οἴκοι μένων βελτίων, τοῦ
δι' ἔνδειαν ἀνάγκῃ τι ποιεῖν αἰσχρὸν ἀπηλλαγμένος.
συμβαίνει τι τοιοῦτον οἷον καὶ τὰ νῦν· στρατιώτης
αὐτὸς ὑπάρχων ἀπὸ τῶν αὐτῶν τούτων λημμάτων,
ὥσπερ ἐστὶ δίκαιον ὑπὲρ τῆς πατρίδος. ἔστι τις ἔξω
τῆς ἡλικίας ἡμῶν· ὅσ' οὗτος ἀτάκτως νῦν λαμβάνων
οὐκ ὠφελεῖ, ταῦτ' ἐν ἴσῃ τάξει λαμβάνων, πάντ'
ἐφορῶν καὶ διοικῶν ἃ χρὴ πράττεσθαι. ὅλως δ' οὔτ' 35
ἀφελὼν οὔτε προσθεὶς πλὴν μικρῶν, τὴν ἀταξίαν
ἀνελὼν εἰς τάξιν ἤγαγον τὴν πόλιν τὴν αὐτὴν τοῦ
λαβεῖν, τοῦ στρατεύεσθαι, τοῦ δικάζειν, τοῦ ποιεῖν
τοῦθ' ὅ τι καθ' ἡλικίαν ἕκαστος ἔχοι καὶ ὅτου καιρὸς
εἴη [τάξιν ποιήσας]. οὐκ ἔστιν ὅπου μηδὲν ἐγὼ
ποιοῦσι τὰ τῶν ποιούντων εἶπον ὡς δεῖ νέμειν, οὐδ'
αὐτοὺς μὲν ἀργεῖν καὶ σχολάζειν καὶ ἀπορεῖν, ὅ τι δ'
οἱ τοῦ δεῖνος νικῶσιν ξένοι, ταῦτα πυνθάνεσθαι·
ταῦτα γὰρ νυνὶ γίγνεται. καὶ οὐχὶ μέμφομαι τὸν 36
ποιοῦντά τι τῶν δεόντων ὑπὲρ ὑμῶν, ἀλλὰ καὶ ὑμᾶς
ὑπὲρ ὑμῶν αὐτῶν ἀξιῶ πράττειν ταῦτ' ἐφ' οἷς ἑτέρους τιμᾶτε, καὶ μὴ παραχωρεῖν, ὦ ἄνδρες Ἀθηναῖοι,
τῆς τάξεως, ἣν ὑμῖν οἱ πρόγονοι τῆς ἀρετῆς μετὰ
πολλῶν καὶ καλῶν κινδύνων κτησάμενοι κατέλιπον.

Σχεδὸν εἴρηχ' ἃ νομίζω συμφέρειν· ὑμεῖς δ'
ἕλοισθ' ὅ τι καὶ τῇ πόλει καὶ ἅπασι συνοίσειν ὑμῖν
μέλλει.

COMMENTARY

FIRST OLYNTHIAC

1. This exordium reappears, with some minor alterations, as the third in the collection of Demosthenic *Prooemia* and was sufficiently well known in antiquity to have been parodied by Lucian (Ζεὺς Τραγῳδός 15) in a speech addressed to an assembly of the Gods.

   ἀντὶ πολλῶν χρημάτων: literally 'in exchange for' or 'in preference to much money'.

   ὦ ἄνδρες Ἀθηναῖοι: the regular method of addressing the *ecclesia*, since this is a deliberative speech - in contrast to ὦ ἄνδρες δικασταί which is used in a forensic speech addressed to a jury.

   ἑλέσθαι: 2nd aorist infinitive middle, from αἱρέω 'I take'. The middle voice of this verb commonly means 'choose' and its passive 'be chosen'.

   ἄν . . . ὑμᾶς ἑλέσθαι νομίζω, εἰ φανερὸν γένοιτο: γένοιτο is aorist optative of γίγνομαι; the construction is that of a future condition, less vivid form (*G*. 1408), in indirect statement, where the infinitive with ἄν represents what would in direct speech be ἄν with the optative (*G*. 1308) - 'I think that you would choose in exchange for a great deal of money (i.e. I think that you would give a great deal to know) if it were to become clear . . .'.

   συνοίσειν: future infinitive of the impersonal verb συμφέρει + dative - 'it is expedient for', 'it is of interest to'.

   περὶ ὧν σκοπεῖτε: for περὶ ἐκείνων ἃ σκοπεῖτε: - 'concerning those matters which you are now considering' - an example of the common practice of 'attracting' a relative pronoun in the accusative to the case of its antecedent, where the antecedent is in the genitive or dative; where the antecedent is a demonstrative pronoun, it is then frequently omitted, especially when unemphatic (*G*. 1032).

   ὅτε: the conjunction has here a causal rather than a temporal force (*G*. 1505) - 'since this is the case'.

   προθύμως: in sense this adverb goes with ἀκούειν but

is taken out of position to give a greater degree of emphasis.

ἀκούειν τῶν βουλομένων: ἀκούω normally takes the accusative when the object is a thing, the genitive when the object is a person (G. 1103).

ἐσκεμμένος: perfect participle of σκοπέω, from the alternative present σκέπτομαι, denoting the present state of the plan - 'if someone has come with an already thought-out useful plan'.

τοῦτ' ἂν ἀκούσαντες λάβοιτε: 'this you would accept, were you to hear it', another example of a less vivid future condition with the protasis taking the form of a participle (ἀκούσαντες is equivalent to εἰ ἀκούσαιτε).

τῆς ὑμετέρας τύχης ὑπολαμβάνω: 'I suppose it to be part of your fortune that . . . ' or 'I suppose it to be the mark / characteristic / nature of your fortune that . . . ', with omission of εἶναι (G. 1094).

ἐκ τοῦ παραχρῆμα: 'on the spur of the moment'.

ἐπελθεῖν ἄν: this represents a direct ἐπέλθοι ἄν. ἐπελθεῖν with the dative here means 'to occur to one', 'to come into one's head'. In this passage Demosthenes is contrasting orators who make premeditated speeches with those who speak *ex tempore*. The most celebrated contemporary example of the latter was Demosthenes' fellow demesman Demades; Demosthenes himself rarely spoke without studied preparation (Plutarch, *Demosthenes* 8.2-5 and 10.1).

2. λέγει φωνὴν ἀφιείς: a rare example in Demosthenes of personification. ἀφιείς is the present participle active of ἀφίημι 'I let go', 'I release', 'I utter'.

ἀντιληπτέον: verbal adjective of ἀντιλαμβάνω 'I seize', 'I take control of'. The verbal adjective in -τέος -τέον (the Greek equivalent of the Latin gerundive) expresses obligation or necessity. Here it is used impersonally and the agent is the dative case - 'it is necessary for you yourselves to take control of' (G. 1597).

ἐκείνων: 'those affairs there', i.e. the affairs of Olynthus and in the northern Aegeam in general. Note the deliberate separation of πραγμάτων from ἐκείνων and of ὑμῖν from αὐτοῖς. This device (*hyperbaton*) is generally used in an atmosphere of passion or excitement,

when the orator wishes to emphasise or give greater
prominence to the words concerned. Here the emphasis
is intended to fall above all on the word αὐτοῖς,
since the personal involvement of the Athenians in the
war lies at the heart of Demosthenes' policies. See
Introduction II 4 f(xiii).

ἡμεῖς δ' οὐκ οἶδ' ὅντινά μοι δοκοῦμεν ἔχειν τρόπον
πρὸς αὐτά: 'but we seem in my opinion to be taking I
don't know what attitude with regard to this'.

δή: frequently in Demosthenes this particle is used to
introduce a specific proposal. In this case the proposal is twofold: (a) the immediate preparation and
despatch of an expeditonary force to Olynthus, and
(b) the sending of an embassy to report on the Athenian
decision and to watch events.

βοηθήσητε: the reading (aorist subjunctive) of all manuscripts save one. If this reading is adopted the object
of παρασκευάσασθαι must be either τὴν βοήθειαν or ὑμᾶς
αὐτούς to be supplied from the context, and the ὅπως
clause would be a final clause with the retention of
the subjunctive mood in historic sequence (G. 1369-70).
Some editors prefer the reading βοηθήσετε (future indicative), found in only one manuscript. If this reading is preferred the ὅπως clause must be construed as
being itself the object of παρασκευάσασθαι. ὅπως and the
future indicative is regularly found as an object clause
after a verb denoting striving, effort, taking care etc.
(G. 1372) - 'to make preparations for the sending of
help'.

τὴν ταχίστην: adverbial accusative (G. 1060) - 'in the
quickest way possible'.

ἐνθένδε: 'from here', i.e. 'from Athens'.

καὶ μὴ πάθητε ταὐτὸν ὅπερ καὶ πρότερον: 'and not to have
the same experience as we have had in the past'. πάσχω
denotes not only 'suffer', but is used to cover situations where something less drastic happens. It is essentially a neutral word indicating only 'to have something happen to one' whether for good or for evil.
'Experience' is perhaps the most suitable translation
here. If βοηθήσητε is adopted in the previous clause
μὴ πάθητε can be taken either as a parenthetical injunction addressed by Demosthenes to his audience or
as a second object clause. Certainly there are examples
of the use of a subjunctive or an optative in an object
clause in preference to a future indicative (G. 1374),
but it would be odd, though not unparalleled, for both
constructions to appear in the same sentence.

ἥτις ταῦτ' ἐρεῖ καὶ παρέσται τοῖς πράγμασι: a relative clause introduced by ὅς or ὅστις frequently denotes purpose when followed by a future indicative (G. 1442). ἐρῶ serves as a future for λέγω alongside the regular λέξω, and other forms from the same root are the perfect active εἴρηκα, the perfect middle εἴρημαι and the aorist passive ἐρρήθην.

3. ὡς ἐστι τοῦτο δέος μή . . . τρέψηται: δέος is here predicative - 'this is our chief fear'. δέος ἐστι is given the normal construction of a verb of fearing, to which it is equivalent; the verb is in the subjunctive in primary sequence (as it would be optative in historic sequence) when the fear is for the future (G. 1378).

πανοῦργος: this word is used as both adjective ('evil', 'villainous', 'unscrupulous') and noun ('a rogue').

δεινὸς πράγμασι χρῆσθαι: 'clever at using events to his own advantage', an appreciation of Philip's accomplishments that comes as close to praise as anything in Demosthenes. For a similar appreciation of Philip in Demosthenes, see 2nd Olynthiac 15. For the use of the infinitive with adjectives denoting ability, fitness, sufficiency, willingness etc., see G. 1526.

ἄνθρωπος: 'the fellow', where ἄνθρωπος is used in a slightly perjorative manner. The form represents ὁ ἄνθρωπος (crasis).

τὰ μὲν εἴκων . . . τὰ δ' ἀπειλῶν: 'sometimes by yielding, at other times by threatening'. Here the article retains its original demonstrative force, and survives in Attic chiefly in contrasts with μέν and δέ (ὁ μὲν . . . ὁ δὲ . . . - 'the one . . . the other'). The neuter, in both singular and plural, is used adverbially ('partly . . . partly', 'now . . . now'); see G. 982.

ἡνίκ' ἂν τύχῃ (sc. εἴκων): 'whenever he happens to yield'. ἄν with the subjunctive is regularly used in indefinite temporal, relative and conditional clauses referring to the present (G. 1431).

ἀξιόπιστος δ' ἂν εἰκότως φαίνοιτο: a parenthetical expression of the sort for which Demosthenes had a particular fondness; see Introduction II 4 e(i). It is to be taken closely with ἀπειλῶν - 'and his threats might reasonably be believed'. The optative with ἄν is here potential (G. 1327).

τρέψεται: the middle voice (present, future and 2nd aorist) of τρέπω means 'turn oneself to', 'have recourse to', 'flee', but the 1st aorist middle in Attic is normally transitive, differing very little in meaning from the active ἔτρεψα. Here, if the text is correct, the word must mean somthing like 'turn to one's own advantage' or 'overturn' but there are no parallels for such meanings in Attic prose. The sense of 'overturn' is regularly found in the compound ἀνατρέπω, hence Dobree amends τρέψηται to ἀνατρέψῃ τε.

παρασπάσηται: aorist middle subjunctive of παρασπάω, with the meaning 'draw aside', 'detach someone from one side and attach him to the other', 'divert for one's own use of advantage'. Presumably the verb is here intended to suggest the forcible wresting from Athens of some advantage which Philip seeks to divert to his own use.

τι τῶν ὅλων πραγμάτων: 'some part of our vital interests'.

4. οὐ μὴν ἀλλά: a combination of particles used in an adversative sense, 'not but what', 'however', denoting that what is said is not to be denied, however strong the arguments to the contrary. See J.D. Denniston, *Greek Particles* 28-30.

ἐπιεικῶς: here placed early in the sentence for emphasis - 'however one may with some justification hold that what is the most impregnable point of Philip's position is at the same time the best of all for us', a typically Demosthenic paradox, designed at the same time to alarm and to encourage his audience.

τὸ γὰρ εἶναι . . . τῷ στρατεύματι: the whole phrase takes the form of a lengthy articular infinitive (*G*. 1542) serving as the subject of the verbs προέχει and ἔχει at the end of the sentence - 'the fact that he thought one individual is the master of everything . . . all this is a great advantage'. Note the effective use made by Demosthenes in the passage of *polysyndeton* in order to build up an impressive list of Philip's advantages; see Introduction II 4 f(vi).

πρὸς μὲν τὸ τὰ τοῦ πολέμου . . . πράττεσθαι: another articular infinitive, this time serving as a substitute for a noun in the accusative case after a preposition (*G*. 1546).

κατὰ καιρόν: 'opportunely', 'at the right time'.

τὰς καταλλαγὰς ἃς ἂν ἐκεῖνος ποιήσαιτ' . . . : 'the compact

which he would gladly make'. Here the optative with ἄν once again represents the less vivid form of the future condition, though in this instance the protasis is suppressed (G. 1413). We have to supply a clause such as 'if the Olynthians were to agree'. The use of the middle voice ποιήσαιτ' in expressions denoting the making of peace, truces, treaties etc. is regular when the reference is to the cities or states concerned (the active voice is found with reference to the individual acting as agent), and here Philip is rightly identified with the Macedonian state; when Philip makes a treaty, he is no mere agent for the Macedonian state but *is* the state.

προέχει . . . ἐναντίως ἔχει: an example of the rhetorical figure known as *antistrophe;* see Introduction II 4 f(ix).

The entire section presents a vivid and forceful picture of Philip's superiority over the Athenians in the military field. The monarchical system, giving as it did to Philip absolute control, a unified command and the ability to make all decisions at all times at will, undoubtedly did enable him to act speedily, as Demosthenes realises only too well. In this passage, the orator is thinking of the contrast between Philip's speed and the lengthy and complicated decision making process at democratic Athens. The contrast, though not made explicit here, occurs in several other passages of Demosthenes, notably *2nd Olynthiac* 23, *2nd Philippic* 3-4 and, above all, *On the Crown* 235-6.

5. δῆλον γάρ . . . ὅτι: an iambic trimeter, followed immediately by a 'limping iambic' or *scazon* (νῦν οὐ περὶ δόξης . . . χώρας). Since Aristotle maintains that the iambic metre is close to ordinary speech (ὁ δὲ ἴαμβός αὐτή ἐστιν ἡ λέξις ἡ τῶν πολλῶν· διὸ μάλιστα πάντων τῶν μέτρων ἰαμβεῖα φθέγγονται λέγοντες, *Rhetoric* 3.8.3; cf. Cicero, *Orator* 56.189 - *senarios vero et Hipponacteos effingere vix possumus: magnam enim partem ex iambis nostra constat oratio*), Demosthenes' use of verse is certainly unintentional, and not without parallel. For other examples of iambic trimeters, see *Against Meidias* 165 and *Against Lacritus* 22; for dactylic hexameter, see *1st Philippic* 6, *On the Crown* 114, 143, 192, 198 and 251, *On the Embassy* 75 and 174, *Against Leptines* 60, 67, 121, 125 and 129, and *Against Meidias* 146 and 179.

οὐ περὶ δόξης οὐδ' ὑπὲρ μέρους χώρας: οὐδέ is emphatic - 'not for glory or even for a portion of their territory'.

κινδυνεύουσι: 'run a risk', preferred by some editors to the manuscript reading πολεμοῦσι, on the grounds that Demosthenes is arguing from a hypothesis that Philip might come to terms with Olynthus. However, the change is unnecessary, for there is no reason to doubt that the fighting had begun before Demosthenes delivered the speech. See 7 below and Introduction, Appendix A.

ἀλλ' ἀναστάσεως καὶ ἀνδραποδισμοῦ τῆς πατρίδος: 'to avoid the destruction and enslavement of their country'. περί or ὑπέρ is to be supplied from the previous phrase.

ἅ . . . ἐποίησε τοὺς παραδόντας αὐτῷ τὴν πόλιν: 'what he did to those who handed over their city to him'. A double accusative is found after the verb ποιέω in the sense of 'treat', 'do something to someone', especially in the phrases ἀγαθὰ ποιεῖν τινα 'to treat someone well' and κακὰ ποιεῖν τινα 'to treat someone badly'; see G. 1073.

Ἀμφιπολιτῶν: the reference here is to Philip's capture (357 B.C.) of Amphipolis, a city on the river Strymon of considerable strategic and economic importance. The language used suggests that treachery on the part of a pro-Macedonian faction contributed to the city's fall, but it was in fact taken by storm (Diodorus 16.8.2). We have no other evidence that Philip treated his Amphipolitan partisans badly. Certainly the anti-Macedonian supporters had their property confiscated when the city fell but Diodorus expressly states that the rest of the population was treated with consideration. Demosthenes may be thinking of the later status of Amphipolis as it gradually lost its automomy and declined to the status of little more than a Macedonian provincial capital and naval base. Cf. Aeschines (*On the Embassy* 27), when he contrasts the wretched condition of the city in 343 B.C. with its heyday in 368/7 B.C., some ten years before its capture by Philip - Ἀμφιπολιτῶν αὐτῶν ἐχόντων τότε (i.e. in 368/7) τὴν πόλιν καὶ τὴν χώραν καρπούντων.

Πυδναίων: the inhabitants of Pydna, a Greek city situated a few miles inland from the west coast of the Thermaic Gulf, an ally of Athens which fell to Philip soon after Amphipolis, late in 357 B.C., apparently by treachery; cf. *Against Leptines* 63 - οἱ προδόντες τὴν Πύδναν τῷ Φιλίππῳ. We have no other evidence as to the fate of its inhabitants, though it is likely that the city was treated in much the same way as Amphipolis.

ὅλως: 'speaking generally', 'as a rule'. The meaning 'wholly' is rare.

ἄπιστον: note the neuter gender - 'tyranny is an object of mistrust'.

ταῖς πολιτείαις: the word here refers to states governed in accordance with the rule of law and is used as the opposite of τυραννίς - 'free states' or 'constitutional governments'.

6. ἐγνωκότας: perfect participle active of γιγνώσκω.

ἃ προσήκει: supply ἐνθυμεῖσθαι, from the following participle ἐνθυμουμένους.

παροξυνθῆναι: aorist infinitive passive of παροξύνω 'I urge on', 'I arouse'.

τῷ πολέμῳ προσέχειν: supply τὸν νοῦν - 'give your attention to the war'.

εἰσφέροντας: this is the verb derived from εἰσφορά, a property tax imposed on Athenians in time of war to help defray military expenses. See Introduction, Appendix B.

καὶ αὐτοὺς ἐξιόντας: the word αὐτοὺς is emphatic. Demosthenes was a strong adherent of the belief that the Athenians must do their own fighting if they were to achieve success in war, and not rely on mercenaries. For similar sentiments in Demosthenes, see Introduction I 2, note 34.

οὐδὲ γὰρ λόγος οὐδὲ σκῆψις ἔτι ὑμῖν: 'you have no longer indeed a reason, nor have you even an excuse'. The words λόγος and σκῆψις are contrasted, the former giving a genuine reason, the latter a mere pretext.

τοῦ μὴ τὰ δέοντα ποιεῖν ἐθέλειν: 'for refusing to do your duty'. The articular infinitive is here used in the genitive dependent on the nouns λόγος and σκῆψις (*G.* 1547). ἐθέλω is generally a weak verb meaning 'to consent to', 'to acquiesce in' but, when accompanied by the negative, it has a much stronger significance; οὐκ ἐθέλω normally means 'I refuse'.

7. ἐθρύλουν τέως: from θρυλέω 'I keep talking about', 'I have constantly on my lips', while τέως means 'hitherto', 'up till then'. Some manuscripts read ἐθρυλεῖτε ὡς which would give the meaning 'the events you all keep

talking about, namely that the Olynthians must become
embroiled in war with Philip'.

γέγον' αὐτόματον: 'it has happened of its own accord'.
γέγονε is the 3rd person singular perfect from γίγνομαι.

καὶ ταῦθ': 'and that too', adding a further element to
the situation.

ὡς ἂν ὑμῖν μάλιστα συμφέροι: 'in such a way as to suit
your interest above all'. ὡς is to be construed here
as a comparative conjunction - 'in the manner that',
while ἂν is to be taken not with ὡς but with συμφέροι
(potential optative; G. 1327-9).

εἰ . . . ἀνείλοντο τὸν πόλεμον . . . σφαλεροὶ σύμμαχοι . . .
ἂν . . . ἦσαν: 'if they had embarked upon the war
. . . they would now be untrustworthy allies'. Here
we have an unreal condition, with an aorist indicative
in the protasis referring to the past, and an imperfect
indicative with ἂν in the apodosis referring to
the present (G. 1397).

καὶ μέχρι του ταῦτ' ἐγνωκότες: 'being resolved up to
a point', i.e. only in part. Unaccented του serves
as the genitive singular of the indefinite pronoun, as
an equivalent of τινος. Similarly τῳ is used for the
dative singular, equivalent of τινι.

ἐκ τῶν πρὸς αὐτοὺς ἐγκλημάτων: 'in consequence of
grievances which they themselves feel'. πρός + accusative
is often used with nouns meaning 'goodwill',
'hatred', 'accusation', in place of the genitive (whether
subjective, as here, or objective). Among examples of
the idiom in Demosthenes may be mentioned the following:-
(a) Subjective: *On the Peace* 17 - ἔγκλημα πρὸς ἅπαντας
- 'a ground of complaint made by everyone'; *2nd Philippic*
3 - τὴν πρὸς ὑμᾶς ἀπέχθειαν ὀκνοῦντες - shrinking from
the hatred you feel'; (b) Objective: *3rd Philippic* 38
- οὐκ ἦν πρίασθαι . . . οὐδὲ τὴν πρὸς τοὺς τυράννους οὐδὲ
τοὺς βαρβάρους ἀπιστίαν - it was not possible to purchase
the mistrust which is felt towards tyrants and barbarians'.
The prepositional phrase is preferred to the genitive
in this passage on grounds of euphony, to avoid the
juxtaposition of two words with the same genitive
plural ending.

ὑπὲρ ὧν φοβοῦνται: 'in regard to what they fear', for
ὑπὲρ ἐκείνων ἃ φοβοῦνται, with attraction and omission
of the antecedent (see on περὶ ὧν σκοπεῖτε, 1 above).

8   παραπεπτωκότα: accusative singular of perfect participle of παραπίπτω 'occur', 'happen', 'fall to one'.

ἀφεῖναι: 2nd aorist infinitive active of ἀφίημι 'I dismiss', 'I let go'.

πεπόνθατε: 2nd person plural perfect tense of πάσχω.

Εὐβοεῦσι: the reference here is to the Euboean expedition of 357 B.C., when the Athenians under Diocles took advantage of strife in the Euboean cities to detach the island from its Boeotian alliance and to enrol it once again in the Second Athenian Confederacy from which it had seceded in 371 B.C.. In this expedition Demosthenes served as a volunteer trierarch. The island remained an Athenian ally till several months after the delivery of this speech.

παρῆσαν: 3rd person imperfect of παριέναι 'to come forward to speak'. This is Dobree's conjecture in place of the manuscript reading παρῆσαν (from παρεῖναι) 'they were present'. However some examples are found elsewhere of the use of παρεῖναι with the construction appropriate to a verb of motion (i.e. where it has the meaning 'to arrive at') followed by the prepositions εἰς, ἐπί or πρός + accusative. In Demosthenes we find πρὸς τοῦτο πάρεστι (*2nd Olynthiac* 8) and ἐφ' οὓς ἂν αὐτῷ δόξῃ πάρεστι (*On the Chersonese* 11), and the manuscript reading could well be retained here.

Ἱέραξ καὶ Στρατοκλῆς: the leaders of the anti-Macedonian faction in Amphipolis who, when Philip's attack was imminent, came to Athens and offered to hand over the city in return for military assistance against Macedonia. Following the capture of the city, the fate of Hierax is unknown, but Stratocles, and a certain Philon, had their property confiscated and were condemned to perpetual exile by a decree of the Amphipolitan *demos*; the decree is still extant (Tod, *Greek Historical Inscriptions* Vol. II, no.150).

εἰ γὰρ . . . τὴν αὐτὴν περιειχόμεθ' ἡμεῖς . . . προθυμίαν . . . εἴχετ' ἂν Ἀμφίπολιν: 'if you had continued to show the same enthusiasm . . . you would have held possession of Amphipolis'. The sentence in form is a past unreal condition, with verbs in the imperfect indicative rather than the aorist because the action is extended over a period of time. (G. 1397)

ἡμεῖς ὑπὲρ ἡμῶν αὐτῶν: the repetition of the reflexive pronoun in two cases emphasises the words - 'if it had been for ourselves that we showed enthusiasm'.

ἂν ἦτ' ἀπαλλαγμένοι: 'you would have got rid of'; this
is the periphrastic form of the pluperfect middle and
passive, equivalent to ἀπήλλαχθε. In all perfect subjunctives and optatives and in the third person plural
perfect and pluperfect indicative of verbs with consonantal stems, the periphrastic form is the only one
that occurs, while it is frequently used in the indicative also in place of the simple form. The use
of the pluperfect indicative in past unreal conditions
is rare, but occurs when, as here, emphasis is placed
on the completed state of some past activity (G. 1397).

πραγμάτων: 'bother', 'trouble'. This meaning occurs
frequently, especially in the phrases πράγματ' ἔχειν
('to have annoyance') and πράγματα παρέχειν τινι ('to
cause trouble for someone').

9. Πύδνα: see on Πυδναίων, 5 above.

Ποτείδαια: a Corinthian colony, situated on the narrow
isthmus connecting the peninsula of Pallene and
Chalcidice (see map). Though the city had been in the
fifth century a member of the Delian league, in the
fourth century it was an Athenian possession for 8 years
only, from the capture by Timotheus in 364 till its
loss to Philip in 356 B.C. Philip handed the city over
to the Chalcidian League, with which he was then in
alliance.

Μεθώνη: a Greek city on the Macedonian seaboard, on the
western coast of the Thermaic Gulf, a few miles north
of Pydna. Captured by Athens in 364, it was besieged
and taken by Philip in 354 B.C. It was in the course
of this siege that Philip lost the use of his right eye,
pierced by an arrow.

Παγασαί: a Thessalian city, situated at the northern end
of the gulf of the same name. It served as the port of
Pherae and as the principal harbour for the whole of
Thessaly. The city, together with Pherae, was captured
by Philip in 352 B.C., in the course of the Sacred War.
Unlike the three other cities named by the orator,
Pagasae had not been an Athenian possession before its
capture but had belonged to Lycophron of Pherae.
Demosthenes mentions it here because his list is not
one of lost Athenian possessions but of places that
might have been kept out of Philip's hands had Athens
sent a naval force in time to assist them. The cities
are mentioned in the chronological order of their capture by Philip, and reappear in similar lists of his
acquisitions at *1st Philippic* 4, *On the Crown* 69 and in
12 below.

ἵνα μὴ καθ' ἕκαστα λέγειν διατρίβω: 'so as not to waste your time by mentioning each one individually', a final clause in primary sequence with the verb in the subjunctive (G. 1365). Here we have an example of the rhetorical figure *parasiopesis;* see Introduction II 4 e(iv).

τούτων ἑνὶ τῷ πρόπῳ: 'any one of these in the first instance', where ἑνί is used indefinitiely, as if it were accompanied by τινι.

εἰ τότε . . . προθύμως . . . ἐβοηθήσαμεν . . . ῥᾴονι νῦν ἂν ἐχρώμεθα τῷ Φιλίππῳ: 'if at that time we had sent help enthusiastically, we would at the present time have a Philip who was easier and more humble to deal with'. This is an unreal condition, with an aorist indicative in the protasis referring to a past event, and ἄν + imperfect is the apodosis to indicate the present (G. 1397). χράομαι followed by a dative of the person is used to mean 'I treat with', 'I have to deal with'.

νῦν δέ: 'but as it is', 'but as the situation now stands', a very frequent meaning of this phrase.

τὸ παρὸν . . . τὰ μέλλοντα: 'the present . . . the future', where the participles are used with the article to represent nouns (G. 1560).

τὰ μέλλοντ' αὐτόματ' οἰόμενοι σχήσειν.καλῶς: 'believing that the future will come right of its own accord', an indirect statement referring to the future. σχήσειν is the future infinitive of ἔχω, coexisting with the more usual ἕξειν. In as far as the two forms can be distinguished, ἕξω is used in a durative or continuative sense ('I shall have and hold on to'), whereas σχήσω is generally ingressive or inceptive ('I shall come to have', 'I shall acquire'). ἔχω with an adverb is, as here, intransitive, being equivalent to εἰμί with the corresponding adjective (σχήσειν καλῶς = ἔσεσθαι καλά).

τηλικοῦτος ἡλίκος οὐδείς πω βασιλεὺς γέγονε: 'to such a position of importance as no king has yet reached'. τηλικοῦτος, with its correlative ἡλίκος, regularly refers to size, age or, as here, degree.

10 δοκεῖ τις ἄν: this ἄν is not construed with δοκεῖ but is picked up later in the sentence by a second ἄν, to be taken with ἔχειν. The first is not to be translated but is there only to serve as a warning that an ἄν will eventually be required in construing the sentence.

The repetition of ἄν in a long apodosis is common;
it may occur twice or even three times (G. 1312).

δίκαιος λογιστὴς καταστάς: 'who has set himself up as a
just appraiser'. καταστάς is the second aorist participle
active of καθίστημι. The second aorist of ἵστημι and
its compounds is always intransitive, in contrast to
the 1st aorist ἔστησα which is transitive.

τῶν παρὰ τῶν θεῶν ἡμῖν ὑπηργμένων: 'of the things that
have accrued to us at the hands of the gods'. ὑπηργμένων is the genitive plural of the perfect participle
passive of ὑπάρχω. In addition to the significance
'begin', this verb can mean 'to be from the beginning',
'to be already in existence', and sometimes differs
little from εἶναι. Here the meaning is 'the things
that have come to us from the gods', i.e. 'the benefits
which the gods have bestowed upon us'.

μεγάλην ἂν ἔχειν αὐτοῖς χάριν: 'he would be exceedingly
grateful', 'he would have much cause for gratitude'.
ἂν ἔχειν is used in indirect speech to represent the
direct ἂν ἔχοι.

τὸ μὲν ἀπολωλεκέναι . . . τὸ δὲ . . . πεπονθέναι:
'our losses . . . our sufferings', where ἀπολωλεκέναι
and πεπονθέναι are perfect infinitives of ἀπόλλυμι
and of πάσχω respectively, used with the article to
serve as nouns. The perfect tense, as usual, indicates
the present state resulting from completed action in
the past (G. 1273). ἀπόλλυμι, in addition to a transitive perfect ἀπολώλεκα, has an intransitive 2nd perfect ἀπόλωλα 'I am undone'.

τῆς ἡμετέρας ἀμελείας ἄν τις θείη δικαίως: 'one might
with justification regard as a mark of (or 'ascribe this
to') our carelessness'. Potential optative with ἄν, as is
ἂν ἔγωγε θείην at the end of the sentence. For the genitive ἀμελείας, see on τῆς ὑμετέρας τύχης ὑπολαμβάνω, 1 above.

πεφηνέναι τέ τιν' ἡμῖν συμμαχίαν: 'the fact that an alliance
has presented itself to us'. πεφηνέναι is the 2nd perfect
infinitive active of φαίνω, a verb with two perfects: the
1st perfect πέφαγκα is transitive ('I have shown'), whereas the 2nd perfect πέφηνα is intransitive ('I have shown
myself', 'I have appeared').

τούτων ἀντίρροπον: 'as a counterweight to these' (i.e.
'to our losses'), a phrase in apposition to συμμαχίαν.
As a compound adjective, ἀντίρροπος has no separate
feminine forms (G. 304).

ἂν βουλώμεθα χρῆσθαι: 'if we are willing to avail ourselves of it'. ἄν here is not the particle but a contracted form of the conjunction ἐάν (εἰ + ἄν), used with the subjunctive to indicate a future condition (G. 1403).

11 παρόμοιόν ἐστιν ὅπερ καὶ περὶ τῆς τῶν χρημάτων κτήσεως: 'the situation is much the same as it is with regard to the acquisition of money too'. παρόμοιος is usually followed by a dative and, we should therefore understand a word like τούτῳ or ἐκείνῳ as antecedent to ὅπερ. We must further supply a verb like ἐστι or γίγνεται in the clause beginning with ὅπερ. The phrase is used to introduce a simile borrowed from money-making. Just as a spendthrift cannot make good use of his gains and thus loses his sense of gratitude, so (καὶ περὶ τῶν πραγμάτων οὕτως at the beginning of the next sentence) we fail both to count our blessings and to feel grateful for them.

ἂν μὲν γάρ, ὅσ' ἂν τις λάβῃ, καὶ σώσῃ: 'if ever anyone keeps all that he obtains'. The first ἄν is again equivalent to ἐάν and is followed by a subjunctive in a protasis expressing a present general supposition, where the apodosis expresses a repeated act or a general truth (G. 1393). ὅσ' ἂν τις λάβῃ is an indefinite relative clause, construed in much the same way as the preceding conditional clause (G. 1431).

ἂν δ' ἀναλώσας λάθῃ: 'but if he loses it unawares'. ἀναλώσας is the aorist participle of ἀναλίσκω 'I spend', 'I waste'. λανθάνω ('I escape notice') is very often used with the participle in cases where the participle expresses the leading idea in the phrase. Such phrases are best rendered in English by translating λανθάνω as 'secretly' or 'unawares'. In Greek the same idea could be expressed by ἂν δ' ἀναλώσῃ λαθών, with ἀναλίσκω as the principal verb and λανθάνω in participial form. In this construction with λανθάνω (as also with φθάνω and τυγχάνω) the participle is 'timeless', i.e. an aorist participle denotes time contemporaneous with, rather than anterior to, the action of the main verb. The aorist participle is regularly used when the principal verb is itself an aorist (G. 1586).

συνανήλωσε καὶ τὸ μεμνῆσθαι τὴν χάριν: 'he loses along with it also all memory of the favour'. συνανήλωσε is a gnomic aorist, i.e. an aorist used in a principal clause to denote a general truth, where English uses a present (G. 1292). μεμνῆσθαι is perfect infinitive middle of μιμνήσκω 'I remind'. The perfect tenses of this verb have in the middle voice the meaning 'remember', and are followed by the accusative as here or, more commonly, by the genitive (G. 1102). Note the repetition of τὴν χάριν at the end of two parallel clauses, i.e. *antistrophe*; see Introduction II 4 f(ix).

οἱ μὴ χρησάμενοι τοῖς καιροῖς ὀρθῶς: 'such people as fail to make proper use of their opportunities'. οἱ μὴ χρησάμενοι is equivalent to ὅσοι ἂν μὴ χρήσωνται. The negative μή is found with the participle when, as here, it is used as a substitute for an indefinite relative clause ('generic participle', G. 1512).

πρὸς γὰρ τὸ τελευταῖον ἐκβὰν ἕκαστον τῶν πρὶν ὑπαρξόντων κρίνεται: 'for each of the previous advantages is judged by the standards of what happened last'. ἐκβάν is the aorist participle neuter of ἐκβαίνω, used here with the article as the equivalent of a noun - 'what has happened', 'the issue', 'the outcome'. τελευταῖον is adverbial - 'in the last instance'. πρός + accusative, with verbs of assessing and judging, denotes the criterion in accordance with which the assessment is made. τῶν ὑπαρξόντων denotes 'things that we already have', 'previous advantages' (see on τῶν ὑπηργμένων, 10 above). πρίν is usually a temporal conjunction meaning 'before' or 'until'. Here, if correct, it must be used adverbially, but as no other example of the adverbial use occurs in Demosthenes, some editors prefer to read, with the inferior manuscripts, τῶν προυπαρχόντων, with the same meaning.

ἵνα . . . ἀποτριψώμεθα: 'in order to obliterate', a final clause with the verb in the subjunctive in primary sequence (G. 1365). ἀποτρίβω ('I rub off') is used in the middle voice with its literal meaning of 'wipe away pollution from one's body', and metaphorically of effacing the taint of disgrace, shame etc.

12. εἰ δὲ προησόμεθα καὶ τούτους τοὺς ἀνθρώπους: 'but if we forsake these men also' (i.e. the Olynthians, as well as the inhabitants of Pydna, Methone etc.). προησόμεθα is the future middle of προΐημι 'I send forward', 'I dismiss'. The protasis of a conditional clause referring to the future is generally expressed by ἐάν + subjunctive, but εἰ with the future indicative is found, as here, in threats, warnings and admonitions, in the interest of vividness (G. 1405).

εἶτα: 'and then in consequence'.

φρασάτω τις: 'let someone tell me', 3rd person singular aorist imperative of φράζω. Demosthenes is fond of inviting his audience to participate in the argument, in order to retain their attention; see Introduction II 4 c.

τὸ κατ' ἀρχάς: 'originally', 'in the first place', as at *2nd Olynthiac* 6 below. The neuter of the article is frequently used with adverbs and with adverbial phrases of time (e.g. τὸ πάρος, τὸ πρίν, τὸ νῦν).

Ἀμφίπολιν, Πύδναν, Ποτείδαίαν, Μεθώνην: see on 9 above.

Θετταλίας: Philip had intervened in Thessaly on three occasions prior to the composition of this speech but since Demosthenes is listing events in chronological order, he must be referring to the expedition of 352 B.C., when he assisted the Thessalian League against Lycophron of Pherae and his brother Peitholaus, who were allied to the Phocians. After his victory over the Phocians at the battle of the Crocus Field, Philip was able to expel Lycophron and Peitholaus from Pherae and to capture Pagasae, its port. See Introduction I 2 above.

13 Μαγνησίαν: one of the perioecic territories subject to Thessaly, a mountainous area with a long rocky barren coastline along the Aegean. Philip seems to have detached this area from Thessaly in 352 B.C. and to have administered it for a time as part of his own realm (Isocrates 5.21). In 349 (*2nd Olynthiac* 7 and 11) and in 346 B.C. (*2nd Philippic* 22), he was holding out the prospect of its restoration as a means of securing Thessalian goodwill.

Θρᾴκην: the vast geographical area stretching from Philip's eastern border to the Black sea, against which Philip conducted an expedition in 352 B.C. Politically Thrace was divided into three kingdoms ruled respectively by Cetriporis, Amadocus and Cersobleptes. As a result of this expedition, all the parts were reduced to varying degrees of dependence on Macedonia.

τοὺς μὲν ἐκβαλών: if the plural is purely rhetorical, the reference may be to Cetriporis, who disappears from history about this time and whose territory was annexed to Macedonia, to which it was adjacent.

τοὺς δὲ καταστήσας: 'having installed others'. The 1st aorist of καθίστημι (κατέστησα, as opposed to the 2nd aorist κατέστην) is transitive. Demosthenes may here be alluding to the younger Amadocus who assisted Philip against Cersobleptes in this campaign (Theopompus, fgt.

101 - Jacoby) and who seems to have supplanted his anti-Macedonian father of the same name around this time.

ἠσθένησε: 'he became ill', an ingressive aorist, to be contrasted with the imperfect, which means 'he was ill'. The aorist of verbs representing a state or condition denotes entry into that state. Thus ἐπλούτησα 'I grew rich', ἐβασίλευσα 'I became king', ἔσχον 'I came to have', 'I acquired' (see G. 1260).

Ἰλλυριοὺς καὶ Παίονας: Balkan peoples living respectively to the north-west and north of the Macedonian kingdom. The terms are ethnic rather than political, since each nation had several tribes, each with its own king. These barbarian tribes were a constant threat to Macedonian security and were accordingly made the objective of several expeditions during Philip's reign. By the date of this speech, there had been two expeditions against Illyrian tribes, in 358 and 356 B.C., and two against Paeonians, in 358 and 355 B.C. The context of this speech strongly suggests a further campaign directed against both some time in 351 B.C. (cf. *1st Philippic* 48, delivered in that year).

Ἀρύββαν: a king of the Molossians, an Epirot tribe living across the Pindus due west of Macedonia. In 360, Arybbas succeeded his brother Neoptolemus whose daughter Olympias was marrried to Philip in 357 B.C. The motive for Philip's attack in 351 is unknown, though it is probable that the Molossians had lent support to the Illyrians and Paeonians in this year. At all events Philip weakened Arybbas' position, deprived him of some territory, and removed his nephew, Alexander, young brother of Olympias, to be brought up at the Macedonian court. Arybbas was eventually dethroned in favour of this Alexander in 343 B.C. and was granted refuge by the Athenians, whose decree in his honour is still extant (Tod. *Greek Historical Inscriptions* no. 173).

ὅποι τις ἂν εἴποι: 'and in whatever possible direction one might mention', a potential optative used with ἄν.

παραλείπω: 'I pass over', a clear sign of the rhetorical figure *paraleipsis*; see Introduction II 4 e (iii).

14 ἄν τις εἴποι: a formula used by Demosthenes to introduce an imaginary objection, which he then proceeds to refute. The order is more frequently εἴποι τις ἄν (e.g. *3rd Olynthiac* 10 and 19; *2nd Phillipic* 13). Goodwin (G. 1315) goes as far as to assert that ἄν never begins a

sentence or a clause but ἄν τις εἴποι does in fact recur in 19 below and Plato (Phaedo 87A) uses the expression τί οὖν, ἂν φαίη ὁ λόγος, ἔτι ἀπιστεῖς. Hence some grammarians hold that ἄν can only begin a sentence or clause when it is used after a weak mark of punctuation.

νῦν: 'why tell us this *now*?', where the word's final position shows it to be emphatic.

ἵνα γνῶτε . . . καὶ αἴσθησθε: final aorist subjunctives, from γιγνώσκω and αἰσθάνομαι respectively. For the construction, cf. on ἵνα μὴ καθ᾽ ἕκαστα λέγειν διατρίβω, 9 above. These final clauses supply the answer of the orator to the imaginary objector.

καὶ τὸ προίεσθαι καθ᾽ ἕκαστον ἀεί τι τῶν πραγμάτων ὡς ἀλυσιτελές: (sc. ἐστιν) 'both how unprofitable is the neglect of one thing after another, as each one takes place'. προίεσθαι is articular infinitive, serving as subject of the sentence. τι is the object of προίεσθαι and καθ᾽ ἕκαστον is an adverbial phrase meaning 'in turn', 'one after the other', 'individually'. ἀεί ('always') is frequently used, as here, in the sense of 'from time to time'. Cf. 2nd Olynthiac 7 - τὴν ἑκάστων ἄνοιαν ἀεὶ τῶν ἀγνοούντων - 'the folly of each set of people who for the time being happen to be ignorant'; and at Against Meidias 223 - οἱ ἀεὶ δικάζοντες - 'the jurymen who from time to time happen to be on the panel'.

φιλοπραγμοσύνην: literally 'fondness for action' but with the implication that it is carried to excess. The word regularly denotes 'meddlesomeness', 'inability to remain inactive', 'restless activity', and is used by Demosthenes elsewhere of his enemy Meidias (Against Meidias 137) and of Philip again at 1st Philippic 42. The orator here shrewdly seizes upon one of the 'key' factors in Philip's character: for an elaboration of Philip's φιλοπραγμοσύνη, see 2nd Olynthiac 15 - ὁ μὲν δόξης ἐπιθυμεῖ καὶ τοῦτ᾽ ἐζήλωκε καὶ προῄρηται πράττων καὶ κινδυνεύων, ἂν συμβῇ τι, παθεῖν, τὴν τοῦ διαπράξασθαι ταῦθ᾽ ἃ μηδεὶς πώποτ᾽ ἄλλος Μακεδόνων βασιλεὺς δόξαν ἀντὶ τοῦ ζῆν ἀσφαλῶς ᾑρημένος.

ᾗ χρῆται καὶ συζῇ Φίλιππος: 'which is part of Philip's habit and very nature'.

οὐκ ἔστιν ὅπως ἀγαπήσας τοῖς πεπραγμένοις ἡσυχίαν σχήσει: 'it cannot be that he will remain content with what he has done and be at peace'. πεπραγμένοις is the dative plural neuter of perfect participle passive of πράττω; on σχήσω as future of ἔχω, cf. on σχήσειν, 9 above. οὐκ ἔστιν ὅς and οὐκ ἔστιν ὅπως introduce relative clauses of result (consecutive relative clauses), which take the indicative mood. The tense depends on the time to which the clause refers; examples occur of the present and aorist, but the future, as here, is particularly common.

εἰ δ' ὁ μὲν ὡς ἀεί τι μεῖζον τῶν ὑπαρχόντων δεῖ πράττειν ἐγνωκὼς ἔσται: 'but if he shall have resolved that he must always aim at achieving something greater than he already possesses', a future condition in the more vivid form, with a future indicative expressing an admonition (cf. on εἰ προήσομεθα, 12 above). ἐγνωκὼς ἔσται serves as the future perfect tense of γιγνώσκω. The active voice of the future perfect is expressed periphrastically by the future of εἰμί accompanied by the perfect participle of the verb. Only two non-periphrastic forms of the future perfect active occur in Attic Greek: ἑστήξω (from ἵστημι) 'I shall stand', and τεθνήξω (from θνῄσκω) 'I shall be dead'.

ἡμεῖς δ' ὡς οὐδένος ἀντιληπτέον ἐρρωμένως τῶν πραγμάτων: 'and we, that we must not apply ourselves resolutely to any of our affairs'. ἀντιληπτέον is the verbal adjective from ἀντιλαμβάνω, expressing necessity (cf. on ἀντιληπτέον, 2 above). ἐρρωμένως is an adverbial form of ἐρρωμένος, perfect participle passive of the verb ῥώννυμι 'I strengthen'.

σκοπεῖσθ' εἰς τί ποτ' ἐλπὶς ταῦτα τελευτῆσαι: 'consider what issue they can possibly be expected to have'. ποτε frequently accompanies interrogative pronouns and adverbs with intensive force, e.g. τίς ποτε; 'who in the world?' and τί ποτε; 'what on earth?' (cf. τί ποτ' at *3rd Olynthiac* 30 below). Verbs of hoping, promising, threatening and swearing are regularly followed by the accusative and *future* infinitve, when they refer to the future, but they also admit the construction of the prolative infinitive, as in English (i.e. they can be followed by a present or aorist infinitive, with no distinction of time between the two, the normal construction with verbs such as βούλομαι, πειράομαι etc.); see *G*. 1286. Here τελευτήσειν might be expected, but in fact Demosthenes seems to prefer a prolative infinitive with the phrase ἐλπίς ἐστι (cf. *1st Philippic* 2 - ἐλπίς ἦν αὐτὰ βελτίω γενέσθαι).

15 πρὸς θεῶν: 'in heaven's name', common in adjurations, where a verb such as ἱκετεύω or ἀντιβολέω is to be understood.

ὅστις ἀγνοεῖ: a consecutive relative clause equivalent to ὥστε ἀγνοεῖν; cf. on οὐκ ἔστιν ὅπως, 14 above.

τὸν ἐκεῖθεν πόλεμον δεῦρο ἥξοντα: 'that the war from Olynthus will come to Attica'. Verbs of perceiving,

knowing, remembering and their opposites, prefer the
construction of accusative and participle to the
accusative and infinitive in indirect discourse (see
G. 1588).

ἂν ἀμελήσωμεν: 'if we pay no attention', where ἂν is
once again equivalent to ἐάν (cf. on ἂν βουλώμεθα χρῆσθαι,
10 above).

εἰ τοῦτο γενήσεται: cf. on εἰ δὲ προησόμεθα, 12 above.

τὸν αὐτὸν τρόπον ὥσπερ οἱ δανειζόμενοι . . . οὕτως καὶ
ἡμεῖς: 'in the same way as people who borrow money . . .
so too we', a simile derived from money-lending. Just as
those who borrow money recklessly at high rates of
interest enjoy temporary benefits, only to forfeit their
security in the end, so the Athenians are in danger of
borrowing the temporary leisure of leaving Philip
unchecked only to pay a heavy price in the long run and
forfeit their autonomy. δανείζω in the active voice
means 'I lend', in the middle 'I borrow'.

ῥᾳδίως: 'thoughtlessly', 'not showing a sufficiently
serious purpose'.

ἐπὶ τοῖς μεγάλοις: (sc. τόκοις) 'at a high rate of
interest'

μικρὸν εὐπορήσαντες χρόνον: 'becoming prosperous for a
short time', an ingressive aorist (cf. on ἠσθένησε, 13
above).

ὕστερον καὶ τῶν ἀρχαίων ἀπέστησαν: 'subsequently they
lose their original security'. καὶ here denotes 'on
top of the money they have borrowed'. τῶν ἀρχαίων,
literally 'what they had at the beginning', referring
to the original property or estate which they had offered
as security for the loan. ἀπέστησαν is the intransitive
2nd aorist of ἀφίστημι (see on δίκαιος λογιστὴς καταστὰς,
10 above); this is a further example of gnomic aorist (see
on συνανήλωσε, 11 above).

ἐπὶ πολλῷ: 'at a heavy cost', picking up ἐπὶ τοῖς μεγάλοις.

δέδοικα . . . μὴ . . . ὑμεῖς . . . φανῶμεν ἐρραθυμηκότες:
'I'm afraid that we may be seen to have been idle'. Verbs
of fearing, when the fear is expressed for the future, are
followed by the subjunctive in primary sequence (hence
φανῶμεν, ἔλθωμεν and κινδυνεύσωμεν) and by the subjunctive
or optative in historic sequence (G. 1378). φανῶμεν
is the 1st person plural 2nd aorist subjunctive passive of
φαίνω. The 1st aorist passive of φαίνω (ἐφάνθην) is
passive in meaning ('I was shown'), the second aorist

passive (ἐφάνην) is middle ('I appeared'). When
followed by the infinitive, φαίνομαι means 'I seem to
be what I am not' but with the participle, as here, the
meaning is 'I am clearly seen to be what I really am'
(G. 1592).

ἅπαντα πρὸς ἡδονὴν ζητοῦντες:(sc. ποιεῖν) 'seeking to do
everything with a view to our pleasure'.

πολλὰ καὶ χαλεπὰ ὧν: here ὧν represents τούτων ἃ (cf. on
περὶ ὧν σκοπεῖτε, 1 above).

κινδυνεύσωμεν περὶ τῶν ἐν αὐτῇ τῇ χώρᾳ: 'and endanger our
position in Attica itself'.

16. φήσαι τις ἄν: formula used to introduce an objection which
the orator imagines a member of his audience might be
likely to make (see on ἄν τις εἴποι, 14 above). φήσαι
is 3rd person singular aorist optative of φημί. Here
the phrase is not parenthetical but is followed by the
accusative and infinitive of indirect discourse.

τὸ ἐπιτιμᾶν . . . τὸ ἀποφαίνεσθαι: articular infinitives,
used as nouns in the accusative case, as the subjects of
the infinitive mood in indirect discourse.

παντὸς εἶναι: 'characteristic of anyone', 'the mark of
anyone', 'within the ability of anyone'. For this
genitive, cf. τοῦτ'εἶναι συμβούλου ('this is the part of
a true adviser') below and see on τῆς ὑμετέρας τύχης
ὑπολαμβάνω, 1 above.

ἄν τι μὴ κατὰ γνώμην ἐκβῇ: (ἄν = ἐάν) 'if ever something
turns out otherwise than in accordance with your will',
where ἐκβῇ is aorist subjunctive of ἐκβαίνω, and the
clause is a general supposition relating to the present
(G. 1393).

οὐ μὴν οἶμαι δεῖν τὴν ἰδίαν ἀσφάλειαν σκοποῦνθ'ὑποστείλασθαι
περὶ ὧν ἡμῖν συμφέρειν ἡγοῦμαι: 'yet I do not think that
even when a speaker is looking to his own personal safety,
he should withhold what I believe to be in accordance with
your interests'. Note the accusative σκοποῦνθ'; if
Demosthenes were thinking only of himself, he would have
written σκοπῶν, in accordance with the requirement that
when the subject of an infinitive is the same as that of
the verb on which it is dependant, it should be in the
nominative, not the accusative (G. 895 and 927). The orat-
or's use of the accusative indicates that he is thinking of
people in general, himself included. ὑποστείλασθαι is
aorist infinitive middle of ὑποστέλλω, meaning literally

'furl one's sails', 'shorten sail'. Here it is used in the common metaphorical sense 'to draw back', 'to restrict oneself', 'to have reservations' and means 'refrain from speaking', as at 1st Philippic 51 - οὐδὲν ὑποστειλάμενος - 'placing no restrictions on what I say', 'holding nothing back'. περὶ ὧν is used for περὶ ἐκείνων ἃ (see on περὶ ὧν σκοπεῖτε, 1 above).

17. φημὶ δὴ διχῇ βοηθητέον εἶναι τοῖς πράγμασιν ὑμῖν: 'I say then that you must assist the situation in two distinct ways'. φημὶ δή is the regular formula for introducing a specific proposal (cf. 2nd Olynthiac 11 and 27). On the verbal adjective βοηθητέον, see on ἀντιληπτέον, 2 above. Here τοῖς πράγμασι is the regular dative of the person or thing assisted and ὑμῖν is dative of the agent ('by you').

τῷ τε τὰς πόλεις σῴζειν . . . καὶ τῷ τὴν ἐκείνου χώραν κακῶς ποιεῖν: 'both by saving their cities . . . and by damaging Philip's territory', explaining what the orator means by διχῇ.

τοῦτο ποιήσοντας: 'to do this', future participle expressing purpose (G. 1288 and 1563).

στρατιώταις ἑτέροις: 'by a second land force', i.e. in addition to the one sent for purely defensive purposes, to save the Chalcidian cities.

εἰ δὲ θατέρου τούτων ὀλιγωρήσετε: 'but if you neglect either of the two of these', where θατέρου represents τοῦ ἑτέρου (crasis). On the future indicative in the protasis of a conditional clause, see on εἰ δὲ προησόμεθα, 12 above.

ὀκνῶ μὴ μάταιος ἡ στρατεία γένηται: 'I fear that the expedition may prove to be in vain'. For the construction after verbs of fearing, see on ἐστι δέος μὴ τρέψηται, 3 above. Though a distinctive feminine form occurs occasionally in Aeschylus, μάταιος is in general declined as a two termination adjective (G. 304). Compound adjectives are almost invariably of this type, as are a few single adjectives such as ἐρῆμος (barren), ἔτυμος (true), ἥμερος (tame), ἥσυχος (quiet), πάτριος (ancestral) and φρόνιμος (sensible).

18. εἴτε γάρ . . . παραστήσεται . . . ἀμυνεῖται: refers to the second of the alternatives outlined in the preceeding section, the ravaging of Philip's territory. For the future παραστήσεται, cf. on εἰ προησόμεθα, 12 above. παραστήσεται is future middle of παρίστημι, meaning 'bring over to one's side by force', 'reduce'.

ὑμῶν τῶν ἐκείνου κακῶς ποιούντων: 'while you are damaging Philip's territory', genitive absolute with temporal force (G. 1152 and 1568).

ἀμυνεῖται: future middle of ἀμύνω. In the active ἀμύνω with the dative of the person only means 'I help', with the dative of the person and the accusative of the thing, 'I ward off something from someone'. In the middle with the accusative of the thing it means 'I guard myself against something', but with the accusative of the person, 'I punish', 'I take revenge on'. Here it is used absolutely, with the meaning 'I protect myself', 'I act in self-defence'.

εἴτε . . . προσκαθεδεῖται . . . περιέσται: this second alternative refers to the first of the two mentioned in the preceding section, i.e. the despatch of an Athenian force to aid Olynthus.

ἀκινδύνως ἔχοντα: equivalent to ἀκίνδυνα ὄντα (see on σχῆσω καλῶς, 9 above).

τὰ οἴκοι: (sc. πράγματα), literally 'the things at home', where the article is used with an adverb to qualify a noun which is not expressed (G. 952); cf. *On the Crown* 247 - οἱ ἐπὶ τῶν πραγμάτων (sc. ἄνθρωποι) - 'the men in power'. οἴκοι ('at home') is an adverb derived from the noun οἶκος and is in fact a relic of the lost locative case (cf. Latin *domi*) which survives in a few words such as χαμαί ('on the ground'), θύρασι ('at the door'), and in various place names (e.g. Ἐλευσῖνι, Μαραθῶνι, Ἰσθμοῖ, Μεγαροῖ, Πειραιοῖ, Ἀθήνησι, Θήβησι, Πλαταιᾶσι, etc.).

προσκαθεδεῖται καὶ προσεδρεύσει: 'will sit down alongside the city and remain on watch', an example of the characteristically Demosthenic figure of *pleonasm*; see Introduction II 4 f(xii). It is used here to emphasize Philip's powers of perseverance. προσκαθεδεῖται is the so-called 'Attic' future (see G. 665) of προσκαθέζομαι.

περιέσται τῷ χρόνῳ τῶν πολιορκουμένων: 'in time he will prove superior to the besieged'. περίειμι with the genitive means 'I am left over', 'I survive' or, most frequently, as here, 'I have an advantage over'.

19. ἔστιν ὅσ' οὐδενὶ τῶν ἄλλων ἀνθρώπων στρατιωτικά: 'you have as much as is possessed by no other men for military purposes', i.e. you have much greater funds at your disposal than anyone else in the world for military purposes. The word στρατιωτικά poses a problem. If it is really part of Demosthenes' address it is perhaps to be taken to pick up

χρημάτων earlier in the sentence but it is separated and placed at the end for emphasis. On this interpretation, however, it is difficult to see why the orator should in the very next sentence call for the distribution to troops on active service. Alternatively, στρατιωτικά might be construed as part of the relative clause only, i.e. Demosthenes would be claiming that the various Athenian funds are collectively greater than is the military fund of any one individual state. Such a claim would be singularly pointless in the context; it may well be that some scholars are correct in deleting the word entirely, as in the Oxford text.

ταῦτα δ'ὑμεῖς οὕτως ὡς βούλεσθε λαμβάνετε: 'you appropriate these monies as you please', a euphemistic allusion to the Theoric Fund, the contents of which the orator would like to see transferred to the military fund, but which he does not dare to propose openly. On the Stratiotic and Theoric Funds, see Introduction, Appendix B.

εἰ μὲν οὖν ταῦτα τοῖς στρατευομένοις ἀποδώσετε, οὐδένος ὑμῖν προσδεῖ πόρου: 'if then you pay these monies to men on active service (i.e. if you divert theoric funds to the war chest), you have no need of any further (προσ-) supply'. For the future ἀποδώσετε, cf. on εἰ προησόμεθα, 12 above.

εἰ δὲ μή (sc. ἀποδώσετε), προσδεῖ: 'but if you fail to do this, there *is* a need for more funds'.

μᾶλλον δ'ἅπαντος ἐνδεῖ τοῦ πόρου: 'or rather there is a lack of any funds at all'.

τί οὖν: 'well then', a question (literally 'what then?') used at the commencement of an imaginary objection, and forming part of it. Cf. *3rd Philippic* 63 - τί οὖν ποτ'αἴτιον, θαυμάζετ'ἴσως; and *On the Crown* 220 - τί οὖν; εἴποι τις ἄν· σὺ τοσοῦθ'ὑπερῆρας ῥώμῃ ὥστε πάντα ποιεῖν αὐτός;

ἄν τις εἴποι: see on same phrase, 14 above.

γράφεις: here used with the meaning of 'propose a decree'.

μὰ Δί'οὐκ ἔγωγε: 'by Heaven I most certainly do not'. Adverbs of swearing (ναί or νή 'yes, by . . . ' and μὰ 'no, by . . . ' are followed by the accusative case (*G.* 1066-67). Demosthenes is at pains to make clear that he is not actually proposing a decree on a subject which aroused so much passion and which would undoubtedly lose him the goodwill of his fellow citizens. For the fate of Apollodorus, who did move such a decree in this very year, see Introduction, Appendix B.

20. ἐγώ . . . ἡγοῦμαι στρατιώτας δεῖν κατασκευασθῆναι καὶ ταῦτ' εἶναι στρατιωτικά: 'my own personal opinion is that a force of soldiers must be made ready and that this money should come from a war-fund'. Scholars who find it impossible to believe that Demosthenes can ever have put forward such a view - even as an expression of a personal opinion (note ἡγοῦμαι) rather than a formal proposal - delete the last four words (so Butcher in the Oxford text).

καὶ μίαν σύνταξιν εἶναι τὴν αὐτὴν τοῦ τε λαμβάνειν καὶ τοῦ ποιεῖν τὰ δέοντα: 'and that there must be one and the same arrangement for receiving payment and for doing one's duty', i.e. military payments should be made only to those performing military service.

ὑμεῖς δ'(sc. ἡγεῖσθει δεῖν) οὕτω πως ἄνευ πραγμάτων λαμβάνειν εἰς τὰς ἑορτάς: 'whereas you think that you should continue to receive the money in some such way as you do now, without incurring any trouble, for the festivals', i.e. you believe that these monies should continue to be distributed as at present from the Theoric Fund. For the meaning of πραγμάτων here see on ἦτ'ἀπηλλαγμένοι πραγμάτων, 8 above.

εἰσφέρειν: to pay the *eisphora* or property tax.

ἂν πολλῶν δέῃ: (ἂν = ἐάν) 'if a large sum is required', where δεῖ is used impersonally with the genitive to mean 'there is need of'.

ἔστι: here the accented form of the verb means 'it is possible' in place of the more usual ἔξεστι or πάρεστι. The simple verb is most frequently used in this sense when it is negative.

λέγουσι δὲ καὶ ἄλλους τινας ἄλλοι πόρους: 'different people suggest different sources of supply'. ἄλλος followed by another of its cases or by an adverb derived from itself (e.g. ἀλλοθεν, ἄλλοτε, ἄλλως) is generally expressed in English by two clauses. Thus ἄλλοι ἄλλα λέγουσι, literally 'different people say different things', is more naturally translated into English as 'some people say one thing, others another'. καί here means 'in addition to those suggested by me'.

ὧν ἔλεσθε: ἔλεσθε, the 2nd aorist middle of αἱρέω means 'choose' (cf. ἔλεσθαι, 1 above). In a usage alien to English, Greek permits the use of an imperative in a subordinate (especially a relative) clause. Here ὧν is equivalent to καὶ τούτων and in English the relative would be most naturally translated by a demonstrative, beginning a new sentence.

ἕως ἐστι καιρός, ἀντιλάβεσθε τῶν πραγμάτων: 'while there is still time, apply yourselves to the matter'. ἀντιλάβεσθε is 2nd aorist middle of ἀντιλαμβάνω, a favourite word of Demosthenes (cf. its use in 2 and 14 above).

21. ἄξιον (sc. ἐστι) . . . ἐνθυμηθῆναι . . . τὰ πράγματ' ἐν ᾧ καθέστηκε νῦν τὰ Φιλίππου: 'it is worthwhile reflecting how Philip's affairs now stand', where τὰ πράγματα τὰ Φιλίππου is split up by a subordinate clause - *hyperbaton*, cf. Introduction I 4 f(xiii),- τὰ Φιλίππου being given the emphatic position at the end. In English, 'Philip's affairs' would be expressed most naturally as the subject of the subordinate clause, but Greek prefers to make them the object of the principal clause ('consider Philip's affairs how they stand'); cf. *3rd Olynthiac* 17 - τοὺς αἰτίους οἵτινες τούτων ζητήσομεν; καθέστηκε is the perfect active of καθίστημι, always used with an intransitive meaning.

ὡς δοκεῖ καὶ φήσειέ τις ἂν μὴ σκοπῶν ἀκριβῶς: 'as seems to be the case and as one who did not examine them carefully might assert'. φήσειε ἂν is potential optative; the negative with the participle σκοπῶν is μή, not οὐ, because the participial phrase is equivalent to a hypothetical conditional or conditional relative clause (G. 1612).

εὐπρεπῶς ἔχει: 'in a fair-seeming condition'. For this idiom, cf. on σχήσειν καλῶς, 9 above.

οὐδ' ὡς ἂν κάλλιστ': (sc. ἔχοι) 'nor are they at all as satisfactory as they might be', another potential optative with ἄν, tacked on to εὐπρεπῶς ἔχει by way of amplification.

οὔτ' ἂν ἐξήνεγκε τὸν πόλεμον τοῦτον . . . εἰ πολεμεῖν ᾠήθη δεήσειν αὐτόν: 'nor would he have embarked upon this war . . . if he had thought he would have to fight it himself', a past 'unreal' condition with an aorist indicative in the protasis and an aorist indicative with ἂν in the apodosis (G. 1397). ἐξήνεγκε is aorist of ἐκφέρω in the sense of 'bring about', 'begin', and δεήσειν is future infinitive of impersonal δεῖ, 'it is necessary'. It should be noted that the orator is here indulging in a piece of special pleading; he does scant justice to Philip, who was never afraid of a fight to gain his objectives.

ὡς ἐπιών: (sc. ἀναιρεῖταί τις τὰ πράγματα) εἶμι ('I go') in the indicative serves in Attic as future to the present ἔρχομαι but the dependant moods (including the participle here) have a present meaning. Here, if ἐπιών refers to the present, the meaning should be 'as one masters the situation when one approaches' (or possibly 'when one attacks') i.e. 'on his very first approach (or attack)', 'by his mere approach'. Some scholars give ἐπιών a future meaning, by analogy with the indicative - 'by being on the point of approach (or attack).

τότε: 'then', i.e. at the moment of the outbreak of war between Philip and Olynthus.

ἤλπιζε τὰ πράγματ' ἀναιρήσεσθαι: 'he expected to master the situation', the regular construction of accusative and future infinitive, after a verb of hoping, when the hope is for the future (G. 1286). For contrast, see on ἐλπὶς τελευτῆσαι, 14 above.

διέψευσται: 'he has been proved mistaken', perfect middle of ψεύδω 'I deceive'.

παρὰ γνώμην γεγονός: 'having happened contrary to his expectation', where γεγονός is perfect participle of γίγνομαι.

τὰ τῶν Θετταλῶν: 'the affairs of the Thessalians' or 'the attitude of the Thessalians'.

22. ταῦτα γὰρ ἄπιστα μὲν ἦν δήπου φύσει καὶ ἀεὶ πᾶσιν ἀνθρώποις: 'for they have always been treacherous, I suppose by nature and constant habit, to all men'. The faithlessness of Thessalians was proverbial in ancient Greece. See scholiast on Aristophanes, *Plutus* 521 - ἀεὶ γὰρ τὰ Θετταλῶν ἄπιστα; Eur. fgt. 426 Nauck - πολλοὶ παρῆσαν ἀλλ' ἄπιστα Θετταλῶν; Demosthenes' *Against Aristocrates* 112 - ὑμεῖς μὲν . . . οὐδένα προὐδώκατε πώποτε τῶν φίλων, Θετταλοὶ δ' οὐδένα πώποθ' ὄντιν' οὔ. Much of this reputation was acquired as a result of the interplay of Thessalian factions, each pursuing its own policies when the opportunity offered. Above all, the Thessalian League, the central government, was frequently at odds with the aristocratic leaders in various individual cities, who tended to adhere to policies contrary to those of the League.

κομιδῇ δ' (sc. ἄπιστα) ὥσπερ ἦν, καὶ ἔστι νῦν τούτῳ: 'exactly as they were in the past, so they are now also to him', the contrast being between the general pattern of unreliability in the past and the particular instance which they are currently displaying in their attitude to Philip. κομιδῇ (in origin the dative of the noun κομιδή), meaning 'with care' is used to denote 'quite', 'entirely', 'all together', usually with verbs (e.g. κομιδῇ μεθύων 'dead drunk'), with adjectives (e.g. νέος κομιδῇ 'quite young'), or in dialogue (with γε or μὲν οὖν) to provide an affirmative answer to a question.

Παγασάς: see on 9 above. Philip had kept Pagasae ever since its capture in 352 B.C. and, so far as is known, retained it permanently because of its great economic and strategic importance.

Μαγνησίαν: see on 13 above. Like Pagasae, a Pheraean possession captured in 352 B.C., but probably returned to the Thessalian League at some time. Certainly in the course of negotiations that took place in or shortly before 346 B.C., Philip expressed a willingness to restore this territory to the Thessalians (*2nd Philippic* 22), though he had already promised to do so in 349 B.C. (*2nd Olynthiac* 7 and 11).

ἤκουον δ' ἔγωγε τινων: cf. on τοῦτ' ἂν δ' ἀκούσαντες λάβοιτε, 1 above.

ὡς οὐδὲ τοὺς λιμένας καὶ τὰς ἀγορὰς ἔτι δώσοιεν αὐτῷ καρποῦσθαι: 'that they would no longer grant him even the enjoyment of (the revenues from) the harbours and market places'. δώσοιεν is future optative of δίδωμι used in indirect discourse in historic sequence to represent what would have been a future indicative in direct speech (*G*. 1287 and 1487). οὐδέ 'not even', i.e. in addition to their refusal to recognise his ownership of Pagasae and Magnesia. In the sense of 'and not', οὐδέ is generally used only if a negative precedes. καρποῦσθαι is an infinitive of purpose (*G*. 1532), commonly used after verbs of giving, choosing, taking and receiving. The harbour and market dues referred to in this section probably came to Philip in his capacity as *archon* of Thessaly (i.e. Head of the Thessalian League), the post he had held since 352 B.C., and they may well have been intended to help defray the expenses incurred in running the League.

τὰ γὰρ κοινὰ . . . λαμβάνειν: a further accusative and infinitive, still part of the reports which the orator had heard. Clearly some Thessalians felt that Philip was diverting these funds for his own personal use.

εἰ ἀποστερήσεται: for the construction, see on εἰ προησόμεθα, 12 above.

εἰς στενὸν κομιδῇ τὰ τῆς τροφῆς τοῖς ξένοις αὐτῷ καταστήσεται: 'the means of maintenance for his mercenaries will be reduced to very narrow limits indeed'. κομιδῇ here qualifies the adjective στενόν. οἱ ξένοι (literally 'foreign troops' as opposed to citizen soldiers) is regularly used to mean 'mercenaries', as a synonym for μισθόφοροι. καταστήσεται is future middle of καθίστημι, used in a passive sense as an equivalent to the less common κατασταθήσεται.

23. τὸν Παίονα καὶ τὸν Ἰλλυριόν: see on 13 above. Probably collective singulars, though some scholars, who hold that barbarian peoples ruled by a despot could not be described as ἀήθεις τοῦ κατακούειν τινος, maintain that Demosthenes must be alluding to Paeonian and Illyrian *rulers* (cf. his use of τὸν Κᾶρα in *On the Peace* 25 to refer to Idrieus satrap of Caria, and of τὸν Θρᾶκα at *Against Aristocrates* 133 with reference to Cersobleptes).

καὶ ἁπλῶς τούτους ἅπαντας: ' and in a word any other of these tribes', i.e. other Balkan tribes subdued by Philip, such as the Thracians.

αὐτονόμους ἥδιον ἂν . . . εἶναι: 'that they would more gladly be free', where the infintive with ἂν represents a potential optative of direct discourse.

ἄνθρωπος: for ὁ ἄνθρωπος (crasis) 'the fellow'.

μὰ Δία: for oaths, see on μὰ Δί' οὐκ ἔγωγε, 19 above.

τὸ γὰρ εὖ πράττειν παρὰ τὴν ἀξίαν ἀφορμὴ τοῦ κακῶς φρονεῖν τοῖς ἀνοήτοις γίγνεται: 'for success beyond one's merits (i.e. greater than one deserves) becomes in the weak-minded the starting point of folly'.

πολλάκις δοκεῖ τὸ φυλάξαι τἀγαθὰ τοῦ κτήσασθαι χαλεπώτερον εἶναι: contrast *2nd Olynthiac* 26 below - πολὺ ῥᾷον ἔχοντας φυλάττειν ἢ κτήσασθαι πάντα πέφυκεν: Clearly Demosthenes is by no means reluctant to contradict himself when it suits his purposes to do so.

24. τὴν ἀκαιρίαν τὴν ἐκείνου καιρὸν ὑμέτερον νομίσαντας: 'having regarded his embarrassment as your opportunity'.

συνάρασθαι τὰ πράγματα: 'to join in carrying the burden', aorist infinitive middle of συναίρω, meaning 'to take part in', 'take something along with someone else', 'help in bearing'.

ἐφ' ἃ δεῖ: an elliptical expression for ἐπὶ ταῦτα ἐφ' ἃ δεῖ: (*sc.* πρεσβεύσασθαι) 'for those purposes for which embassies need to be sent'.

στρατευομένους αὐτούς: a concept that lies at the very core of Demosthenes' political advice (cf. 6 above).

λογιζομένους . . . πῶς ἂν αὐτὸν οἴεσθ' . . . ἐλθεῖν: 'considering that if Philip were to obtain so great an opportunity against us and that if war were to come about on the borders of our land, how readily do you suppose that he would march against you?', an example of *anacoluthon* (see Introduction II 4 e ii (a)), where the construction is broken off after λογιζομένους because of the addition of the two conditional clauses, and λογιζομένους is then picked up not by a statement, as might be expected, but by the question πῶς οἴεσθε; For the construction of εἰ λάβοι . . . καὶ γένοιτο . . . ἂν ἐλθεῖν, cf. on ἂν ὑμᾶς ἐλέσθαι νομίζω εἰ φανερὸν γένοιτο etc., 1 above. In the phrase πρὸς τῇ χώρᾳ, πρὸς with the dative signifies 'near', i.e. 'on the frontiers of'.

εἶτ' οὐκ αἰσχύνεσθε . . . οὐ τολμήσετε: 'then are you not ashamed that even if what you would have had done to you if he had the power - will you not venture to do this when *you* have the opportunity?'. εἰ is used quite frequently in place of ὅτι or an accusative and infinitive, after verbs indicating emotion, such as θαυμάζω, ἀγανακτέω, αἰσχύνομαι, μέμφομαι, φθονέω, δεινόν ἐστι, δεινὸν ποιοῦμαι (*G.* 1423)'. In this sentence we have yet another *anacoluthon*, where the construction of the clause dependent on αἰσχύνεσθε εἰ is broken off after εἰ δύναιτ' ἐκεῖνος, and no verb is supplied. Instead the orator continues with a new energetic question (οὐ τολμήσετε) and even changes the negative from μή (in μηδ' ἃ πάθοιτ' ἂν) to οὐ. It is most unusual to find *anacoluthon* in two consecutive sentences and this instance is probably a deliberate attempt to create the impression of *ex tempore* speaking. For the use of εἶτα to introduce an indignant question, cf. on εἶθ' οὕτως ἀγνωμόνως ἔχετε, *2nd Olynthiac* 26 below.

25. ἐὰν μὲν γὰρ ἀντέχῃ τὰ τῶν Ὀλυνθίων: (*sc.* πράγματα) 'for if the power of the Olynthians holds out', a condition referring to the future with ἐάν + subjunctive in the protasis (*G.* 1403 and 1434).

τὴν ἐκείνου: (*sc.* γῆν or χώραν) 'his territory'.

τὴν ὑπάρχουσαν καὶ τὴν οἰκείαν: 'the land which is already yours, and which belongs to you'. For ὑπάρχουσαν cf. on τῶν ὑπηργμένων, 10 above, and on τῶν ὑπαρχόντων, 11 above.

ἂν δ' ἐκεῖνα Φίλιππος λάβῃ, τίς αὐτὸν κωλύσει δεῦρο βαδίζειν: (ἂν=ἐάν) 'but if Philip takes Olynthus, who will stop him marching hither?'. Demosthenes uses question in this passage as a change from mere statement, to keep the audience alert, and he goes on to use yet further questions to provide the answer. These answers are presented in such a way as to suggest that they are emanating from members of the audience; see also Introduction II 4 b.

26. Θηβαῖοι; . . . Φωκεῖς: since Philip was *archon* of Thessaly, Phocis and Boeotia were the only independent states left between the frontiers of his domains and Attica.

μὴ λίαν πικρὸν εἰπεῖν ᾖ: 'perhaps this is a very harsh thing to say, but . . . ', the sole example in Demosthenes of μή with the subjunctive used to express a cautious assertion either because the statement is considered to be of doubtful veracity or, as here, as a sort of apology for making a statement which is regrettable but nevertheless true (*G*. 1350). A cautious assertion referring to the past is generally expressed by μή with the indicative (*G*. 1351); the construction in both cases is that after a verb of fearing. Both constructions are particularly common in Platonic dialogue, but rare elsewhere. On the use of the infinitive after πικρόν, see *G*. 1528.

καὶ συνεισβαλοῦσιν ἑτοίμως: 'they will actually join wholeheartedly in the invasion', where συνεισβαλοῦσιν is the future of συνεισβάλλω. Relations between Athens and Thebes were bad for most of the fourth century, except during brief periods of alliance (395- 387 and 378-371 B.C.). The two states were currently fighting on opposite sides in the Sacred War. For other instances of anti-Theban sentiment in Demosthenes, cf. *Against Leptines* 109 - μεῖζον Θηβαῖοι φρονοῦσιν ἐπ᾽ ὠμότητι καὶ πονηρίᾳ ἢ ὑμεῖς ἐπὶ φιλανθρωπίᾳ; *On the Symmories* 33 - Θηβαίους . . . διὰ γὰρ τὸ μισεῖν αὐτοὺς οὐδ᾽ ἂν ἀληθὲς οὐδὲν ἡδέως ἀγαθὸν περὶ αὐτῶν ἀκούσαιτε; *On the Peace* 15 - Θηβαίους οὐχ ὡς ἡδέως ἔχουσιν ἡμῖν, οὐδ᾽ ὡς οὐκ ἂν χαρίζοιντο Φιλίππῳ, ἀλλ᾽ ἴσασιν ἀκριβῶς, εἰ καὶ πάνυ φησί τις αὐτοὺς ἀναισθήτους εἶναι etc.; *On the Crown* 43 - οἱ κατάπτυστοι Θετταλοὶ καὶ ἀναίσθητοι Θηβαῖοι.

ἐὰν μὴ βουλήσηθ᾽ ὑμεῖς: 'unless you come to their assistance', probably a reference to the Athenian occupation of Thermopylae in 352 B.C., which kept Philip out of Phocis after his victory at the Battle of the Crocus Field. The orator's use of the construction of a general supposition (ἐάν + subjunctive) may however indicate that he is thinking of Athenian assistance in general, not just of the events of 352 B.C.

ἢ ἄλλος τις: to be construed as part of the preceding sentence, and parallel to ὑμεῖς. If Demosthenes had anyone in particular in mind, he may be thinking of the Spartans and Achaeans who, like Athens, sent help to Phocis in 352 B.C. Some scholars detach ἢ ἄλλος τις from this sentence and interpret it as yet another question parallel to Θηβαῖοι and Φωκεῖς, and providing yet another possible answer to the original question, 'who will stop Philip marching on Attica?'. However, though the orator answers the questions about the Thebans and Phocians, he does not do so in this particular instance and, in any case, a third question ought to be couched in the form ἀλλ' ἄλλος τις; rather than ἢ ἄλλος τις; (cf. above ἀλλὰ Φωκεῖς; rather than ἢ Φωκεῖς;).

ἀλλ', ὦ τᾶν, οὐχὶ βουλήσεται: 'but, my good sir, he will not wish to do so', put into the mouth of another imaginary member of the audience. ὦ τᾶν, 'my good fellow', is a common form of address, especially in Plato and comedy, used by Demosthenes above all to introduce an imaginary objection (cf. *3rd Olynthiac* 29 below; *On the Crown* 312).

τῶν ἀποπωτάτων μεντἄν εἴη: 'however it would be one of the strangest things of all', partitive genitive. μεντἄν is crasis of μέντοι ἄν, the optative with ἄν being potential.

εἰ ἃ νῦν ἄνοιαν ὀφλισκάνων ὅμως ἐκλαλεῖ, ταῦτα δυνηθεὶς μὴ πράξει: 'if, though he has the power, he does not carry out the threat he is now blurting out, despite the reputation for folly which he is acquiring'. ἃ . . . ταῦτα is an instance of an inverted relative sentence with the antecedent omitted; in such cases the principal clause frequently contains a demonstrative pronoun referring back to the omitted antecedent (G. 1030). ὀφλισκάνω (literally 'I owe') is used with δίκην in the judicial sense of 'lose one's case', 'be convicted'; from this usage comes the metaphorical use with objects such as δειλίαν, μωρίαν, αἰσχύνην etc. to mean 'incur a charge of'. This sentence takes the form of a mixed condition, with εἰ + future indicative in the protasis and potential optative with ἄν in the apodosis (G. 1421).

27. ἡλίκα: for the use of ἡλίκος 'as big as', 'as old as', as correlative to τηλικοῦτος, see on τηλικοῦτος ἡλίκος οὐδείς πω βασιλεὺς γέγονε, 9 above. Here the word is used as an indirect interrogative, with the meaning 'how great?'.

οὐδὲ λόγου προσδεῖν ἡγοῦμαι: 'I don't think that it even requires the addition of an argument', where οὐδέ means 'not even' rather than 'and not' (cf. on οὐδὲ τοὺς λιμένας, 22 above).

ἔξω: (*sc.* τῆς πόλεως) 'outside the city walls'.

καὶ ὅσ' ἀνάγκη (*sc.* ἐστι λαμβάνειν) στρατοπέδῳ χρωμένους τῶν ἐκ τῆς χώρας λαμβάνειν: 'and if you had to take from the

country such things as are necessary for men in camp
(*sc.* to take)', where λαμβάνειν is governed by δεήσειν but
must also be understood after ἀνάγκη. τῶν ἐκ τῆς χώρας
means 'the produce of the countryside'.

μηδένος ὄντος ἐν αὐτῇ πολεμίου λέγω: 'I mean supposing that
there is no enemy in the countryside', a parenthetical
clause containing a genitive absolute equivalent to a
conditional clause (hence the negative is μή, not οὐ;
cf. *G*. 1612).

τοὺς γεωργοῦντας ὑμῶν: 'those among you who are farmers',
where ὑμῶν is a partitive genitive.

τὸν πρὸ τοῦ πόλεμον: 'the war that has been going on up
to now', i.e. the war over Amphipolis, in which the
Athenians had been engaged ever since 357 B.C. In the
expression πρὸ τοῦ we have a survival of the demonstrative
use of the article, in what had become a standard phrase
(*G*. 984).

δεδαπάνησθε: 2nd person plural perfect middle of δαπανάω,
with the meaning 'spend in one's own interest'.

εἰ δὲ δὴ πόλεμός τις ἥξει: 'but of a war *does* come here'
(cf. on εἰ δὲ προησόμεθα, 12 above).

ζημιώσεσθαι: future infinitive middle, with passive sense
(cf. καταστήσεται, 22 above), in place of the rare
ζημιωθήσεσθαι. Grammar books advise that in so far as
there is a difference, the middle form is durative, the
true passive aoristic. Here the middle may perhaps
indicate that the effects of the damage to be inflicted
will be lasting.

καὶ πρόσεσθ': 'and there is in addition (πρόσεστι)', i.e.
'to this there is to be added'.

τῶν πραγμάτων αἰσχύνη: 'the disgrace of being in the position
in which we would find ourselves'.

τοῖς γε σώφροσι: 'to men of sense at least' (if not to all),
an example of the dative of reference, which is used to
denote the person in whose opinion a statement holds good.
(cf. Aristophanes, *Birds* 445-6 – πᾶσι νικᾶν τοῖς κριταῖς/
καὶ τοῖς θεαταῖς πᾶσι – 'to be victorious in the eyes of
all the judges and all the spectators'; and see *G*. 1172).

28. ἵν' ὑπὲρ τῶν πολλῶν ὧν καλῶς ποιοῦντες ἔχουσι μίκρ' ἀναλίσκοντες τὰ λοιπὰ καρπῶνται ἀδεῶς: 'so that they, having spent a little in defence of the great wealth which they are fortunate enough to possess, may enjoy the remainder in security', a final clause with the verb in the subjunctive in primary sequence. ὑπὲρ τῶν πολλῶν ὧν (for ἅ) is an example of the attraction of a relative pronoun in the accusative to the case of an antecedent in the genitive or dative (G. 1031), the first example of such attraction in the *Olynthiacs* in which the antecedent is not an omitted demonstrative pronoun. καλῶς ποιοῦντες is a colloquial phrase used to indicate an ungrudging appreciation of some fact 'I am happy to say', 'to which they are welcome'. The phrase is common in Plato and Aristophanes, and occurs elsewhere in Demosthenes, e.g. *Against Leptines* 110 - ὅτε δ' ὑμεῖς, καλῶς ποιοῦντες . . . ἄμεινον ἐκείνων πράττετε - 'when you are more prosperous than they, and I do not grudge you your prosperity'; *On the Crown* 231 - τῆς φιλανθρωπίας ὑμεῖς καλῶς ποιοῦντες τοὺς καρποὺς κεκόμισθε - 'you have enjoyed the fruits of his humanity, to which you are welcome'.

τοὺς ἐν ἡλικίᾳ: 'those of an age for military service', i.e. men aged from 18-60.

ἵνα . . . φοβεροὶ φύλακες τῆς οἰκείας ἀκεραίου γένωνται: 'so that they may become formidable guardians of a country, their own country, which remains unspoilt'. φοβερός is an adjective which can be used both actively, as here, with the meaning 'causing fear', 'terrible', and in the passive significance of 'afraid'. ἀκέραιος, being a compound adjective, has only two terminations. It is sometimes used in the sense of 'unmixed', 'pure', as if derived from κεράννυμι 'I mix', but occurs more frequently in the sense of 'unravaged', as if from κείρω or κεραΐζω 'I plunder'. In this passage, the word is used proleptically to mean 'so that it may remain inviolate'.

ἵν' αἱ τῶν πεπολιτευμένων αὐτοῖς εὔθυναι ῥᾴδιαι γένωνται: 'so that they might find it easy to render an account for their political activities'. εὐθύνη was the name given to the official audit undergone by Athenian magistrates when they laid down office (cf. δοκιμασία, the official scrutiny for in-coming magistrates which ensured that they were fit to hold office). Here the word is extended from magistrates to politicians in general, in a purely metaphorical sense. τῶν πεπολιτευμένων αὐτοῖς ('what has been done by them in the course of their political career') is an instance of the dative of the agent (=ὑπ' αὐτῶν), found only with verbal adjectives in -τέος and with the perfect and pluperfect passive of certain verbs (G. 1186). In the latter case it occurs chiefly with the neuter participle of πράττω and similar verbs (τὰ πεπραγμένα, τὰ εἰργασμένα, τὰ πεπολιτευμένα, τὰ πεπρεσβευμένα etc.) and with the perfect and pluperfect indicative where the subject is a neuter adjective or pronoun (e.g. *2nd Olynthiac* 27 - ἐξεστάσαι τί πέπρακται τοῖς ἄλλοις; *On the Embassy* 205 = πάντα τἀναντί' ἐμοὶ καὶ τούτοις πέπρακται - 'my conduct and theirs have been completely different'.

ὡς ὁποῖ' ἄττ' ἂν ὑμᾶς περιστῇ τὰ πράγματα: a relative sentence with ἄν + subjunctive referring to the future (G. 1434). περιστῇ is 3rd person singular 2nd aorist subjunctive of περιίστημι 'I get something around someone', used intransitively, 'stand around'.

τῶν πεπραγμένων αὐτοῖς: for the dative, see on τῶν πεπολιτευμένων αὐτοῖς in the preceding sentence.

χρηστὰ δ' εἴη παντὸς ἕνεκα (sc. τὰ πράγματα) 'may the circumstances be happy, on every ground', a wish for the future, expressed by the optative mood (G. 1507).

COMMENTARY

SECOND OLYNTHIAC

1. ἐπὶ πολλῶν: 'on many occasions'.

   ἄν τις ἰδεῖν . . . δοκεῖ μοι: 'it seems to me that one might see', where ἄν + infinitive, representing the potential optative (ἴδοι ἄν τις), is dependent on the verb δοκεῖ, used here in the personal construction (G. 1522.2).

   τὸ . . . τοὺς πολεμήσοντας Φιλίππῳ γεγενῆσθαι: 'the fact that Philip has men who are ready to fight him'. γεγενῆσθαι is perfect infinitive of γίγνομαι, used here as an articular infinitive serving as the subject of the verb ἔοικεν at the end of the sentence.

   τὴν ὑπὲρ τοῦ πολέμου γνώμην τοιαύτην ἔχοντας ὥστε τὰς πρὸς ἐκεῖνον διαλλαγὰς πρῶτον μὲν ἀπίστους, εἶτα τῆς ἑαυτῶν πατρίδος νομίζειν ἀνάστασιν: 'having such a sentiment with regard to the war that they regard any reconciliation with him in the first place as untrustworthy, then as the destruction of their country'. Consecutive clauses introduced by ὥστε may take the indicative or, as here, the infinitive; when there is a difference between the two, the infinitive designates a result that the principal verb tends to produce, the indicative a result that the principal verb really does produce (G. 1450). When πρῶτον μέν is followed by εἶτα or ἔπειτα, the δέ is often, though not invariably, omitted. The infinitive νομίζειν is to be taken with both the πρῶτον μέν and the εἶτα clauses.

   δαιμονίᾳ τινὶ καὶ θείᾳ παντάπασιν ἔοικεν εὐεργεσίᾳ: 'is like a benefaction that one might almost say came from heaven, one in every way divine', an example of *pleonasm* (see Introduction II 4 f(xii)). The indefinite τις is used here, much as *quidam* in Latin, to tone down or apologise for the rather bold use of a particular word. It is practically equivalent to the English 'if I might use the expression'.

2. δεῖ . . . σκοπεῖν . . . ὅπως μὴ χείρους περὶ ἡμᾶς αὐτοὺς εἶναι δόξομεν τῶν ὑπαρχόντων: 'we must see to it that we do not appear to treat ourselves less well than the circumstances do'. For the use of ὅπως with the future

125

indicative after a verb denoting effort, see G. 1372
(cf. on παρασκευάσασθαι . . . ὅπως . . . βοηθήσετε,
1st Olynthiac 2 above. χείρους is a contracted σ-stem
(for χείροσες) coexisting with χείρονες (cf. G. 358) as
nominative plural of χείρων 'worse', 'inferior', a
comparative adjective which serves as comparative of
κακός. For τῶν ὑπαρχόντων 'existing advantages',
'present circumstances', see on τῶν ὑπηργμένων,
1st Olynthiac 10 above and on τῶν ὑπαρξάντων,
1st Olynthiac 11 above.

ὡς ἐστι τῶν αἰσχρῶν, μᾶλλον δὲ τῶν αἰσχίστων: 'since it
is the mark of shame, or rather, of the very depths of
shame'. For the genitive, see on τῆς ὑμετέρας τύχης
ὑπολαμβάνω and on τῶν ἀτοπωτάτων μεντἂν εἴη, 1st
Olynthiac 1 and 26 respectively above.

μὴ μόνον πόλεων καὶ τόπων ὧν ἧμέν ποτε κύριοι προϊεμένους:
'abandoning not only the cities and places of which we
once were the masters'. Here we would expect πόλεις καὶ
τόπους as objects of προϊεμένους but instead we have an
instance of 'inverse attraction', where, in place of
the attraction of the relative to the case of its
antecedent, the antecedent is attracted to the case
of the relative (G. 1035). This construction is not
at all common and occurs only when the antecedent
would have been in the nominative or accusative; in
such cases the antecedent is usually placed immediately
in front of the relative to whose case it is attracted.

φαίνεσθαι προϊεμένους: 'to be seen openly to abandon'.
For the construction φαίνομαι + participle, cf. on
δέδοικα μὴ . . . ἡμεῖς . . . φανῶμεν ἐρραθυμηκότες,
1st Olynthiac 15 above.

ἀλλὰ καὶ τῶν ὑπὸ τῆς τύχης παρασκευασθέντων συμμάχων καὶ
καιρῶν: 'but also abandoning the allies and the
opportunities which have been provided for us by
fortune'. Since the nouns συμμάχων and καιρῶν also
form part of προϊεμένους, accusatives would be expected.
There is no good reason for the use of genitives here,
except that the two nouns πόλεων and τόπων in the
preceding clause, to which they are exactly parallel,
are themselves in the genitive.

3. τὸ μὲν οὖν . . . ἡγοῦμαι: this is picked up again with
ταῦτα μὲν οὖν παραλείψω at the beginning of 4 below,
and is intended to balance ἃ δὲ καὶ χωρὶς τούτων . . .
ταῦτ' εἰπεῖν πειράσομαι at the end of 4 below.

προτρέπειν: to encourage, exhort, urge on, persuade someone to do something.

καλῶς ἔχειν: ≠καλὸν εἶναι (cf. on σχήσειν καλῶς 1st Olynthiac 9 above.

διὰ τί: a question which the orator affects to believe a member of the audience to have asked, and to which he immediately provides an answer; see Introduction II 4 d.

ὑπὲρ τούτων: 'concerning these topics', i.e. τὴν Φιλίππου ῥώμην καὶ ... προτρέπειν τὰ δέοντα ποιεῖν ὑμᾶς.

ἐκείνῳ ἔχειν φιλοτιμίαν: 'bring credit to him'. φιλοτιμία normally means 'ambition' but can also mean, as here, 'distinction', 'honour', as the virtual synonym for δόξα.

ἡμῖν δ' οὐχὶ καλῶς πεπρᾶχθαι: 'but failure for us', a slightly euphemistic way of saying what Demosthenes states openly at the end of the next sentence (αἰσχύνην ὠφλήκατε). οὐχὶ καλῶς is equivalent to κακῶς, the use of a negative in place of a positive expression (the figure of speech called *litotes*). πεπρᾶχθαι is the perfect infinitive middle of πράττω.

ὅσῳ πλεῖον' ὑπὲρ τὴν ἀξίαν πεποίηκε τὴν αὐτοῦ, τοσούτῳ θαυμαστότερος παρὰ πᾶσι νομίζεται: 'the more he has accomplished beyond his real worth, the more marvellous he is held to be in the eyes of all'. ὅσῳ ... τοσούτῳ with comparative (literally 'by as much ... by so much') corresponds to the English 'the more ... the more'.

ὑμεῖς δ' ὅσῳ χεῖρον ἢ προσῆκε κέχρησθε τοῖς πράγμασι τοσούτῳ πλεῖον' αἰσχύνην ὠφλήκατε: 'the more you have failed to make proper use of your opportunities, the greater the disgrace you have incurred'. ὠφλήκατε is perfect tense of ὀφλισκάνω, for the use of which, see on ἄνοιαν ὀφλισκάνων, 1st Olynthiac 26 above.

4. ταῦτα μὲν οὖν παραλείψω: this phrase indicates that the whole of the preceding section is an example of the rhetorical device called *paraleipsis* (see Introduction II 4 e (iii).

εἰ μετ' ἀληθείας τις ... σκοποῖτο ἐνθένδ' ἂν αὐτὸν ἴδοι μέγαν γεγενημένον, οὐχὶ παρ' αὐτοῦ: 'if one were to examine the matter correctly, one could see that he has become great from here (i.e. Athens, or, more specific- ally, from the Athenian *ecclesia*) and not in himself', an example of a future conditional sentence in the less vivid form (G. 1387 and 1408).

ὧν οὖν ἐκεῖνος μὲν ὀφείλει τοῖς ὑπὲρ αὐτοῦ πεπολιτευμένοις χάριν, ὑμῖν δὲ δίκην προσήκει λαβεῖν, οὐχὶ νῦν ὁρῶ τὸν καιρὸν τοῦ λέγειν: 'of those activities for which Philip feels grateful to those whose political activities have been in his interest, and for which it is right for you to exact punishment, I do not at present see that this is the occasion to speak'. ὧν, to be taken with χάριν and δίκην, here introduces an inverted relative clause, the antecedent to which has to be supplied. On the most probable interpretation, we should supply ταῦτα, as the object of λέγειν at the end of the sentence, though some inferior manuscripts, followed by the Oxford Text, supply τούτων to be inserted immediately before the words οὐχὶ νῦν ὁρῶ. If correctly introduced, τούτων would have to be construed as one of two genitives dependent on καιρόν, the other being τοῦ λέγειν. For the inverted relative clause, cf. on εἰ νῦν . . . ἐκλαλεῖ, ταῦτα . . . μὴ πράξει, 1st Olynthiac 26 above (see G. 1032). τοῖς ὑπὲρ αὐτοῦ πεπολιτευμένοις should be translated 'to those whose political career has been pursued in his interest', a clear reference to the pro-Macedonian faction at Athens.

ἃ δὲ καὶ χωρὶς τούτων ἔνι: (sc. λέγειν) – 'but it is possible for me to mention topics other than these', picking up τὰ μὲν οὖν . . . τὴν Φιλίππου ῥώμην διεξιέναι καὶ προτρέπειν τὰ δέοντα ποιεῖν ὑμᾶς in the previous section. ἔνι, a poetic form of the preposition ἐν, is frequently used as equivalent to the impersonal verb ἔνεστι ('it is possible'). Strictly speaking it is an adverbial use of the preposition, with which the verb ἐστι is to be supplied; cf. the similar uses of μέτα and πάρα (note the change of accent) as equivalents for μέτεστι and πάρεστι respectively and, in verse, of ἄνα for ἀναστῆθι ('stand up').

καὶ βέλτιόν ἐστιν ἀκηκοέναι πάντας ὑμᾶς: 'it is better that you should all have heard'. ἀκηκοέναι is perfect infinitive of ἀκούω, with the significance 'to have heard and to know well as a result'.

καὶ μεγάλ' . . . κατ' ἐκείνου φαίνοιτ' ἂν ὀνείδη βουλομένοις ὀρθῶς δοκιμάζειν: 'things which to those willing to examine them properly would be revealed as a grave reproach against him'. The subject of φαίνοιτ' ἂν is ἃ (nominative), to be supplied from ἃ (accusative) at the beginning of the sentence. When two relative pronouns referring to the same antecedent (here ταῦτ')

have different cases, the second is usually either
replaced by a personal or demonstrative pronoun
(e.g. *3rd Olynthiac* 24 οἷς οὐκ ἐχαρίζονθ' οἱ λέγοντες
οὐδ' ἐφίλουν αὐτούς 'whom the speakers neither gratified
nor liked, where οὐδ' ἐφίλουν αὐτούς represents
οὓς οὐδ' ἐφίλουν) or, as here, simply omitted (*G.* 1040).
φαίνοιτ' ἄν is a potential optative.

5. τὸ μὲν οὖν ἐπίορκον καὶ ἄπιστον καλεῖν: articular infinitive, serving as the subject of the verb φήσειε.

   ἄνευ τοῦ τὰ πεπραγμένα δεικνύναι: 'without shedding light
   on his actions', another articular infinitive, this time
   dependent on the preposition ἄνευ.

   ἄν φήσειε: (aorist optative of φημί) 'one might say',
   potential optative.

   δικαίως: 'and with justice', 'and quite right too',
   placed emphatically at the end.

   τὸ δὲ πάνθ' ὅσα πώποτ' ἔπραξε διεξιόντ' ἐφ' ἅπασι τούτοις
   ἐλέγχειν: 'but to go through all the actions he has
   ever carried out and to convict him in every case'.
   The articular infinitive τὸ ἐλέγχειν serves as subject
   to συμβαίνει δεῖσθαι in the following clause, while the
   participle διεξιόντ' agrees with the pronoun (τινα)
   that has to be supplied as subject of ἐλέγχειν; cf. οὐκ
   ἔνι δ' αὐτὸν ἀργοῦντα (sc. τινα) οὐδὲ τοῖς φίλοις
   ἐπιτάττειν ('it is not possible for someone who is
   himself idle to give orders to his friends'), 23 below.

   βραχέος λόγου συμβαίνει δεῖσθαι: 'requires, as it happens,
   only a short speech', i.e. 'fortunately requires only
   a short speech'.

   δυοῖν ἕνεχ' ἡγοῦμαι συμφέρειν εἰρῆσθαι: 'I think that it
   is worthwhile for it to be told for two reasons', where
   εἰρῆσθαι is the perfect infinitive passive from the root
   of the future ἐρῶ and the aorist passive ἐρρήθην, which
   serves to supplement the various tenses of the verb
   λέγω. The use of the perfect infinitive here signifies
   that the action is to be decisive and permanent ('for
   it to be told once and for all'); cf. *G.* 1275).

   ὅπερ καὶ ἀληθὲς ὑπάρχει: 'as in actual fact too (i.e.
   in addition to the revelation of his baseness - φαῦλον
   φαίνεσθαι) is the case', where ὑπάρχει differs but
   little from ἔστι; cf. on παρὰ τῶν θεῶν ἡμῖν ὑπηργμένων,

1st Olynthiac 10, above.

τοὺς ὑπερεκπεπληγμένους ὡς ἄμαχόν τινα τὴν Φιλίππου: 'those who are excessively alarmed at Philip as being someone who is invincible'. The form ὑπερεκπεπληγμένους is the perfect participle passive of ὑπερεκπλήττω, where the prefix ὑπερ- is intensive, denoting 'very much', 'excessively'. Though passive in form, the verb is occasionally used with a direct object because in sense it is equivalent to the transitive verb 'I fear'.

ἰδεῖν ὅτι ταῦτα διεξελήλυθεν οἷς πρότερον παρακρουόμενος μέγας ηὐξήθη: 'see that he has run through everything on which he fraudulently grew great in the past'. διεξελήλυθεν is perfect indicative of διέρχομαι, in the sense of 'go through and exhaust in the process', while παρακρουόμενος is the participle of παρακρούομαι, regularly used in the sense of 'deceive', 'cheat'. This meaning is said by the lexicographer Harpocration to be derived from the practice of dishonest merchants who struck off (παρακρούω) too much from the top of the contents of a measure in order to defraud the purchaser, but no example of this use of the verb occurs in extant Greek literature. ηὐξήθη is the aorist passive of αὐξάνω, 'I exalt', 'I increase'; πρότερον is to be taken with both παρακρουόμενος and ηὐξήθη.

6. σφόδρ' ἂν ἡγούμην . . . φοβερὸν τὸν Φιλίππον καὶ θαυμαστόν, εἰ τὰ δίκαια πράττονθ' ἑώρων ηὐξημένον: 'I would regard Philip as being very much an object of fear and wonder, if I saw that he had become great as a result of doing what was right', an unreal condition in present time, with εἰ + imperfect indicative in the protasis and the imperfect with ἄν in the apodosis (*G.* 1397). σφόδρα is to be taken with both φοβερόν and θαυμαστόν, from which it is separated for emphasis. On φοβερόν, see *1st Olynthiac* 28 above. ηὐξημένον is the perfect participle passive of αὐξάνω.

νῦν δέ: 'but as it is'.

θεωρῶν καὶ σκοπῶν: another instance of pleonasm (see Introduction II 4 f(xii)).

εὑρίσκω τὴν μὲν ἡμετέραν εὐήθειαν . . . τῷ τὴν Ἀμφίπολιν φάσκων παραδώσειν . . . καὶ τὸ θρυλούμενόν ποτ' ἀπόρρητον ἐκεῖνον κατασκευάσαι, τούτῳ προσαγαγόμενον, τὴν δ' Ὀλυνθίων φιλίαν τῷ Ποτείδαιαν ἐξελεῖν . . .

Θετταλοὺς δὲ . . . τῷ Μαγνησίαν παραδώσειν ὑποσχέσθαι: 'I find that he has won over our guilelessness by saying that he would hand over Amphipolis and by fabricating that well-known secret . . . that he further won the friendship of the Olynthians by storming Poteidaea and that he conciliated the Thessalians by promising to hand over Magnesia'. τὴν ἡμετέραν εὐήθειαν, τὴν ᾿Ολυνθίων φιλίαν and Θετταλοὺς are all objects of the verb προσαγαγόμενον, distinguished in turn by the temporal phrases τὸ κατ᾽ ἀρχάς ('in the first place'; cf. 1st Olynthiac 12 above), μετὰ ταῦτα and νῦν τὰ τελευταῖα, and by the instrumental datives τῷ φάσκειν παραδώσειν (subsequently picked up by τούτῳ immediately preceding προσαγαγόμενον), τῷ Ποτείδαιαν ἐξελεῖν and τῷ Μαγνησίαν παραδώσειν ὑποσχέσθαι. Note Demosthenes' willingness to include himself among the Athenians who were duped by Philip (ἡμετέραν rather than ὑμετέραν εὐήθειαν). ἐνθένδε means 'from here', i.e. from the Athenian *ecclesia*, as in 4 above. ὅτ᾽ ᾿Ολυνθίους ἀπήλαυνόν τινες ('when certain persons were for driving off the Olynthians') refers to the existence of the leaders of a pro-Macedonian faction who were determined to undermine any possibility of a rapprochement with the Chalcidians.

βουλομένους ὑμῖν διαλεχθῆναι: 'who were desirous of negotiating with you', i.e. with reference to the conclusion of an alliance, in the course of the diplomatic negotiations of 357 B.C. initiated by the Chalcidians in response to Philip's siege of Amphipolis.

τὸ θρυλούμενόν ποτ᾽ ἀπόρρητον ἐκεῖνο: 'that notorious secret which was on everyone's lips', a sort of oxymoron (see Introduction II 4 f (vii)) justified to some extent by the fact that, though the nature of the secret may have been unknown to the general public, it was a matter of common knowledge that Philip was negotiating some secret deal. The content of this passage strongly suggests, though does not prove, that this secret had something to do with Amphipolis; Theopompus (fgt. 30 Jacoby) states quite specifically that Philip was involved in some sort of secret negotiations with two Athenian envoys, Antiphon and Charidemus who had suggested that, if Philip were to agree to hand over Amphipolis after its capture, the Athenians might be willing to give him in exchange Pydna, a city near the Macedonian seaboard with which they were currently in alliance. The secret negotiations were, on this interpretation, necessary to

allay the suspicions of the citizens of Pydna, who
would be guaranteed to object most strongly to the
deal were they to learn of it. This view was generally
accepted by modern scholars till the appearance of an
article by G.E.M. de Ste.-Croix (*The Alleged Secret
Pact between Athens and Philip II concerning Amphipolis
and Pydna*, Classical Quarterly 13 (1963) 110-119) who
rejected it on the grounds that there can be no place
for secret diplomacy in a democracy. However, it is
clear from Theopompus that there were negotiations
between Philip and Athens about the time of the fall
of Amphipolis and that Philip did at some time openly
express the intention of handing the city over to
Athens (τὴν 'Αμφίπολιν φάσκειν ἀποδώσειν, confirmed
by Demosthenes, *Against Aristocrates* 116 and *On
Halonnesus* 27), though the real nature of the secret,
if there ever was one, and if indeed it is connected
in time with the fall of Amphipolis, cannot be
determined. At all events the Athenians, while still
willing to believe in Philip's good will, rejected
the Chalcidian overtures, and by the time they
discovered the nature of Philip's real intentions, the
opportunity for concluding a Chalcidian alliance had
gone. The Euboean situation and the outbreak of the
Social War (see Introduction I 2, p.8) were
further distractions for Athens at this time.

7. Ποτείδαιαν: see on *1st Olynthiac* 9 above. Following
the city's capture in 356 B.C., Philip handed it over
to the Chalcidians, in accordance with the terms of
their alliance of the previous year. The verb ἐξελεῖν,
from ἐξαιρέω, means 'to take completely', 'to take by
storm', but the meaning 'destroy' is equally possible.
The extent of the destruction is by no means clear from
the one account of its fall to survive (Diodorus 16.8.5).

καὶ τοὺς μὲν πρότερον συμμάχους ὑμᾶς ἀδικῆσαι: if the
text is sound and ὑμᾶς is retained, the translation
would be 'he was wronging you, his former allies', and
the passage would be a reference to the alliance
concluded by Philip and the Athenians in the negotiations of 359 B.C. that followed the abortive rising led
by the Athenian-backed pretender Argaeus. This
alliance is attested elsewhere only by [Demosthenes] *On
Halonnesus* 10 - 'Ἀθηναίων οἱ ἐν Ποτειδαίᾳ κατοικοῦντες
οὐκ ὄντος αὐτοῖς πολέμου πρὸς Φίλιππον ἀλλὰ συμμαχίας,
and is not mentioned by Diodorus in his account of the
negotiations (16.4.1). Scholars who reject the alliance

delete the word ὑμᾶς and understand the orator to be
referring to the Potidaeans. But since Potidaea was
closely allied to Athens at the time and the home of
a large number of Athenian cleruchs, it is difficult
to believe that Potidaea could have been an ally of
Philip if the Athenians themselves were not.

Μαγνησίαν: on this territory, see on *1st Olynthiac*
13 and 22 above.

τὸν Φωκικὸν πόλεμον: the Sacred War of 356-346 B.C.,
in which Philip became involved in 354. See
Introduction pp.9-10.

ὅλως: 'in a word', 'in short'.

τῶν αὐτῷ χρησαμένων: 'of those who have come into contact
with him', 'of those who have had dealings with him'.
On this use of χράομαι, see on ἐχρώμεθα τῷ Φιλίππῳ,
1st Olynthiac 9 above.

τὴν γὰρ ἑκάστων ἄνοιαν ἀεὶ τῶν ἀγνοούντων ἐξαπατῶν καὶ
προσλαμβάνων οὕτως ηὐξήθη: 'for by deceiving and
conciliating the ignorance of each people in turn who
did not know him, in this way he increased his power'.
The plural of ἕκαστος is used to indicate 'each set' or
'each group' of people. ἀεί denotes 'in turn', 'from
time to time'; see on ἀεί τι τῶν πραγμάτων ὡς ἀλυσιτελές,
1st Olynthiac 14, above.

8. ὥσπερ . . . διὰ τούτων ἤρθη μέγας . . . οὕτως ὀφείλει διὰ
τῶν αὐτῶν τούτων καὶ καθαιρεθῆναι πάλιν: 'just as he
has been raised up by these deceits, so too it is
inevitable that by these very same deceits he will be
brought down', where ὥσπερ and οὕτως are used to
introduce the two parts of a comparative sentence.
ἤρθη is aorist passive of αἴρω 'I raise', καθαιρεθῆναι
of καθαιρέω, 'I pull down'.

ἐπειδὴ πάνθ᾽ ἕνεχ᾽ ἑαυτοῦ ποιῶν ἐξελήλεγκται: 'now that he
stands convicted of doing everything for his own sake',
where ἐξελήλεγκται is perfect passive of ἐλέγχω, 'examine',
'test', 'prove', 'convict'. ἕνεκα 'for the sake of'
normally, though not invariably, follows the word which
it governs.

καιροῦ . . . πρὸς τοῦτο πάρεστι Φιλίππῳ τὰ πράγματα:

'Philip's affairs have come to the present critical position', 'this is the critical situation to which Philip's fortunes have reached', where καιροῦ depends on πρὸς τοῦτο.

ἢ παρελθών τις ἐμοί, μᾶλλον δ᾽ ὑμῖν δειξάτω: 'otherwise let someone come forward and prove to me, or rather to you'. The first ἢ is not to be taken as the first of three alternatives, and is quite distinct from the two examples of the word which occur later in the sentence. The first ἢ means 'or else', 'or if not', 'failing which' (cf. ἢ φρασάτω τις ἐμοὶ παρελθών, 3rd *Olynthiac* 28 below).

δειξάτω ὡς οὐκ ἀληθῆ ταῦτ᾽ ἐγὼ λέγω, ἢ ὡς οἱ τὰ πρῶτ᾽ ἐξηπατημένοι τὰ λοιπὰ πιστεύουσιν, ἢ ὡς οἱ παρὰ τὴν αὑτῶν ἀξίαν δεδουλωμένοι [Θετταλοί] νῦν οὐκ ἂν ἐλεύθεροι γένοιντ᾽ ἄσμενοι: 'let him prove that what I say is false, or that those who have been deceived at first will trust him in future or that those who have been enslaved contrary to what they deserve would not now wholeheartedly welcome becoming free'. Here the two clauses linked by ἢ . . . ἢ are alternatives. Θετταλοί, though found in the manuscripts, was probably not part of Demosthenes' original text, but crept into the text as an explanatory gloss. οὐκ ἂν γένοιντ᾽ is a potential optative. ἄσμενοι ('glad') is emphasised by its final position in the sentence.

9. οἴεται δὲ βίᾳ καθέξειν αὑτὸν τὰ πράγματα: 'he thinks that Philip will retain his position by force'.

τῷ τὰ χωρία καὶ λιμένας καὶ τὰ τοιαῦτα προειληφέναι: 'through his prior occupation of the fortresses and harbours and positions such as these', an articular infinitive in the dative (instrumental usage, *G*. 1181), equivalent to 'because he is already in occupation of'. χωρία are 'fortified places', such as Pydna and Amphipolis, while λιμένας certainly includes Pagasae - places whose acquisition by Philip has been mentioned in several earlier passages (*1st Olynthiac* 9 and 12, *2nd Olynthiac* 6-7 above).

ὅταν μὲν γὰρ ὑπ᾽ εὐνοίας τὰ πράγματα συστῇ καὶ πᾶσι ταὐτὰ συμφέρῃ τοῖς μετέχουσι τοῦ πολέμου, καὶ συμπονεῖν καὶ φέρειν τὰς συμφορὰς καὶ μένειν ἐθέλουσιν ἄνθρωποι: 'for whenever power is consolidated by goodwill and all those

participating in the war have the same interests, men
are willing to share in the labour, endure the mis-
fortunes and remain steadfast'. This is an indefinite
temporal sentence denoting repetition, with ἄν +
subjunctive in the subordinate clause (G. 1431).
συστῇ is the second aorist subjunctive, with intransitive
meaning, of συνίστημι, 'I keep together'.

ὅταν δ' ἐκ πλεονεξίας καὶ πονηρίας τις ὥσπερ οὗτος
ἰσχύσῃ, ἡ πρώτη πρόφασις καὶ μικρὸν πταῖσμ' ἅπαντ'
ἀνεχαίτισε καὶ διέλυσεν: 'but whenever someone has
grown powerful through aggression and crime, as Philip
has, the first pretext, the merest stumble, throws him
to the ground and breaks his power'. ἰσχύσῃ is an
ingressive aorist (see on ἠσθένησε, 1st Olynthiac 13
above). ἀνεχαίτισε and διέλυσεν are gnomic aorists
(see on συνανήλωσε, 1st Olynthiac 11 and ἀπέστησαν,
1st Olynthiac 15 above). ἀναχαιτίζω, when used literally,
refers to a horse throwing its rider, a metaphor picked
up from the word πταῖσμα ('fall', 'stumble') while
διαλύω is used to refer to the dissolution of the power
base which Philip has constructed.

10. οὐ γάρ ἐστιν, οὐκ ἔστιν: an example of the rhetorical
figure anadiplosis (see Introduction II 4 f (xi))
used for emphasis in an emotional context, in which the
orator, in an outburst of moral indignation, passionately
insists that injustice cannot remain triumphant for long.

τὰ τοιαῦτ' εἰς μὲν ἅπαξ καὶ βραχὺν χρόνον ἀντέχει, καὶ
σφόδρα γ' ἤνθησεν ἐπὶ ταῖς ἐλπίσιν, ἂν τύχῃ, τῷ χρόνῳ δὲ
φωρᾶται καὶ περὶ αὑτὰ καταρρεῖ: 'such things endure
indeed for a moment, for a brief period, by reason of
the hopes they inspire; they blossom it may be, bravely,
but in time are found out and wither away', a moving
passage in which Philip's power based on injustice
is metaphorically depicted as a plant which is basically
unhealthy but which, for a time at least, may flourish
and even blossom, only to wither away when its unhealthy
condition is exposed. ἤνθησε is another gnomic aorist;
with ἂν τύχῃ we must supply ἀνθοῦντα or ἀνθήσαντα, 'if
ever they happen to bloom'. περὶ αὑτὰ καταρρεῖ, ('they
wither away around themselves') refers to the falling
off of blossoms around the plant; it implies that the
unsoundness lies in the internal condition of the plant
and is not the result of some purely external agency.

ὥσπερ γὰρ οἰκίας . . . καὶ πλοίου καὶ τῶν ἄλλων τῶν
τοιούτων τὰ κάτωθεν ἰσχυρότατ' εἶναι δεῖ, οὕτω καὶ τῶν
πράξεων τὰς ἀρχὰς καὶ τὰς ὑποθέσεις ἀληθεῖς καὶ δικαίας
εἶναι προσήκει: 'for just as in a house or in a vessel
or in any other structure of that kind, the lower parts
must be the most solid, so too must the beginnings and
foundations of actions be based on truth and justice' -
a simile derived from building which vividly draws the
parallel between the physical foundations of the material
object and the moral principles on which conduct is
based. The unusual combination of elaborate metaphor
followed by memorable simile illustrates clearly the
strength of feeling which the orator wishes to commun-
icate. In few passages of the *Olynthiacs* are his fervid
emotions conveyed more strikingly.

11. φημὶ δή: the regular formula in Demosthenes for
   introducing a specific proposal; cf. φημὶ δὴ διχῇ
   βοηθητέον εἶναι etc. *1st Olynthiac* 17 and φημὶ δὴ δεῖν
   εἰσφέρειν χρήματα, *2nd Olynthiac* 27.

   ὅπως τις λέγει κάλλιστα καὶ τάχιστα, οὕτως ἀρέσκει μοι:
   'the best and quickest method proposed by anyone, that
   is the method I approve'.

   Θετταλούς: hostility to Philip in Thessaly is also
   mentioned in *1st Olynthiac* 22 (see on that passage and
   on *2nd Olynthiac* 8 above).

   πρεσβείαν . . . ἣ τοὺς μὲν διδάξει ταῦτα, τοὺς δὲ παροξυνεῖ:
   the future indicative is used with the relative pronouns
   ὅς and ὅστις to express purpose (*G.* 1442). παροξυνεῖ
   with circumflex on the last syllable is future, as
   opposed to the present παροξύνει, which is paroxytone.

   εἰσιν ἐψηφισμένοι: periphrastic perfect middle from
   ψηφίζομαι. Such forms are regularly used in the third
   person plural of the perfect and pluperfect middle of
   verbs with consonantal stems, since the simple form
   would be unpronouncable (*G.* 486ff.).

   Παγασάς, Μαγνησίας: see on *1st Olynthiac* 9 and 12, *2nd
   Olynthiac* 7 above.

   περὶ Μαγνησίας λόγους ποιεῖσθαι: 'to open negotiations
   concerning Magnesia', i.e. to raise with Philip the
   question of his continued occupation of the territory.

Nothing in fact seems to have resulted from these negotiations if indeed they were ever held.

12. σκοπεῖσθε . . . ὅπως μὴ λόγους ἐροῦσιν μόνον οἱ παρ' ἡμῶν πρέσβεις: 'see to it that our ambassadors do not confine themselves to talk', an example of an object clause with verb in the future indicative after a verb of striving (G. 1372). ἐρῶ serves as future to λέγω, as well as λέξω.

ἀλλὰ καὶ ἔργον τι δεικνύειν ἕξουσι: 'but that they are also able to indicate some deed'. δείκνυω is a rare verbal form used in place of the much commoner δείκνυμι, presumably here to avoid the hiatus δεικνύναι ἕξουσι.

ἐξεληλυθότων ὑμῶν ἀξίως τῆς πόλεως καὶ ὄντων ἐπὶ τοῖς πράγμασιν: 'as a result of your having marched out in a manner worthy of the city, and being engaged in action'. ἐξεληλυθότων is perfect participle of ἐξέρχομαι, the favourite word of Demosthenes to indicate the despatching of an Athenian military force (cf. 1st Olynthiac 6 above and 2nd Olynthiac 13 below).

ἅπας . . . λόγος, ἂν ἀπῇ τὰ πράγματα, μάταιόν τι φαίνεται καὶ κενόν: 'all words, if not accompanied by action, are seen to be in vain and empty', where ἂν (=ἐάν) is used with the subjunctive in the protasis of a conditional clause denoting a general truth (present general condition, G. 1393 and 1431). μάταιον . . . καὶ κενόν is yet another example of pleonasm (see Introduction II 4 f(xii). ὅσῳ γὰρ ἑτοιμότατ' αὐτῷ δοκοῦμεν χρῆσθαι, τοσούτῳ μᾶλλον ἀπιστοῦσι πάντες αὐτῷ: literally 'by as much as we are thought to make use of it (i.e. words as opposed to deeds) most readily, by so much more do all men mistrust it'. i.e. 'the more we are thought to make use of words, the more distrustful all men become'. The regular construction is ὅσῳ + comparative in the subordinate clause with τοσούτῳ + comparative in the principal clause (G. 1184) but examples of a superlative in both clauses or, as here, a comparative in one clause and a superlative in the other occur occasionally. See e.g. [Demosthenes], On the Letter 23 ἅπας . . . ἐστι λόγος μάταιος πράξεως ἄμοιρος γενόμενος, τοσούτῳ δὲ μάλισθ' ὁ παρὰ τῆς ἡμετέρας πόλεως, ὅσῳ δοκοῦμεν αὐτῷ προχειρότατα χρῆσθαι τῶν ἄλλων Ἑλλήνων; Demosthenes, Against Polycles 15, ὅσῳ . . . ἄμεινον ἐπληρωσάμην τὴν ναῦν, τοσούτῳ μοι πλείστη ἀπόλειψις ἐγένετο. The

Athenian preference for words over deeds is also
mentioned at *3rd Olynthiac* 14-15 below and at
2nd Philippic 4, ἐν οἷς ἑκάτεροι διατρίβετε καὶ περὶ
ἃ σπουδάζετε, ταῦτ' ἄμεινον ἑκατέροις ἔχει, ἐκείνῳ
μὲν (sc. Φιλίππῳ) αἱ πράξεις, ὑμῖν δ' οἱ λόγοι.

13. πολλὴν δὴ τὴν μετάστασιν καὶ μεγάλην δεικτέον τὴν
μεταβολήν: 'you must show a great change and a great
reformation', where δεικτέον is the verbal adjective
from δείκνυμι, expressing necessity (cf. on
ἀντιληπτέον, *1st Olynthiac* 2 above). μετάστασιν . . .
μεταβολὴν is yet another example of *pleonasm*; so far
as the two words can be distinguished, the former may
indicate the state resulting from change 'changed
attitude', while the latter denotes the act of change.

εἰσφέροντας, ἐξιόντας: on εἰσφορά, see on *1st Olynthiac*
6 above and Introduction, Appendix B. With the
sentiments expressed in this sentence, cf. Introduction
I 2, note 34. The participles εἰσφέροντας, ἐξιόντας
and ποιοῦντας agree with ὑμᾶς, which is to be supplied as
accusative of the agent with the verbal adjective
δεικτέον, 'by you'. Though the dative is the normal
case for expressing the agent with the verbal adjective,
examples of the accusative occur (*G*. 1597).

εἴπερ τις ὑμῖν προσέξει τὸν νοῦν: 'if indeed anyone pays
any attention to you', 'if anybody takes you seriously'.
For the use of the future indicative in the protasis
of a conditional clause expressing an appeal to the
feelings or indicating a threat or warning, see *G*. 1405.
Cf. on εἰ δὲ προησόμεθα καὶ τούτους τοὺς ἀνθρώπους,
1st Olynthiac 12 above.

κἂν ταῦτ' ἐθελήσηθ' ὡς προσήκει καὶ δὴ περαίνειν: 'and
if you consent to accomplish this at once as it ought
to be accomplished'. καὶ δὴ approximates in sense to
the adverb ἤδη (see Denniston, *Greek Particles* 252).
For the meaning of ἐθέλω, cf. on τοῦ μὴ τὰ δέοντα ποιεῖν
ἐθέλειν, *1st Olynthiac* 6 above.

τὰ συμμαχικὰ ἀσθενῶς καὶ ἀπίστως ἔχοντα φανήσεται Φιλίππῳ:
'Philip's alliances will be seen to be in a weak and
precarious state'. For the use of ἔχω with an adverb
as equivalent to εἶναι with the corresponding adjective,
see on σχήσειν καλῶς *1st Olynthiac* 9 above. For the
meaning of φαίνομαι with the participle, see on φανῶμεν

ἐρραθυμηκότες, 1st Olynthiac 15 above.

τὰ τῆς οἰκείας ἀρχῆς καὶ δυνάμεως κακῶς ἔχοντ' ἐξελεγχθήσεται: 'the poor and weak state of his own power and position will be revealed'. For τά with the genitive (sc. πράγματα), cf. 1st Olynthiac 21 τὰ τῶν Θετταλῶν. οἰκεῖος denotes here either 'one's own', 'belonging to oneself', 'personal', or 'domestic', 'belonging to one's household'. The meaning here is either 'his personal power and position', or 'his power and position at home'. ἐξελεγχθήσεται is future passive, from ἐξελέγχω; for the meaning of this verb, see on ἐξελήλεγκται, 2nd Olynthiac 8 above.

14. ὅλως: 'on the whole', 'speaking generally', 'in a word' (cf. on 1st Olynthiac 5 above), used here to summarise the position of the Macedonian monarchy. The first μέν in this sentence, used here with ὅλως and without any following δέ to which it marks a contrast, has the function of emphasising the word which it accompanies (the so-called μέν solitarium; cf. Denniston, Greek Particles 380-84).

ἐν μὲν προσθήκῃ μερίς ἐστιν οὐ μικρά: 'as an accessory it is a not unimportant factor', an example of the negative expression of a positive idea (litotes). προσθήκῃ denotes something added, 'an addition', 'a supplement', 'an adjustment', while μερίς means 'part', 'portion', 'share', 'contribution'.

ὑπῆρξε: for the use of the verb ὑπάρχω as a virtual synonym for εἰμί, cf. 1st Olynthiac 10 τῶν ὑπηργμένων, 11 τῶν ὑπαρξάντων, 14 τῶν ὑπαρχόντων, 25 τὴν ὑπάρχουσαν and 2nd Olynthiac 2 τῶν ὑπαρχόντων, 5 ὑπάρχει. With οἷον ὑπῆρξε, μερίς οὐ μικρά is to be understood from the previous clause.

ἐπί Τιμοθέου: 'in the time of Timotheus'. The reference is to the famous Athenian general Timotheus son of Conon who in the course of the campaigns of 364 B.C. captured Pydna, Potidaea and Torone and detached Philip's elder brother Perdiccas III from his alliance with the Chalcidians. A pupil of the orator Isocrates, Timotheus and his services to Athens are praised by his teacher in the Antidosis (Isocrates 15.107-113).

πάλιν αὖ πρὸς Ποτείδαιαν Ὀλυνθίοις ἐφάνη τι τοῦτο συμαμφότερον: 'again on another occasion, this united power proved to be of some importance to the Olynthians against Potidaea', where συναμφότερον (literally 'both together') is used exceptionally as an equivalent to σὺν ἄλλῳ γενόμενον ('in combination with one another'). The reference is to Philip's capture, with Chalcidian support, of Potidaea in 356 B.C. See on *1st Olynthiac* 9 above; and cf. *1st Olynthiac* 12 and *2nd Olynthiac* 6-7.

νυνὶ δὲ Θετταλοῖς νοσοῦσι καὶ στασιάζουσι καὶ τεταραγμένοις ἐπὶ τὴν τυραννικὴν οἰκίαν ἐβοήθησεν: 'and recently the Macedonian power has come to the assistance of the Thessalians who are plagued by faction and strife and are disordered, to help them against the tyrant house'. The orator is here referring to the dissensions between the central government of the Thessalian Confederacy and the ruling house of Pherae. The two tyrants of Pherae, Lycophron and Peitholaus, fought as Phocian allies in the Sacred War, while the Thessalian Confederacy was hostile to Phocis. Philip entered the Sacred War in 353 B.C. on the side of the Thessalian Confederacy and in the following year expelled Lycophron and Peitholaus from Pherae (see Introduction I 2, p.10); cf. on Πάγασαι *1st Olynthiac* 9 and Θετταλίας *1st Olynthiac* 12 above. The manuscript reading νοσοῦσι καὶ στασιάζουσι καὶ τεταραγμένοις provides an exception to the orator's usual preference for a pleonasm consisting of two nearly synonymous words. It is probable that either νοσοῦσι or στασιάζουσι has entered the text as an explanatory gloss and that one or other of these participles should be deleted. Two manuscripts, including the best, in fact omit the words νοσοῦσι καί.

καὶ ὅποι τις ἄν, οἶμαι, προσθῇ κἂν μικρὰν δύναμιν, πάντ᾽ ὠφελεῖ: 'and whenever anyone makes an addition to a force, however small that addition may be, it helps in every way'. The subjunctive with ἄν is here used in a conditional relative clause denoting repetition in a generalising statement (G. 1431). When the particle is used with a subjunctive, it either coalesces with the relative or conjunction (to become ἐάν, ὅταν, etc) or is separated from it only by a monosyllabic particle such as τε, δέ, γάρ. The insertion of τις, as here, is quite exceptional. κἂν μικρὰν δύναμιν is best explained as an ellipse, representing κἂν (=καὶ ἐάν) τις προσθῇ μικρὰν δύναμιν. πάντ᾽ is an internal accusative after ὠφελεῖ, 'it helps in every way' (G. 1054).

αὕτη δὲ καθ᾽ αὑτήν: 'by itself', as opposed to ἐν μὲν προσθήκῃ at the beginning of 14 above.

15. καὶ γὰρ οὗτος ἅπασι τούτοις, οἷς ἄν τις μέγαν αὐτὸν ἡγήσαιτο, τοῖς πολέμοις καὶ ταῖς στρατείαις, ἔτ' ἐπισφαλεστέραν ἢ ὑπῆρχε φύσει κατεσκεύακεν αὐτῷ: 'for by his wars and expeditions and all those things in which one might suppose him to be great, he has rendered Macedonia still more insecure for himself than it naturally was'.

καὶ τοῦτ' ἐζήλωκε: 'and has made this his ambition', where τοῦτ' means τὸ δόξης ἐπιθυμεῖν. ζηλόω with the accusative of the person means 'I envy' or 'I emulate', with the cause of rivalry, if any, being expressed by the genitive, e.g. ζηλῶ σε τοῦ νοῦ, 'I envy you your mind' (Sophocles, *Electra* 1027; cf. *G*. 1126). With the accusative of the thing, ζηλόω means 'I strive to attain' (some desirable quality).

καὶ προῄρηται πράττων καὶ κινδυνεύων, ἂν συμβῇ τι, παθεῖν: 'and has chosen to suffer in a life of action and danger, whatever may befall him'. συμβῇ is second aorist subjunctive of συμβαίνει ('it happens'), used with ἄν (=ἐάν) in a general supposition (*G*. 1393). προαιρέομαι is regularly used to indicate a deliberate choice on someone's part to follow one out of several possible courses of action.

τὴν τοῦ διαπράξασθαι ταῦθ' ἃ μηδεὶς πώποτ' ἄλλος Μακεδόνων βασιλεὺς δόξαν ἀντὶ τοῦ ζῆν ἀσφαλῶς ᾑρημένος: 'having chosen in preference to a life of safety the glory of accomplishing such things as no other king of Macedonia ever accomplished'. The article τὴν is to be taken with δόξαν some ten words later, which in turn governs its articular infinitive τοῦ διαπράξασθαι. ᾑρημένος is perfect participle middle for αἱρέω, meaning 'choose'. With the relative clause ἃ μηδεὶς πώποτ' ἄλλος Μακεδόνων βασιλεύς we must supply the verb διεπράξατο from the infinitive διαπράξασθαι above. The negative in the relative clause is here μή rather than οὐ because the clause is general in sense (*G*. 1428 and 1610). This passage, like *1st Olynthiac* 3, shows a somewhat grudging appreciation of Philip's accomplishments, and comes as close to praise of Philip, as any passage in Demosthenes' work. Cf. *On the Crown* 67 - Φίλιππον . . . ὑπὲρ ἀρχῆς καὶ δυναστείας τὸν ὀφθαλμὸν ἐκκεκομμένον, τὴν κλεῖν κατεαγότα, τὴν χεῖρα, τὸ σκέλος πεπηρωμένον, πᾶν ὅ τι βουληθείη μέρος ἡ τύχη τοῦ σώματος παρελέσθαι, τοῦτο προϊέμενον ὥστε τῷ λοιπῷ μετὰ τιμῆς καὶ δόξης ζῆν, 'Philip for the sake of power and supremacy has had his eye cut out, his collar bone shattered, his hand and leg

maimed and has lost whatever part of his body fortune
might wish to take from him, provided that he could live
with the rest intact in glory and renown'.

16. τοῖς δέ: refers to τοὺς ἀρχομένους above.

ἄνω κάτω: 'up and down', 'to and fro', 'all over the place'.
The phrase also occurs in the form ἄνω καὶ κάτω, but the
omission of the connective (*asyndeton*) makes for
vividness in suggesting the idea of constant campaigning.

λυποῦνται καὶ συνεχῶς ταλαιπωροῦσιν: yet another instance
of *pleonasm*.

οὔτ᾽ ἐπὶ τοῖς ἔργοις οὔτ᾽ ἐπὶ τοῖς αὐτῶν ἰδίοις ἐωμένοι
διατρίβειν: 'allowed to spend time neither on their
work nor on their own personal affairs'. ἔργον here
means 'occupation', 'employment'.

οὔθ᾽ ὅσ᾽ ἂν ποιήσωσιν οὕτως ὅπως ἂν δύνωνται ταῦτ᾽ ἔχοντες
διαθέσθαι: 'unable to dispose of the little they are
able to produce, in whatever way they can', with
reference primarily to the agricultural produce of their
land. The relative clauses in the subjunctive mood with
ἄν are indefinite (*G*. 1431).

κεκλειμένων τῶν ἐμπορίων τῶν ἐν τῇ χώρᾳ, διὰ τὸν πόλεμον:
'the trading posts in the country being closed on
account of the war', genitive absolute. κεκλειμένων
is perfect participle passive from κλήω, κλείω, 'I shut'.
Demosthenes is referring here to the difficulties faced
by the Macedonians in trying to conduct maritime trade
at a time when the hostile Athenians were in command
of the sea: so little trade would have been carried
on in the event of an Athenian blockade that it would
have been unprofitable to keep the trading stations
open. However as Macedonia was agriculturally self-
sufficient, any damage inflicted on her economy by such
means can scarcely have been as serious as the orator
claims.

17. πῶς ἔχουσι Φιλίππῳ, ἐκ τούτων ἄν τις σκέψαιτ᾽ οὐ χαλεπῶς:
'one would not have any difficulty in finding out how
they are disposed to Philip', i.e. 'what attitude they
have towards him', 'in what light they regard him' -
potential optative with ἄν (*G*. 1327ff.).

ξένοι: literally, 'foreign troops', i.e. mercenaries hired by Philip in large numbers, thanks to the rich deposits of gold and silver in the areas which he controlled.

πεζέταιροι: 'Foot Companions'. In the reign of Alexander the Great this term was applied to the entire native Macedonian infantry, as distinct from the Companion Cavalry and the mercenaries. According to Theopompus (fgt. 348 Jacoby), the *pezetairoi* were an elite group of infantry who served as the Royal Bodyguard, i.e. they were the men called *hypaspists* in the reign of Alexander. Since Theopompus was neither a Macedonian nor a military expert, it is likely that he simply confused the terms *pezetairoi* and *hypaspists*, but if his evidence is accepted, we have to postulate a transfer of the title from the Bodyguards to the entire *phalanx* about the time of Alexander's accession. In view of this uncertainty we cannot tell whether the term *pezetairoi* in Philip's reign referred to the entire *phalanx* or to the elite bodyguard only; and Demosthenes probably had no definite information on the subject. To him the word was an obscure, if rather exotic name, and no more.

συγκεκροτημένοι τὰ τοῦ πολέμου: (*sc*. πράγματα) 'well trained in the affairs of war'. συγκροτέω, (literally 'I knock together') is used by Demosthenes to indicate the fashioning of a group of inexperienced individuals into a skilled company. Cf. *Against Meidias* 17, Τηλεφάνης . . . αὐτοὺς συγκροτεῖν καὶ διδάσκειν ᾤετο δεῖν τὸν χόρον, with reference to the training of a tragic chorus.

ὡς δ' ἐγὼ τῶν ἐν αὐτῇ τῇ χώρᾳ γεγενημένων τινος ἤκουν: an attempt by the orator to establish a greater degree of credibility by claiming to have first-hand information on the subject. Such a claim is not without precedent in Demosthenes (cf. *1st Olynthiac* 22 above and *1st Philippic* 24) and his failure to name his authority is fully in accord with oratorical convention. The similarity between Demosthenes' account of the immorality of Philip's court and Theopompus' description (fgt. 225 Jacoby. cf. fgts. 224, 236 and 263) is so close that scholars have been tempted to postulate the historian as Demosthenes' informant. Certainly both men had been pupils of Aesion (Suda, s.v. Demosthenes), but they had totally dissimilar political outlooks, and the orator was criticised both by

Theopompus' teacher Isocrates (*Philip* 73-5, where he
is not mentioned by name), and by Theopompus himself
(Plutarch, *Demosthenes* 13). A close relationship
between the men is unlikely and, while we know that
Theopompus was at the Macedonian court in 343/2 B.C.
(Speusippus, *Letter to Philip*), we have no clear
evidence for an earlier visit around 349. Which
writer is borrowing from the other must remain undet-
ermined.

ἀνδρὸς οὐδαμῶς οἵου τε (*sc.* ὄντος) ψεύδεσθαι: 'a man
wholly incapable of lying'.

οὐδένων εἰσὶ βελτίους: literally 'they are better than
no others', a sort of *litotes*, equivalent to 'they are
no better than anyone else'. The plural of οὐδείς is
rare, but is occasionally found with the meaning 'no
set of individuals', or in the sense of 'nobodies',
'nonentities', 'mere cyphers'.

18. ἀνήρ . . . οἷος ἔμπειρος πολέμου καὶ ἀγώνων: 'such a
man as is skilled in battle and engagements', where
with οἷος we must supply the correlative τοιοῦτος.
The phrase is an elliptical version of the fuller
ἀνὴρ τοιοῦτος οἷος ἐστιν ἔμπειρος. Adjectives denoting the possession or lack of skill, ability, knowledge
etc. (such as ἐπιστήμων, ἔμπειρος, ἀμαθής, ἄπειρος) are
followed by the genitive case.

τούτους μὲν φιλοτιμίᾳ πάντας ἀπωθεῖν αὐτὸν ἔφη: 'he said
that he keeps away all these people through jealousy'.
τούτους is here used to denote a class ('such people
as these') and refers back, though plural, to εἰ μὲν
γάρ τις ἀνήρ. Cf. *3rd Philippic* 61 - τῶν δὲ πολλῶν εἴ
τις αἴσθοιτο, ἐσίγα καὶ κατεπέπληκτο τὸν Εὐφραῖον οἵ
ἔπαθε μεμνημένοι; Xenophon, *Memorabilia* 1.2.62 - ἐάν
τις φανερὸς γένηται κλέπτων . . . τούτοις θάνατος ἐστιν
ἡ ζημία. The subject of ἔφη is Demosthenes' unnamed
informant; αὐτόν refers of course to Philip.

πρὸς γὰρ αὖ τοῖς ἄλλοις καὶ τὴν φιλοτιμίαν ἀνυπέρβλητον
εἶναι: 'furthermore, in addition to his other defects,
he has an ambition that is insatiable', a parenthetical
clause (for Demosthenes' fondness for parenthesis, see
Introduction II 4 e(i)), in *oratio obliqua*, still
forming part of the report of the orator's informant.
ἀνυπέρβλητος means 'unable to be surpassed', from the
verb ὑπερβάλλω, 'I excel'. ἀνυπέρβλητον refers to
Philip, who is to be understood as the unexpressed

subject of εἶναι, with τὴν φιλοτιμίαν as an accusative of respect (G. 1058).

εἰ δέ τις σώφρων ἢ δίκαιος ἄλλως: (sc. ἐστι) 'if there is anyone who is temperate and upright in other respects'. ἄλλως is probably intended to mark the contrast between the moral qualities and the military skills mentioned in the previous sentence.

τὴν καθ' ἡμέραν ἀκρασίαν τοῦ βίου καὶ μέθην καὶ κορδακισμοὺς οὐ δυνάμενος φέρειν: 'unable to endure the wantonness of his daily life, the drunkenness and the lewdness of the dancing', where καθ' ἡμέραν is to be taken not only with ἀκρασίαν but also with μέθην and κορδακισμούς. ἀκρασία means 'licentiousness', 'incontinence', 'inability to master one's desires'. κορδακισμός is the act of dancing the *kordax*, an indecent dance, associated particularly with Old Comedy, involving drunken participants in obscene bodily postures (see Aristophanes, *Clouds* 540 and 557 ff., with scholia; and Theophrastus, *Characters* 6, where the reckless man is said to dance the *kordax* when sober and without a mask on his face). For other references to Philip's drunkenness, see Theopompus, fgts. 27 and 282 Jacoby; Carystus in Athenaeus 10.435D; Diodorus 16.55 and 87; Plutarch, *Demosthenes* 16.2 and 20.3. For his drunken dancing, see Theopompus, fgts. 81 and 162. Though forming part of the protasis of a conditional clause, the participle δυνάμενος is accompanied by οὐ rather than μή because the two are to be taken closely together. οὐ δυνάμενος is virtually equivalent to ἀδύνατος ὤν or ἀδυνατῶν.

παρεῶσθαι καὶ ἐν οὐδένος εἶναι μέρει τὸν τοιοῦτον: 'such a person is thrust aside and is held of no acount' (literally 'is in the category of nothing'). παρεῶσθαι is the perfect infinitive passive of παρωθέω ('I thrust aside') and is an example of the gnomic perfect, i.e. a perfect tense indicative of a general truth, in place of the more common gnomic aorist. For the gnomic perfect, see G. 1295.

19. τοιούτους ἀνθρώπους οἵους μεθυσθέντας ὀρχεῖσθαι τοιαῦθ' οἷ' ἐγὼ νῦν ὀκνῶ πρὸς ὑμᾶς ὀνομάσαι: 'such men as are capable of getting drunk and performing such dances as I would hesitate to mention in your presence'. The

infinitive is regularly used after adjectives denoting fitness, ability and sufficiency (e.g. δεινός, ἄξιος, δυνατός, πρόθυμος, ἱκανός, οἷος); see G. 1526. τοιαῦθ' (τοιαῦτα) with ὀρχεῖσθαι is an internal accusative, where with the neuter plural τοιαῦθ' we have to supply a noun like ὀρχήματα (G. 1051 and 1054). For the link between drunkenness and dancing in antiquity, cf. Herodotus 6.129 (the story of Hippocleides); Aristophanes, Wasps 1476-8; Cicero, Pro Murena 6.13 - *nemo enim fere saltat sobrius, nisi forte insanit;* Theophrastus, Characters 12, where the unseasonable man is described as the sort of person who, after dancing once, seizes as partner someone who is not yet drunk. Demosthenes may be thinking in this passage of dances such as the *sikinnis,* the dance associated with satyric drama (Euripides, Cyclops 37; Athenaeus 1.20E; Lucian, Peri Orcheseos 22) and the *mothon,* a lewd dance mentioned by Aristophanes (Knights 697).

ἐνθένδε: 'from here', i.e. from Athens.

ἀπήλαυνον: the verb probably denotes unofficial banishment from acceptable society, as opposed to formal exile (ἐκβάλλω).

θαυματοποιῶν: the word means literally 'maker of marvels' and is used to refer to public entertainers of various sorts, including acrobats, jugglers and conjurors. The present passage provides a clear indication of the low social position of such men at Athens.

Καλλίαν ἐκεῖνον τὸν δημόσιον: 'that notorious Callias the executioner'. With δημόσιον, literally 'belonging to the public', we have to supply δοῦλον (cf. the similar use of δήμιος). Public slaves were employed in a fairly humble capacity at lower levels of the administration, e.g. as junior accountants, town criers and law enforcement officers (the Scythian archers known from Aristophanes' comedies). In the sense of 'hangman', the δήμιος or δημόσιος worked under the supervision of the Eleven, the board of officials in charge of law and order, prisons and execution. Despite the orator's claim that Callias was well-known, nothing further is known of him.

μίμους γελοίων: 'players of farces'. A μῖμος is an actor or performer in a mime; γελοίων is neuter plural, from the adjective γέλοιος, 'amusing'.

ποιητὰς αἰσχρῶν ᾀσμάτων: 'composers of indecent songs'.

ὧν εἰς τοὺς συνόντας ποιοῦσιν: 'which they direct
against their companions'. ὧν, for ἅ is attracted
to the case of its antecedent ᾀσμάτων (see on περὶ
ὧν σκοπεῖτε, 1st Olynthiac 1 above; G. 1032).
Philip's fondness for the company of low comedians
and scurrilous lampoonists is also attested by
Theopompus, fgts. 81, 162, 224, 225 and 236, where
the word βωμόλοχος ('buffoon', 'coarse jester') is
frequently used to denote men of this sort. These
passages add to the list of Philip's low acquaintances
the names of Aristonicus the player of the *cithara*,
Dorion the piper and Agathocles, the Thessalian serf
(*penestes*).

20. τῆς ἐκείνου γνώμης καὶ κακοδαιμονίας: 'his disposition
and delusion'. κακοδαιμονία, in addition to the common
meaning 'unhappiness', 'misfortune', can be used more
generally to denote the condition of someone possessed
by some infatuate blindness. It is thus capable of
being translated 'delusion', 'infatuation', 'perversity',
'wrong-headedness', or similar words.

ἐπισκοτεῖ τούτοις τὸ κατορθοῦν: 'his success casts a veil
over these things', where ἐπισκοτέω means literally 'over-
shadow', 'cast a shadow upon'. τὸ κατορθοῦν is an articular infinitive (G. 955 and 1542) doing duty for the noun
κατόρθωμα, which is not found in classical Greek.

αἱ γὰρ εὐπραξίαι δειναὶ (sc. εἰσι) συγκρύψαι τὰ τοιαῦθ᾽
ὀνείδη: 'for successes are well able to cover up scandals
such as these'. The plural of abstract nouns is used to
denote specific instances, occurrences or manifestations
of the idea expressed by the abstract. Thus μανίαι would
mean 'concrete examples of madness'. Cf. *On the Crown*
246 - καὶ ἔτι τὰς ἑκασταχοῦ βραδυτῆτας, ὄκνους, ἀγνοίας,
φιλονεικίας . . . ταῦθ᾽ ὡς εἰς ἐλάχιστα συστεῖλαι. For
the infinitive with δεινός, cf. on ἀνθρώπους οἵους
ὀρχεῖσθαι, 2nd Olynthiac 19 above.

εἰ δέ τι πταίσει, τότ᾽ ἀκριβῶς αὐτοῦ ταῦτ᾽ ἐξετασθήσεται:
'if he slips up in any way, all these vices will then be
fully revealed'. For εἰ with the future indicative, see
on εἰ δὲ προησόμεθα, 1st Olynthiac 12 and G. 1405.

δοκεῖ δ᾽ ἐμοίγ᾽ . . . δείξειν οὐκ εἰς μακράν: literally
'it seems to me that it will appear in the not too
distant future', i.e. 'I should imagine that all will
be revealed in due course'. Here the third person
of the verb δείκνυμι is used impersonally and absol-

utely. Cf. Aristophanes, *Frogs* 1261, δείξει δὴ τάχα: 'time will show'.

21. ὥσπερ γὰρ ἐν τοῖς σώμασι . . . οὕτω καὶ τῶν πόλεων καὶ τυράννων: a simile derived from the language of medicine.

   τέως μὲν ἂν ἐρρωμένος ᾖ τις, οὐδὲν ἐπαισθάνεται: 'as long as someone is in a good physical condition, he feels no pain'. τέως is generally an adverb meaning 'for the time being', used as correlative to ἕως; but it is sometimes used, as here, as a substitute for ἕως, as a temporal conjunction with the meaning 'as long as', 'all the time that', 'while'. This meaning occurs elsewhere in Demosthenes, e.g. *On the Embassy* 326 and *Against Leptines* 91. Here it takes the frequentative construction since it means 'on every occasion that', with ἄν and the subjunctive like other conditional, relative and temporal conjunctions (*G.* 1431). ἐρρωμένος is the perfect participle middle of ῥώννυμι 'I strengthen', used frequently as an adjective meaning 'strong', 'healthy'.

   ἐπὰν δ' ἀρρώστημά τι συμβῇ πάντα κινεῖται: 'but whenever some illness comes upon him, everything is set in motion', another frequentative temporal clause (ἐπάν=ἐπεὶ ἄν).

   κἂν ῥῆγμα κἂν στρέμμα κἂν ἄλλό τι τῶν ὑπαρχόντων σαθρὸν ᾖ: 'whether it be a rupture or a sprain or whether it is some other part of his constitution that is unsound'.

   ἕως μὲν ἂν ἔξω πολεμῶσιν, ἀφανῆ τὰ κακὰ τοῖς πολλοῖς ἐστιν: 'as long as they are fighting away from home, these weaknesses are not apparent to the general public'. ἔξω refers to fighting outside the borders of one's country.

   ἐπειδὰν δ' ὅμορος πόλεμος συμπλακῇ, πάντ' ἐποίησεν ἔκδηλα: 'but when a war on their border grapples with them, it reveals all'. συμπλακῇ is second aorist passive from συμπλέκω 'I entangle', used frequently of a wrestler coming to grips with his opponent. The orator may well be thinking of a wrestling metaphor in his picture of a war grappling with a city on its frontier. ἐποίησεν is a gnomic aorist (see on συνανήλωσε, *1st Olynthiac* 11 and *G.* 1292).

22. ταύτῃ φοβερὸν προσπολεμῆσαι νομίζεται: 'considers that in this respect he is a formidable antagonist'. For the ('epexegetic') infinitive limiting the meaning of adjectives, see G. 1528. (Cf. *Against Meidias* 24 - λόγους ἐμοὶ μὲν ἀναγκαιοτάτους προειπεῖν, ὑμῖν δὲ χρησιμωτάτους ἀκοῦσαι - 'words that are most essential for me to speak, and most useful for you to hear'.

μεγάλη γὰρ ῥοπή, μᾶλλον δὲ τὸ ὅλον ἡ τύχη παρὰ πάντ' ἐστι τὰ τῶν ἀνθρώπων πράγματα: 'for throughout all human affairs fortune is a powerful force, or rather it is everything'. ῥοπή denotes literally the fall of one pan on a pair of scales when some object is weighed, but it can also denote one or more of a series of weights added to the balance during the weighing process. Hence comes the metaphorical meaning of 'something able to decide some issue', i.e. 'the decisive influence'.

οὐ μὴ ἀλλ' ἔγωγε: this phrase provides the antithesis to σώφρονος μὲν ἀνθρώπου in the previous sentence.

εἴ τις αἵρεσίν μοι δοίη, τὴν τῆς ἡμετέρας πόλεως τύχην ἂν ἑλοίμην: 'if someone were to give me the choice, I would choose the fortune of our city', a future condition in the less vivid form (G. 1408). δοίη and ἑλοίμην are respectively the second aorist optative of δίδωμι and αἱρέω.

ἐθελόντων ἃ προσήκει ποιεῖν ὑμῶν αὐτῶν καὶ κατὰ μικρόν: 'provided that you are yourselves willing to do your duty even to a limited extent', a genitive absolute with conditional force.

ἢ τὴν ἐκείνου: (sc. τύχην) 'rather than his fortune', with omission of μᾶλλον, which is implied in the verb ἑλοίμην.

πολὺ γὰρ πλείους ἀφορμὰς εἰς τὸ τὴν παρὰ τῶν θεῶν εὔνοιαν ἔχειν ὁρῶ ὑμῖν ἐνούσας ἢ 'κείνῳ: 'for I see that we have far more numerous means open to us for attaining the favour of the gods than he has'. For -ους instead of -ονες and -ονας in the plural of comparative adjectives in -ιων, see G. 358-9. ἀφορμή is a noun meaning 'origin', 'starting point', often used more generally to denote 'resources', 'means to some end'. Cf. on ἀφορμαῖς ἐπὶ τὰ ἔξω τῶν ἀγαθῶν ('a means of obtaining benefits abroad'), *3rd Olynthiac* 33 below.

23. οὐκ ἔνι δ' αὐτὸν ἀργοῦντ' οὐδὲ τοῖς φίλοις ἐπιτάττειν ὑπὲρ

αὐτοῦ τι ποιεῖν, μή τί γε δή τοῖς θεοῖς: 'it is impossible for me who is idle to call upon even his friends to do something on his behalf, far less the gods'.
ἔνι is equivalent to ἔνεστι, 'it is possible' (cf. on ἃ δὲ καὶ χωρὶς τούτων ἔνι, 2nd Olynthiac 4 above. αὐτὸν ἀργοῦντα is to be taken with τινα, which must be supplied as the subject of ἐπιτάττειν. μή τί γε and μή τί γε δή are used in affirmative contexts to mean 'so much the more'; cf. Against Conon 17 - τοιαῦτα ποιοῦντες ἃ πολλὴν αἰσχύνην ἔχει καὶ λέγειν, μή τί γε δὴ ποιεῖν ἀνθρώπους μετρίους - 'performing such acts as would greatly shame decent men merely to mention, to say nothing about actual participation'. In a negative context, as here, the phrase is equivalent to the Latin nedum, meaning 'much less'. Cf. Against Meidias 148 - ἀλλ' οὐδὲ στρατιώτης οὗτος οὐδενός ἐστ' ἄξιος, μή τί γε τῶν ἄλλων ἡγεμών - 'but not even as a private soldier is he of any value, much less as a leader of others'.

οὐ δὴ θαυμαστόν ἐστιν εἰ: 'it is not surprising that'. εἰ is occasionally used instead of ὅτι after verbs and phrases denoting emotion, such as θαυμάζω, ἀγανακτέω, αἰσχύνομαι, φθονέω, δεινόν ἐστι, αἰσχρόν ἐστι (G. 1423).

παρὼν ἐφ' ἅπασι: 'present at all activities', or possibly 'present on all occasions'.

ἡμῶν μελλόντων καὶ ψηφιζομένων καὶ πυνθανομένων περιγίγνεται: he gets the better of us as we delay and pass resolutions and ask questions'. The orator once again contrasts the speed and personal involvement of Philip with the apathy of democratic Athens and the protracted nature of its decision making process. For the sentiment, cf. 1st Olynthiac 4, 2nd Philippic 3-4, 4th Philippic 29 and On the Crown 235-6.

τοὐναντίον γὰρ ἂν θαυμαστόν, εἰ μηδὲν ποιοῦντες ἡμεῖς ὧν τοῖς πολεμοῦσι προσήκει τοῦ πάντα ποιοῦντος περιῆμεν: 'for the opposite would be a source of wonder, if we who do none of the things which people at war ought to do, should prove superior to the man who does all', a present unreal condition with an imperfect indicative in the protasis and an imperfect with ἂν in the apodosis (G. 1397). The protasis of this sentence is a real condition, and not another example of εἰ replacing ὅτι after a verb of emotion. ὧν προσήκει arises from τούτων ἃ προσήκει by attraction (see on περὶ ὧν σκοπεῖτε, 1st Olynthiac 1 above).

24. ἀλλ' ἐκεῖνο θαυμάζω, εἰ . . . οὐκ ἠθελήσατε: cf. on θαυμαστόν ἐστιν εἰ, 23 above. The negative in such clauses can be either οὐ, as in clauses introduced by ὅτι, or μή, as in normal conditional clauses. οὐ is particularly common, as here, where two contrasting clauses introduced by μέν and δέ respectively depend upon one single εἰ.

ὑπὲρ τῶν Ἑλληνικῶν δικαίων: 'in defence of the rights of the Greeks'.

πολλ' ἰδίᾳ πλεονεκτῆσαι πολλάκις ὑμῖν ἐξόν: 'though it is on your power to seize many advantages for yourselves', accusative absolute with an impersonal verb (G. 1569).

ἵν' οἱ ἄλλοι τύχωσι τῶν δικαίων: 'so that others might obtain their rights', a final clause in historic sequence with retention of the subjunctive in place of an optative (G. 1369).

τὰ ὑμέτερ' αὐτῶν ἀνηλίσκετ': 'you spent your *own* money', where ὑμέτερ' αὐτῶν is the possessive adjective of the second person reflexive pronoun. The use of the genitive ὑμῶν αὐτῶν in such contexts is very rare.

νυνὶ δ' ὀκνεῖτ' ἐξιέναι καὶ μέλλετ' εἰσφέρειν: the second εἰ clause after the main verb θαυμάζω, contrasting with εἰ Λακεδαιμονίοις μέν ποτ'. Strictly speaking it is only the present behaviour of the Athenians at which Demosthenes affects surprise but he wishes to emphasise the inconsistency between Athenians of the past and those of the present, to the detriment of the latter. For the use of ἐξιέναι to denote a military expedition, cf. *1st Olynthiac* 6 and *2nd Olynthiac* 13 above; for the *eisphora*, see those two passages together with *1st Olynthiac* 20 and Introduction, Appendix B. Note the chiastic arrangement of εἰσφέροντας καὶ προυκινδυνεύετε στρατευόμενοι . . . ὀκνεῖτ' ἐξιέναι καὶ μέλλετ' εἰσφέρειν. For *chiasmus*, see Introduction II 4 f(iv).

πάντας καὶ καθ' ἕν' αὐτῶν ἐν μέρει: 'all of them together and each one separately in turn'. The salvation of the Greek states collectively refers to the role of Athens during the Persian invasion of 480-79 B.C.. On the salvation of individual states, see e.g. *For the Megalopolitans* 14 - οὐδέν' ἂν ἀντειπεῖν οἴομαι ὡς οὐ καὶ Λακεδαιμονίους καὶ πρότερον Θηβαίους καὶ τὸ τελευταῖον Εὐβοέας ἔσωσεν ἡ πόλις.

κάθησθε: 'just sit about idly', cf. καθήμεθα, 22 above.

25. εἰ μηδεὶς ὑμῶν . . . δύναται λογίσασθαι πόσον πολεμεῖτε χρόνον Φιλίππῳ: 'that none of you is able to realise how long you have been at war with Philip'. The war in fact had lasted eight years, to be reckoned from Philip's seizure of Amphipolis in 357 B.C.. In Greek, the present tense is used where English has a perfect to denote an action which began in the past but is still going on in the present. This usage is commonly found where there is in the clause an adverb or some other expression of time, such as πάλαι, πάρος, πολὺν χρόνον.

τί ποιούντων ὑμῶν: genitive absolute, asking a question. This use of an interrogative subordinate clause is alien to English, where the idea must be expressed in a principal clause: 'what you were doing when this time has elapsed'.

μελλόντων (sc. ὑμῶν) αὐτῶν: 'while you yourselves were procrastinating', to be contrasted with ἑτέρους τινας.

ἐλπιζόντων πράξειν: for the future infinitive with verbs of hoping, promising, threatening and swearing, see on ἐλπὶς ταῦτα τελευτῆσαι, 1st Olynthiac 14 above; G. 1286.

κρινόντων: 'bringing lawsuits against one another'.

26. εἶθ' οὕτως ἀγνωμόνως ἔχετ' . . . ὥστε δι' ὧν ἐκ χρηστῶν φαῦλα τὰ πράγματα τῆς πόλεως γέγονεν, διὰ τούτων ἐλπίζετε τῶν αὐτῶν πράξεων ἐκ φαύλων αὐτὰ χρηστὰ γενήσεσθαι: 'and so are you so senseless that you expect the position of the city to become good instead of bad as a result of the same policies thanks to which it passed from good to bad?'. εἶτα is used to introduce questions expressing surprise, contempt or indignation. Cf. εἶτ' οὐκ αἰσχύνεσθε, 1st Olynthiac 24 above. For ἀγνωμόνως ἔχετε as an equivalent for ἀγνώμονες ἐστε, cf. on σχήσειν καλῶς, 1st Olynthiac 9 above. ὥστε is used in consecutive clauses with the infinitive to denote the result which the action of the principal verb *tends* to produce ('so senseless as to expect') and with the indicative to indicate the result which the principal verb *really does produce* ('so senseless that you really do expect'); see G. 1450. Note the chiastic arrangement of ἐκ χρηστῶν φαῦλα . . . ἐκ φαύλων αὐτὰ χρηστά (see Introduction, II 4 f(iv).

ἔχον φύσιν: 'natural', serving as a parallel to εὔλογον

as an adjective derived from φύσις, in place of φυσικός, which is not found in Classical Attic apart from one occurrence in Xenophon (*Memorabilia* 3.9.1).

πολύ γάρ ῥᾷον ἔχοντας φυλάττειν ἤ κτήσασθαι πάντα πέφυκεν: 'for it is by nature much easier to hold on to all that one has than it is to acquire it in the first place'. φυλάττειν and κτήσασθαι are the subjects of πέφυκεν and πάντα is the object of both infinitives. For the contrary thought, see *1st Olynthiac* 23 - πολλάκις δοκεῖ τὸ φύλαξαι τἀγαθὰ τοῦ κτήσασθαι χαλεπώτερον εἶναι.

νῦν δ' ὅτι μὲν φυλάξομεν οὐδέν ἐστιν ὑπὸ τοῦ πολέμου λοιπὸν τῶν πρότερον: 'but now nothing is left to us by the war to keep of what we formerly possessed'. ὑπο τοῦ πολέμου expresses the agent after the phrase λοιπόν ἐστι, which is equivalent in meaning to the passive λέλειπται. ὅτι φυλάξομεν with the future indicative is a relative clause expressing purpose (G. 1442).

αὐτῶν οὖν ἡμῶν ἔργον τοῦτ' (sc. ἐστιν) ἤδη: 'this is the immediate personal task before us', where αὐτῶν is placed first in the sentence for emphasis.

27. φημί δὴ δεῖν εἰσφέρειν: on φημί δὴ introducing a specific proposal, see *1st Olynthiac* 17 and *2nd Olynthiac* 13 above. On εἰσφορά, see *1st Olynthiac* 6 and 20, *2nd Olynthiac* 13 and 24, with Introduction, Appendix B.

ἐξιέναι: Demosthenes' favourite word for a military expedition involving Athenian citizens. See *1st Olynthiac* 6 and *2nd Olynthiac* 13 and 24 above.

μηδὲν αἰτιᾶσθαι πρὶν ἂν τῶν πραγμάτων κρατήσητε: 'to make no accusations till you have made yourselves masters of the situation'. For πρίν in the sense of 'until', used after a negative, with ἄν + subjunctive with reference to the future, see G. 1470-1.

τὰς προφάσεις δ' ἀφελεῖν καὶ τὰ καθ' ὑμᾶς ἐλλείμματα: 'to get rid of excuses and all failings on your own part'. It is clear from what follows that the excuses which Demosthenes has in mind are those offered by generals for their failures.

οὐ γὰρ ἔστι πικρῶς ἐξετάσαι τί πέπρακται τοῖς ἄλλοις: 'for it is impossible to examine severely what has been done by others'. ἔστι (note the accent) is here used

impersonally with the meaning 'it is possible'.
πέπρακται is the perfect passive of πράττω. On the
use of the dative to express the agent after a perfect
passive, cf. on τῶν πεπολιτευμένων αὐτοῖς,
1st Olynthiac 28 above; G. 1186.

ἂν μὴ παρ' ὑμῶν αὐτῶν πρῶτον ὑπάρξῃ τὰ δέοντα: literally
'when your duty first originates with you yourselves',
i.e. 'unless on the basis of you yourselves doing your
duty first'.

28. τοῦτον . . . τὸν πόλεμον: refers to the war between Philip
and Athens which had been going on since 357 B.C.

πάντας ὅσους ἂν ἐκπέμψητε στρατηγούς: 'all the generals
you send out', a relative clause with indefinite
antecedent, expressed by ἂν with the subjunctive (G. 1431).

ἰδίους δ' εὑρίσκειν πολέμους: 'to find wars of their own',
i.e. 'private wars'.

εἰ δεῖ τι τῶν ὄντων καὶ περὶ τῶν στρατηγῶν: 'if I must
speak something of the truth concerning the generals
too'.

ἐνταῦθα μὲν: 'in this war involving us', i.e. the war
currently being waged by the Athenians, as opposed to
ἐκεῖ δέ at the beginning of the next sentence, which
refers to the private wars being conducted by generals
on their own account.

'Αμφίπολίς γ' ἂν ληφθῇ, παραχρῆμα τ' ὑμεῖς κομιεῖσθε: 'if
(ἂν=ἐάν) Amphipolis at any rate is captured, you yourselves will quickly take it over'. ληφθῇ is aorist
passive of λαμβάνω, κομιεῖσθε future middle from κομίζω.
Amphipolis is mentioned first in the clause for emphasis
and is picked out as the most desirable prize for success
in the war that had been going on ever since its capture
by Philip eight years before. ὑμεῖς is emphatic; what
Demosthenes seems to mean is that the city will not first
be handed over to mercenaries for looting.

οἱ δὲ κίνδυνοι τῶν ἐφεστηκότων ἴδιοι: 'dangers peculiar to
those in command'. ἐφεστηκότων is the perfect participle
of ἐφίστημι, with intransitive meaning.

ἐλάττους: for ἐλάττονες, ('less'), an adjective used to
supply the comparative of ὀλίγος or μικρός. For the
declension of such comparatives, see G. 358-60.

τὰ δὲ λήμματα τῶν ἐφεστηκότων καὶ τῶν στρατιωτῶν . . . τὰ πλοῖ' ἃ συλῶσιν: 'the profits of the commanders and of the soldiers . . . are the vessels which they plunder'. πλοῖον, in contrast to ναῦς, refers to a merchant ship, a trading vessel. As this passage indicates, attacks by Athenian commanders on non-allied merchant shipping were by no means rare, at least in the weakened financial conditions during and after the Sacred War of 357-355 B.C. The motive was on occasion self-enrichment but more frequently stemmed from the failure of the Athenians to provide adequate funds for the sailors' pay. Lack of funding is in fact a partial answer to the question posed by Demosthenes, though he ignores it in this passage. Athenian commanders had not infrequently to devise expedients of their own to raise the necessary money, and we hear of generals extorting what they called εὔνοιαι ('benevolences') from allies, to ensure a safe-conduct for the passage of their ships. These 'benevolences' Demosthenes considers to be little better than λήμματα ('exactions') and he paints (On the Chersonese 25) a picture of generals who behave in the manner of gangsters operating a protection racket. Similar behaviour is attested for the subordinates of the general Chares by Aeschines, On the Embassy 71 - τοὺς μὲν ταλαιπώρους νησιώτας . . . ἑξήκοντα τάλαντα εἰσέπραττον σύνταξιν, κατῆγον δὲ τὰ πλοῖα καὶ τοὺς Ἕλληνας ἐκ τῆς κοινῆς θαλάττης. Cf. Demosthenes, On the Trierarchic Crown 13 - ἐπειδὰν γάρ τις μισθωσάμενος τριηραρχίαν ἐκπλεύσῃ πάντας ἀνθρώπους ἄγει καὶ φέρει. Further malpractices of Chares are mentioned by Diodorus 15.95.3, Aeneas Tacticus 11.13-15 and Plutarch, Phocion 14.2.

Λάμψακος: a Greek city on the north-east coast of Asia Minor, at the north-eastern end of the Hellespont, captured by Chares in 356/5 B.C. while fighting in the service of the rebel satrap Ariobarzanes in order to supplement the funds provided by the Athenians to pay his troops (Diodorus 16.22).

Σίγειον: another city on the north-east coast of Asia Minor, situated at the south-western end of the Hellespont and captured by Chares in the course of the same campaign. It seems to have been retained by him as his personal possession, and became a favourite retreat when he was in disgrace at Athens (Theopompus fgt. 105 Jacoby; Nepos, Chabrias 3.4). He was still in possession of Sigeum as late as 334 B.C., when he set off to visit Alexander the Great at Ilium, presumably to offer submission and secure Alexander's recognition of his rule (Arrian 1.12.1).

ἐπ' οὖν τὸ λυσιτελοῦν αὐτοῖς ἕκαστοι (sc. στρατηγοὶ καὶ στρατιῶται) χωροῦσιν: 'such groups therefore go where their interests lie'. For the plural of words like ἕκαστος, used in the meaning of 'each party', 'each set of individuals', cf. on the use of οὐδένες, *2nd Olynthiac* 17 above (οὐδένων εἰσὶ βελτίους).

29. ὅταν μὲν εἰς τὰ πράγματ' ἀναβλέψητε φαύλως ἔχοντα: 'whenever you devote your attention to the sorry state of your affairs', a temporal clause denoting repetition, with ἄν + subjunctive (G. 1431 b i). On the use of the adverb with ἔχω, see on σχήσειν καλῶς, *1st Olynthiac* 9 above.

τοὺς ἐφεστηκότας κρίνετε: 'you put your commanders on trial'.

δόντες λόγον: 'having given them a hearing', cf. λόγον διδόναι, 31 below.

περίεστι; 'the net result is', an impersonal usage of the verb περίειμι, arising from the meaning 'to be left over'. It occurs elsewhere in Demosthenes (*Against Meidias* 155, and, if genuine, *On Syntaxis* 20).

διεστάναι: 'to be at variance', second perfect infinitive active, with intransitive meaning, from διίστημι, 'I cause to stand apart', i.e. 'I separate', 'set at variance'.

ταῦτα πεπεισμένοις: 'convinced of this', where πεπεισμένοις is the perfect participle passive of πείθω, 'I persuade'. πείθω in the active is occasionally followed by a double accusative, one of the person being persuaded and one of the thing of which he is being persuaded, especially when the latter is a neuter pronoun. The neuter pronoun, as here, can be retained as object of the verb when it is used in the passive (G. 1239).

τὰ κοινὰ δ' ἔχειν φαύλως: 'the interests of the state are in a sorry condition'.

πρότερον μὲν γάρ . . . εἰσεφέρετε κατὰ συμμορίας: 'for in the past you were in the habit of paying your property tax by symmories'. πρότερον seems to suggest not that

symmories were no longer used in the collection of
tax, but that no eisphora had been levied in the years
immediately prior to the delivery of the speech. In
this passage, the orator is referring to the organisation, from 378/7 B.C. onwards, of all Athenians
wealthy enough to be assessed for eisphora into 100
symmories ('boards' or 'syndicates') to which each
paid a fixed proportion of his wealth. The wealthiest member of each symmory was termed hegemon
('president'; Demosthenes, 2nd Against Aphobus 4,
Against Meidias 157); immediately below him in wealth
and importance came the Second Man (ὁ δεύτερος) and
the Third Man (ὁ τρίτος). These three, taken from
each symmory, formed collectively the group mentioned
by Demosthenes (On the Crown 103), which is probably
identical with the three hundred wealthiest men
in the city who underwrote the total amount of the
eisphora paying it themselves in the first instance
from their own resources and recovering most of it
subsequently from the other members of the symmories
(οἱ προεισφέροντες, Demosthenes, Against Phaenippus
4 and 25). The symmory system was extended from the
payment of eisphora to the trierarchy in 357 B.C.
(law of Periander), and from this year to Demosthenes'
reform of 340 B.C., trierarchic symmories comprised
1200 individuals organised in 20 symmories
(Demosthenes, On the Symmories 16-17), each headed
by an epimeletes (Demosthenes, Against Euergus 21ff.).

νυνὶ δὲ πολιτεύεσθε κατὰ συμμορίας: 'now you conduct
your politics by symmories'.

ῥήτωρ ἡγεμὼν ἑκατέρων καὶ στρατηγὸς ὑπὸ τούτῳ καὶ οἱ
βοησόμενοι τριακόσιοι· οἱ δ' ἄλλοι προσνενέμησθε οἱ
μὲν ὡς τούτους, οἱ δ' ὡς ἐκείνους: 'the orator is
the director of each symmory, there is a general
under him, and the Three Hundred to cheer. The rest
of you are assigned, some to one symmory, the rest
to the other'. The orator here introduces a simile
likening politics to the symmory system, whereby
the Athenian factions are compared to two symmories,
each with its own orator, who, like the hegemon of
the symmory, decides on policy and decision making;
then comes the general, who, like the Second Man of
the symmory, implements these decisions, and the
group of supporters, parallel to the Three Hundred
προεισφέροντες, who merely applaud decisions already
taken. Finally there is the populace at large,
which like those too poor to be included in the
symmories have no influence whatever in deciding

and implementing policy, but merely attach themselves to one or the other of the factions. Note
the subordination of the general to the orator in
fourth century Athens. In the fifth century the
strategia was the most important office in the state,
and indeed the same man was usually both orator and
strategos, but in the fourth century the greater
degree of specialisation in the art of both politics
and war necessitated a separation of the two roles
(cf. Plutarch, *Phocion* 7.3). As the present passage
indicates, it was the orator who came to formulate
policy, while the general's role was merely to
implement decisions already formulated by the orator.
There was indeed as close a connection between some
orators and generals as between the *hegemon* and
Second Man in the symmory, as for instance, between
Callistratus and, at various times, Iphicrates,
Chabrias and Timomachus or between Aristophon and
Chares in the early 350s or between Hyperides and
Leosthenes during the Lamian War (cf. Plutarch,
Comparison of Demosthenes and Cicero 3.1 on the
links between Demosthenes on the one hand and Chares,
Diopeithes and Leosthenes on the other). For other
passages linking orators and generals, see
[Demosthenes] 12.19 and Aeschines, *On the Crown* 7.

προσνενέμησθε: perfect passive of προσνέμω 'I assign'.
The passage occurs also in in the doubtfully genuine
speech *On Organisation* 20.

30. δεῖ δὴ ταῦτ' ἐπανέντας καὶ ὑμῶν αὐτῶν ἔτι καὶ νῦν
γενομένους κοινὸν καὶ τὸ βουλεύεσθαι καὶ τὸ λέγειν
καὶ τὸ πράττειν ποιῆσαι: 'it is my opinion that you
must abandon this system and must even now become
your own masters and make deliberation, speech and
action open to all'. ἐπανέντας is aorist participle
passive of ἐπανίημι 'I give up'; ὑμῶν αὐτῶν is
possessive genitive, to be construed with γεγομένους
literally 'becoming of yourselves'. Demosthenes
makes the same criticism of the subordination of
citizens to the orators in his speech *Against
Aristocrates* 209 - τότε μὲν γὰρ ὁ δῆμος ἦν δεσπότης
τῶν πολιτευομένων, νῦν δ' ὑπηρέτης.

εἰ δὲ τοῖς μὲν ὥσπερ ἐκ τυραννίδος ὑμῶν ἐπιτάττειν
ἀποδώσετε: 'if you allow one body of men to issue
orders as if they were tyrants over you', a
conditional clause denoting admonition, with the

verb in the future indicative (G. 1405). The τοῖς μὲν refers in particular to the orators and generals mentioned in 29 above.

τοῖς δ' ἀναγκάζεσθαι τριηραρχεῖν, εἰσφέρειν, στρατεύεσθαι (sc. ἀποδώσετε): 'and if you allow another group to be forced into serving as trierarchs, paying property tax and performing personal military service', a reference to the hoplite classes on whom these burdens normally fell.

τοῖς δὲ ψηφίζεσθαι κατὰ τούτων μόνον: 'and if you permit yet another group only to vote in condemnation of these', i.e. the masses who sit on the juries.

οὐχὶ γενήσεται τῶν δεόντων ὑμῖν οὐδὲν ἐν καιρῷ: 'you will never have anything that needs to be done accomplished by the proper time', the apodosis to which the three preceding clauses serve as protasis.

τὸ γὰρ ἠδικημένον ἀεὶ μέρος ἐλλείψει: 'for the section of the community that is for the time being aggrieved will be in default'. On this use of ἀεί, see on ἀεί τι τῶν πραγμάτων ὡς ἀλυσιτελές, 1st Olynthiac 14, above.

εἶθ' ὑμῖν τούτους κολάζειν ἀντὶ τῶν ἐχθρῶν ἐξέσται: 'then you will always have the privilege of punishing them instead of the enemy', an ironical use of the verb ἔξεστι.

31. λέγω δὴ κεφάλαιον: 'I propose then by way of summing up', where λέγω δή is used much as φημὶ δή (cf. on 1st Olynthiac 17, 2nd Olynthiac 11 and 27 above).

πάντας εἰσφέρειν ἀφ' ὅσων ἕκαστος ἔχει τὸ ἴσον: 'that everyone should pay property tax, each according to what is fair', i.e. 'in proportion to his means'. Since Demosthenes is doing no more than recapitulate what he has already discussed at length, he cannot here be proposing a controversial motion to the effect that all citizens, however poor, should pay *eisphora*: all he is doing is to recommend that all existing tax-payers should continue to do so, on the basis of the system currently in use, which he regards as being as equitable as possible in the circumstances.

πάντας ἐξιέναι κατὰ μέρος, ἕως ἂν ἅπαντες στρατεύσησθε: 'that everyone should march out in turn, until all have performed their military service'. For ἐξέρχομαι in the sense of στρατεύομαι, cf. *1st Olynthiac* 6 and *2nd Olynthiac* 13, 24 and 27 above. The orator is here referring to the κατάλογος or military service roster, containing the names of all citizens eligible for service, arranged by age-groups. From this list troops of some specific age groups might be called upon and individuals summoned in rotation. See Aristophanes, *Knights* 1369-71; Aeschines, *On the Embassy* 168; Demosthenes, *1st Philippic* 21. For temporal clauses containing the subjunctive with ἄν in reference to the future, see *G.* 1434 and 1465.

πᾶσι τοῖς παριοῦσι λόγον διδόναι: 'to give a hearing to all those who came forward to speak', i.e. to the *bema* or orator's platform. Cf. δόντες λόγον, 29 above.

καὶ τὰ βέλτισθ' ὧν ἂν ἀκούσηθ' αἱρεῖσθαι: 'and to choose the best advice from what you hear'. ὧν here represents τούτων ἅ (cf. on περὶ ὧν σκοπεῖτε, *1st Olynthiac* 1 above) and introduces a conditional relative clause with ἄν + subjunctive (*G.* 1431).

μὴ ἃ ἂν ὁ δεῖν' ἢ ὁ δεῖν' εἴπῃ: 'and not merely what this man or that might say'. δεῖνα is an essentially colloquial indefinite pronoun meaning 'such a one', 'so and so', and is always accompanied by the definite article. For the declension of δεῖνα, see *G.* 420.

κἂν τοῦτο ποιῆτε: 'and if you do this', an ordinary conditional clause referring to the future, with ἄν + subjunctive (*G.* 1403).

βέλτιον τῶν ὅλων πραγμάτων ὑμῖν ἐχόντων: 'when the whole position of your affairs improve', a genitive absolute with temporal meaning. Note the characteristically hopeful ending to the speech, parallel to the prayer for prosperity which concludes *1st Olynthiac* and also the *1st* and *3rd Philippics*.

COMMENTARY

THIRD OLYNTHIAC

1. οὐχὶ ταὐτὰ παρίσταταί μοι γιγνώσκειν: literally 'it does not occur to me to know the same things', i.e. 'very different thoughts present themselves to me'.

καὶ ὅταν πρὸς τοὺς λόγους (sc. ἀποβλέψω) οὓς ἀκούω: 'and when I direct my attention to the speeches that I hear'.

τοὺς μὲν γὰρ λόγους . . . ὁρῶ γιγνομένους: 'I see that the speeches that are made are concerned with the punishment of Philip', where ὁρῶ is given the accusative and participle construction common with verbs of perceiving, hearing, knowing, remembering etc. (the participle of indirect discourse, G. 1588). γίγνεσθαι is very often used as the passive of ποιεῖσθαι, when used in periphrasis with a noun (e.g. λόγον ποιοῦμαι, 'I make a speech'; λόγος γίγνεται, 'a speech is made').

τὰ δὲ πράγματα εἰς τοῦτο προσήκοντα, ὥσθ' ὅπως μὴ πεισόμεθ' αὐτοὶ πρότερον κακῶς σκέψασθαι δέον: 'whereas our affairs reach such a condition that we must consider how we may not ourselves be the first to come to harm'. Here the consecutive conjunction ὥστε is used not, as it usually is, with the indicative or the infinitive (G. 1449-51) but with the participle (δέον), by way of assimilation to the participle προσήκοντα, on which the consecutive clause depends. Cf. *Against Theocrines* 23 - νῦν δὲ τούτων οὐδεμίαν ὁρῶ τῶν σκήψεων ὑπόλογον οὖσαν ἐν τοῖς νόμοις . . . ὥστε . . . μυριάκις παρὰ τῶν κρινομένων εἰρημένην - 'as it is, I see that no such excuse is taken into account in the laws, so that on countless occasions it has been used by those who are on trial': cf. also *4th Philippic* 40. πεισόμεθ' here is not from πείθω 'I persuade', but the future of πάσχω 'I suffer'. For the use of σκοπέω with ὅπως and the future indicative, see G. 1372 ('object clauses after verbs of striving'). Cf. on *1st Olynthiac* 2 and *2nd Olynthiac* 2 above. The adverb κακῶς is to be taken colsely with πεισόμεθ', despite its separation, and the hyperbaton is probably intended to emphasise the adverb. Note the chiastic arrangement in this sentence of τὰ πράγματα . . . πρὸς τοὺς

λόγους . . . τοὺς μὲν γὰρ λόγους . . . τὰ δὲ πράγματ'.
The opening section of the sentence reappears at the
beginning of the second *Prooemium* in the extant
Demosthenic collection, while the entire sentence is
parodied in a speech of Rhetoric in Lucian's *Double
Indictment* (Lucian 29.26), and also imitated by
Sallust in a speech put into the mouth of the younger
Cato in the *Catiline* (52.2).

οὐδὲν ἄλλο μοι δοκοῦσιν (*sc.* ποιεῖν) οἱ τὰ τοιαῦτα
λέγοντες ἢ τὴν ὑπόθεσιν περὶ ἧς βουλεύεσθε, οὐχὶ τὴν
οὖσαν παριστάντες ὑμῖν ἁμαρτάνειν: 'those who say
such things (i.e. about the punishment of Philip)
seem to me to be doing nothing more than making the
mistake of putting before you a subject for deliberation which is not the true one', i.e. 'that is
quite unreal'.

2. ἐπ' ἐμοῦ: the preposition is here used in its temporal
sense, 'in my lifetime'.

πέπεισμαι τοῦθ' ἱκανὸν προλαβεῖν ἡμῖν εἶναι τὴν πρώτην,
ὅπως τοὺς συμμάχους σώσομεν: 'I am convinced that it
is quite enough for us to secure this in the first
instance, namely the salvation of our allies', where
the prefix in the verb προλαβεῖν is intended to suggest
'before Philip can prevent us'. On ὅπως . . . σώσομεν,
cf. on ὅπως μὴ πείσομεθ', *3rd Olynthiac* 1 above. The
clause picks up and amplifies the pronoun τοῦθ'. τὴν
πρώτην is an adverbial accusative (*G*. 1060).

ἐὰν γὰρ τοῦτο βεβαίως ὑπάρξῃ: 'for if this is secured'.
On the meaning of ὑπάρχω, see on τῶν παρὰ τῶν θεῶν
ἡμῖν ὑπηργμένων, *1st Olynthiac* 10 above.

τότε καὶ περὶ τοῦ τίνα τιμωρήσεταί τις καὶ ὃν τρόπον
ἐξέσται σκοπεῖν: 'then it will be possible also (i.e.
in addition to saving our allies) to consider whom one
is to punish and in what way', perhaps better translated by nouns - 'the identity of the victims of the
punishment and the method'. The words τίνα τιμωρήσεται
τις καὶ ὃν τρόπον go closely together and are to be
taken with the article τοῦ as a phrase used in place of
a noun (or nouns) in the genitive. Note the distinction
between accented τίνα (interrogative) and unaccented
τις (indefinite). ὃν τρόπον is an example of the use
of a relative pronoun to introduce an indirect question,
in place of an interrogative; this usage normally occurs

after a verb of saying, knowing or perceiving (but never after a verb of asking). Cf. *Against Callippus* 7, ἐκέλευσε . . . δεῖξαι ὃς εἴη, and for the combination of interrogative and relative pronouns, see *1st Philippic* 33 - ἃ μὲν οὖν χρήσεται καὶ πότε τῇ δυνάμει, ὁ τούτων κύριος καταστὰς ὑφ' ὑμῶν βουλεύσεται.

πρὶν δὲ τὴν ἀρχὴν ὀρθῶς ὑποθέσθαι: 'before we lay down the foundation properly'. For the use of ἀρχή, cf. τῶν πράξεων τὰς ἀρχὰς καὶ τὰς ὑποθέσεις, *2nd Olynthiac* 10 above. On the use of πρίν with the infinitive in affirmative sentences, see G. 1470-1.

ματαῖον ἡγοῦμαι περὶ τῆς τελευτῆς ὁντινοῦν ποιεῖσθαι λόγον: 'I consider it futile to say anything at all about the end', i.e. about the ultimate goal, the punishment of Philip. οὖν, δήποτε and δηποτοῦν are frequently added to relative words such as ὅστις and ὅπως to make them more indefinite. Hence ὁστισοῦν means 'anybody at all', 'anybody whatsoever'.

3. φροντίδος καὶ βουλῆς: 'thought and deliberation', another example of pleonasm (see Introduction II 4 f (xii)).

πέπεισμαι γὰρ ἐξ ὧν παρὼν καὶ ἀκούων σύνοιδα: 'I am convinced as a result of what I know, both from personal observation and hearsay evidence'. πέπεισμαι is perfect middle passive of πείθω 'I persuade', and ἐξ ὧν represents ἐξ ἐκείνων ἃ (attraction of relative pronoun to an antecedent left unexpressed). See on περὶ ὧν σκοπεῖτε, *1st Olynthiac* 1 above.

τὰ πλείω τῶν πραγμάτων ἡμᾶς ἐκπεφευγέναι: 'that most of our interests have slipped through our hands', a metaphor from hunting (cf. Introduction II 4 f (i)).

τῷ μὴ βούλεσθαι τὰ δέοντα ποιεῖν ἢ τῷ μὴ συνιέναι: 'through not wanting to do our duty rather than as a result of not understanding it', an articular infinitive in the dative, expressing cause or instrument (see G. 1546-7).

ἀξιῶ δ' ὑμᾶς . . . ὑπομένειν: 'I ask you to bear with me'. ἀξιόω + infinitive expresses a range of meanings such as 'ask', 'require', 'think it right', 'deign', 'expect', 'consent'.

ἵνα τὰ λοιπὰ βελτίω γένηται: 'so that the future may become better', final subjunctive (G. 1365).

ὁρᾶτε γὰρ ὡς ἐκ τοῦ πρὸς χάριν δημηγορεῖν ἐνίους εἰς πᾶν προελήλυθε μοχθηρίας τὰ παρόντα: 'for you see that, in consequence of some people addressing you with a view to pleasing you, the present situation has come to a totality of wretchedness', i.e. 'because some orators are in the habit of addressing you only to give you satisfaction, our affairs have reached their present wholly wretched condition'.
ἐκ τοῦ δημηγορεῖν ἐνίους is an articular infinitive, with the accusative ἐνίους as subject. πρὸς χάριν is to be taken adverbially 'with a view to pleasing'; προελήλυθε is perfect tense of προέρχομαι; μοχθηρίας is to be taken closely with πᾶν - 'a totality of wretchedness'.

4. ἀναγκαῖον δ' ὑπολαμβάνω μικρὰ τῶν γεγενημένων, πρῶτον ἡμᾶς ὑπομνῆσαι: 'I think it necessary to remind you first of a few of the events of the past'. Verbs of reminding (μιμνήσκω and compounds) are regularly followed by two accusatives, one of the person and another of the thing of which he is reminded (G. 1069). μικρά here is equivalent to ὀλίγα, 'a few'.

ἀπηγγέλθη Φίλιππος ὑμῖν ἐν Θράκῃ . . . Ἡραῖον τεῖχος πολιορκῶν: literally ' Philip was reported to you to be in the act of besieging Heraeum Teichos in Thrace'; where Greek prefers the personal construction, English prefers the impersonal - 'it was reported to you that Philip was besieging'. ἀγγέλω is often followed by accusative and participle of indirect discourse (G. 1588).

τρίτον ἢ τέταρτον ἔτος τουτί: literally 'this is now the third or fourth year', i.e. 'two or three years ago'. The accusative is regularly used in expressions of time involving an ordinal number, usually with the demonstrative pronoun οὑτοσί to denote how many years since an event has happened. In reckoning the passage of time, the present day, month or year is included (see G. 1064). Heraeum Teichos was a Thracian fortress, of uncertain location, belonging to Cersobleptes, which Philip captured in 352 B.C. It is perhaps to be identified with Heraeum, on the Propontis, a few miles west of Perinthus (Herodotus 4.90).

μαιμακτηριών: the fifth month of the Athenian year, corresponding roughly to November.

πολλῶν δὲ λόγων καὶ θορύβου γιγνομένου: genitive absolute. If the identification of Heraeum Teichos with Heraeum on the Propontis is correct, the cause of such alarm would be Philip's proximity to the Athenian settlements in the Chersonese at the end of the fighting season.

τοὺς μέχρι πέντε καὶ τετταράκοντ' ἐτῶν αὐτοὺς ἐμβαίνειν: 'that those up to the age of 45 should embark in person', where the pronoun αὐτοὺς stresses that the force was to be composed of citizens rather than mercenaries. Since Athenians aged from 20 to 60 were eligible for military service abroad and were listed according to age (see on *2nd Olynthiac* 37 above), no less than 25 out of the 40 age groups were being mobilised in the present circumstances, a clear indication of the extent of the threat which Philip's proximity was felt to pose to the Chersonese.

τάλανθ' ἑξήκοντ' εἰσφέρειν: 'to raise a property tax of 60 talents'. On *eisphora*, see *1st Olynthiac* 6 and 20, *2nd Olynthiac* 13, and Introduction Appendix B.

5. ἑκατομβαιών, μεταγειτνιών, βοηδρομιών: the first three months of the Athenian calendar, corresponding roughly to July, August and September (351 B.C.).

   μόγις: 'with difficulty', 'with reluctance'.

   τὰ μυστήρια: the Eleusinian Mysteries, held in the month of Boedromion in honour of the goddesses Demeter and Kore. The celebrations took place at Eleusis from the 20th to the 23rd day of the month, though preliminary ceremonies were held at Athens from the 15th to the 19th. Despite the gravity of the situation, it is clear that the Athenians took ten months to act and even then came nowhere near fulfilling the terms of their original resolution.

   δέκα ναῦς . . . κενάς: 'ten ships without crews', i.e. lacking the citizen troops who were to be used in accordance with the resolution of ten months before. Presumably the intention was to use the five talents mentioned by Demosthenes to recruit mercenaries *en* route.

Χαρίδημον: a Euboean mercenary commander, who spent much of his earlier career in the service of Athens' enemies (his native city of Oreus, then Cotys king of Thrace), but when the Athenians reached an understanding with Cotys' son and successor, Cersobleptes, Charidemus, who had recently married Cersobleptes' sister, was granted Athenian citizenship (357 B.C.). In 351 he came to Athens, received a grant of inviolability and secured election to the *strategia*. The command mentioned in this passage is his first in Athenian service but he subsequently commanded at Olynthus (349 B.C.) and became well known in support of the anti-Macedonian cause. When Alexander demanded his surrender in 335, he withdrew from Attica and entered Persian service but, coming under suspicion at court, was put to death by Darius III in 333 B.C. (Curtius 3.2). His reputation as a mercenary commander and general does not stand high and may have been damaged by the accusations made aginst him in Demosthenes' speech *Against Aristocrates*.

ὡς γὰρ ἠγγέλθη Φίλιππος ἀσθενῶν ἢ τεθνεώς: for the construction, cf. ἀπηγγέλθη Φίλιππος πολιορκῶν, *3rd Olynthiac* 4 above. The Athenian procrastination strongly suggests that Philip's illness was not just rumour but actual fact.

ἦλθε γὰρ ἀμφότερα: 'for both reports reached you'.

ἦν δ' οὗτος ὁ καιρὸς αὐτός: 'for that was just the very opportunity'.

εἰ γὰρ τότ' ἐκεῖσ' ἐβοηθήσαμεν . . . οὐκ ἂν ἠνώχλει ἡμῖν ὁ Φίλιππος σωθείς: 'for if we had sent a force there (i.e. to Heraeum Teichos), Philip would not have survived to cause us trouble', a past unreal condition (*G.* 1397).

6. τὰ μὲν δὴ τότε πραχθέντ' οὐκ ἂν ἄλλως ἔχοι: 'well, what was done then could not be otherwise', i.e. 'cannot be undone', a commonplace found also at *Prooemium* 30.2 - τὰ μὲν παρεληλυθότ' οὐκ ἂν ἄλλως ἔχει and *On the Crown* 192 - τὸ μὲν παρεληλυθὸς ἀεὶ παρὰ πᾶσιν ἀφεῖται.

δι' ὃν καὶ περὶ τούτων ἐμνήσθην: 'on account of which
I have recalled those events also', i.e. in addition
to examining the present situation. ἐμνήσθην is
aorist passive of μιμνήσκω 'I remind', used with
middle meaning, 'I reminded myself of', 'I recalled'.

ἵνα μὴ ταὐτὰ πάθητε: 'so that you may not have the
same experience', i.e. 'so that you may not make the
same mistake', a final clause in primary sequence,
with verb in the subjunctive (G. 1365).

τί δὴ χρησόμεθ' . . . τούτῳ: (sc. καιρῷ) 'what use
shall we make of this opportunity?' For rhetorical
questions in Demosthenes, see Introduction II 4 b.

εἰ γὰρ μὴ βοηθήσετε παντὶ σθένει κατὰ τὸ δυνατόν,
θεάσασθ' ὃν τρόπον ὑμεῖς ἐστρατηγηκότες πάντ' ἔσεσθ'
ὑπὲρ Φιλίππου: 'for unless you assist with all your
strength to the best of your ability, observe how
you will be seen to have conducted all military
operations on Philip's behalf'. For the use of εἰ
with the future indicative in the protasis of a
conditional clause to denote a warning or
admonition, cf. on εἰ δὴ προησόμεθα, 1st Olynthiac
12 above and G. 1405. σθένος ('strength') is a poetic
word, for which prose writers use δύναμις or ἰσχύς.
However the phrase παντὶ σθένει does occur occasionally
in prose (e.g. Xenophon, Hellenica 6.5.2 - βοηθήσω
παντὶ σθένει and Cyropaedia 8.5.25 - βοηθήσειν παντὶ
σθένει), though never in the orators. The phrase
κατὰ τὸ δυνατόν, with its five successive short
syllables is equally alien to Demosthenes' vocabulary.
The entire phrase παντὶ σθένει κατὰ τὸ δυνατόν,
usually accompanied by the verb βοηθεῖν is, however,
of frequent occurrence in the text of fourth century
treaties (e.g. Decree of Aristoteles, Tod 123.51;
cf. Tod 101.6, 102.6-7, 118.27, 127.6-7 and 28,
136.16 and 22-3, 144.27-28 and 33-4, 147.16-17 and
26-7). The orator is presumably quoting from the
text of the alliance recently concluded between Athens
and the Chalcidians. For the use of the relative ὃν
in indirect questions, cf. on ὃν τρόπον ἔξεσται σκοπεῖν,
3rd Olynthiac 3 above. ἐστρατηγηκότες ἔσεσθε serves
as a periphrasis for the non-existent future perfect
active (in Attic prose only ἵστημι and θνήσκω have
simple forms of this tense in the active, G. 705-6),
to denote a future state resulting from activity
going on in the past.

7. ὑπῆρχον Ὀλύνθιοι δύναμίν τινα κεκτημένοι: 'the Olynthians were at the beginning in possession of considerable strength'. κεκτημένοι is perfect participle of κτάομαι 'I acquire', the perfect tense of which is used in the sense of 'possess', 'own'. Note the absence of a connecting particle, since the sentence is intended to serve as the first part of the survey promised by the orator at the end of the previous sentence. The absence of connectives in such circumstances goes under the name of 'asyndetic explanation'; see also Introduction II 4 f (v).

οὔτε Φίλιππος ἐθάρρει τούτους οὔθ' οὗτοι Φίλιππον: 'neither did Philip have confidence in them nor did they have confidence in him'. This sentence, together with the two that follow, is likewise written without a connective, since the three together explain the phrase διέκειθ' οὕτω τὰ πράγματα at the end of the sentence immediately preceding.

ἐπράξαμεν ἡμεῖς κἀκεῖνοι πρὸς ἡμᾶς εἰρήνην: 'we made peace with them as they did with us', a reference to the peace of 352 B.C. (see Introduction I iii, p.16.

πόλιν μεγάλην ἐφορμεῖν τοῖς ἑαυτοῦ καιροῖς διηλλαγμένην πρὸς ἡμᾶς: 'namely that a large city reconciled to us should be lying in wait for any opportunity he might provide', an accusative and infinitive serving to explain the pronoun τοῦτο at the beginning of the sentence. ἐφορμέω is a nautical term, neaning 'to lie at anchor over against some place and keep a strict watch over it'. This is the only example in Demosthenes of its metaphorical use, though the literal meaning occurs at *On the Embassy* 322 - τὰς Πύλας ἐφ' ἧν αἱ πεντήκοντα τριήρεις ἐφώρμουν, ἵν' εἰ πορεύοιτο Φίλιππος, κωλύοιθ' ὑμεῖς. διηλλαγμένην is perfect participle passive of διαλλάττω 'I reconcile'.

ἐκπολεμῶσαι δεῖν ᾠόμεθα τοὺς ἀνθρώπους ἐκ παντὸς τρόπου, καὶ ὃ πάντες ἐθρύλουν, πέπρακται νυνὶ τοῦθ' ὁπωδήποτε: 'we thought we must rouse the men to war by every means, and what everyone kept talking about has now been accomplished by some means or other'. The passage recalls *1st Olynthiac* 7 - νυνὶ γάρ, ὃ πάντες ἐθρύλουν τέως, Ὀλυνθίους ἐκπολεμῶσαι δεῖ Φιλίππῳ,

γέγον' αὐτόματον. On ὁπωσδήποτε cf. on μάταιον
ἡγοῦμαι . . . ὁντινοῦν ποιεῖσθαι λόγον, *3rd Olynthiac*
2 above.

8. ἐρρωμένως: 'with all our strength', an adverb derived
   from ἐρρωμένος 'strong', 'powerful' (perfect participle passive of ῥώννυμι 'I strengthen') used adjectivally.

   χωρὶς γὰρ τῆς περιστάσης ἂν ἡμᾶς αἰσχύνης εἰ καθυφείμεθά τι τῶν πραγμάτων: 'for apart from the disgrace
   that would surround us if we were to abandon any of
   our interests', a future condition in the less vivid
   form (*G*. 1408), with a participle accompanied by ἄν
   in the apodosis doing duty for a relative clause in
   the aorist optative with ἄν (*G*. 1308): περιστάσης
   ἂν is equivalent to the relative clause ἣ περισταίη
   ἄν. περιστάσης is the second aorist participle with
   intransitive meaning, of περιΐστημι 'I position
   round about'. καθυφείμεθα is the aorist optative
   middle of καθυφίημι 'I give up'.

   οὐδὲ τὸν φόβον . . . μικρὸν ὁρῶ τὸν τῶν μετὰ ταῦτα:
   'nor is the danger that I see arising from subsequent
   events small', where οὐδὲ τὸν φόβον picks up τῆς
   αἰσχύνης earlier in the sentence.

   ἐχόντων μὲν ὡς ἔχουσι Θηβαίων ἡμῖν: 'the Thebans being
   disposed to us as they are now', genitive absolute.
   For ἔχειν with an adverb equivalent to εἶναι with
   corresponding adjective, cf. on σχήσειν καλῶς
   1st Olynthiac 9 above. In view of the current bad
   feeling between Athens and Thebes that lasted
   since 370 B.C., the orator can only be resorting to
   euphemism.

   ἀπειρηκότων δὲ χρήμασι Φωκέων: 'the Phocians having
   become exhausted in their money', i.e. 'the finances
   of the Phocians having become exhausted', genitive
   absolute. ἀπειρηκότων is the perfect participle of
   ἀπαγορεύω meaning, when used transitively, 'I forbid',
   and, in the intransitive use, 'I grow weary', 'I
   fail'. The Phocians had seized and melted down the
   Delphic treasures in the Sacred War (see Introduction
   I ii, p.9), but even such vast quantities of
   precious metal could not provide them with resources

indefinitely.

μηδενὸς δ' ἐμποδὼν ὄντος: 'there being nothing to prevent', genitive absolute with conditional force (hence negative μή).

τὰ παρόντα καταστρεψαμένῳ: 'having subdued what lies before him now', i.e. 'having conquered Olynthus'.

πρὸς ταῦτ' ἐπικλῖναι τὰ πράγματα: 'to turn towards the situation here', i.e. to Phocis and then to Attica.

9. εἴ τις ὑμῶν εἰς τοῦτ' ἀναβάλλεται ποιήσειν τὰ δέοντα: 'if anyone among you is for postponing doing what is necessary until then'. The use of a prolative infinitive in the future tense is rare and, when found, lays greater emphasis on the idea of futurity than would be indicated be a present or an aorist. Here ποιήσειν signifies 'the wish to do one's duty', 'the intention of doing one's duty' (see G. 1277).

ἐγγύθεν: 'from near at hand'.

ἐξὸν ἀκούειν ἄλλοθ' γιγνόμενα: 'it being permitted to hear of it elsewhere', i.e. 'at a distance'. ἐξὸν is an example of the use of an impersonal verb in the accusative (instead of the genitive) absolute; cf. on πλεονεκτῆσαι πολλάκις ὑμῖν ἐξόν, *2nd Olynthiac* 24 above and G. 1569.

ὅτι γὰρ εἰς τοῦτο περιστήσεται τὰ πράγματα, ἐὰν τὰ παρόντα προώμεθα, σχεδὸν ἴσμεν ἅπαντες δήπου: 'for presumably we are all more or less aware that this is what things will come to if we abandon our present opportunity'. εἰ . . . προώμεθα is an ordinary future condition in the more vivid form (G. 1403); προώμεθα is the aorist subjunctive middle of προίημι 'I let go'.

10. εἴποι τις ἄν: the regular formula for introducing an imaginary interruption from the audience; cf. on ἄν τις εἴποι, *1st Olynthiac* 14 above.

τὸ δ' ὅπως: (sc. βοηθήσομεν) 'but the question *'how''*.

The neuter of the definite article is frequently used
with a word, phrase or clause to turn that word, phrase
or clause into the equivalent of a noun (G.955); cf.
On the Crown 88 - τὸ δ' ὑμεῖς ὅταν λέγω, τὴν πόλιν λέγω
('when I say the word "you" I mean the state') and
Against Aristocrates 220 - ὑπερβὰς τὸ καὶ ἁλῷ φόνου
καὶ τὸ δόξῃ ἀπεκτονέναι καὶ τὸ δικὰς ὑπεχέτω τοῦ φόνου
('omitting the words "and is convicted of murder",
and "is adjudged to have killed" and "let him submit
to judgement for the murder"').

μὴ θαυμάσητε ἂν παράδοξον εἴπω τι τοῖς πολλοῖς: 'don't
be surprised if (ἂν = ἐάν) I say something which will
astound most people'. A negative command is expressed
by μή with either the present imperative or, as here,
the aorist subjunctive (G. 1346).

νομοθέτας καθίσατε: 'appoint a body of law-makers',
from καθίζω 'I give a seat to'. The *nomothetai* were
a board of citizens chosen from the jurors' panel
and appointed by a decree of the assembly to enquire
into cases in which the assembly voted to repeal a
law or to replace it with some new law on the same
subject. *Nomothetai* could sit only in connection
with *nomoi*, as distinct from *psephismata*, decrees
enacted by a simple vote in the council and assembly.
Once appointed, they conducted proceedings very much
along the lines of an ordinary court of law, themselves sitting in judgment on the existing law.
Those in favour of repealing or wishing to propose a
new law on the subject acted as prosecutors, while
five advocates (*synegoroi* or *syndikoi*) were appointed
by the assembly to plead the case of the existing law.
If the *nomothetai* voted in favour of acquittal, the
status quo was preserved, while condemnation resulted
in the annulment of existing legislation and the
automatic enactment of the new proposal.

11. λέγω τοὺς περὶ τῶν θεωρικῶν: 'I mean the laws that
exist on the subject of the Festival Fund', i.e.
the law of Eubulus requiring the transfer to this
fund of the surplus of income over expenditure from
each of the city's treasuries. On the Theoric Fund,
see Introduction, Appendix B. In this passage
Demosthenes comes out openly in favour of the repeal

of Eubulus' law, while at the same time making it
quite clear that he is making a recommendation
only, not a specific proposal to this effect. He
is well aware that if he were to make a specific
proposal, he would inevitably face prosecution
under the γραφὴ παρανόμων, on the grounds that
the proposal was illegal, or under the γραφὴ μὴ
ἐπιτήδειον θεῖναι, on the grounds that it was in-
opportune. Furthermore the complicated and protracted nature of the constitutional process involved
in the repeal of a law would have rendered such a
proposal useless as a measure aimed at the current
critical situation. Proposals for a new *nomos*
could be made only once a year, at the first
regular session of the assembly of the year. Then
the proposer had to arrange for the prominent
publication of his law on a white board in front of
the shrine of the Eponymous Heroes in the agora,
and three regular meetings later, the assembly voted
to establish the board of *nomothetai* and to draw up
their terms of reference. Only then were the
nomothetai free to hear the case and deliver their
verdict. Accordingly Demosthenes cannot have been
making a proposal to deal with the immediate crisis,
but was giving advice for the longer term.

σαφῶς οὑτωσί: literally 'thus plainly', i.e. 'openly',
'in unambiguous language', as contrasted with the
cautious statements he had made on the subject in
earlier speeches (*1st Philippic* 35 and *1st Olynthiac*
19-20).

οἱ μὲν τὰ στρατιωτικὰ τοῖς οἴκοι μένουσι διανέμουσι
θεωρικά: 'the former distribute military funds
to those who remain at home as festival money',
where θεωρικά is predicative, and οἴκοι is the old
locative of οἶκος, used adverbially.

οἱ δὲ τοὺς ἀτακτοῦντας ἀθῴους καθιστᾶσιν: 'the latter
make those who shirk military service immune from
prosecution', i.e. do not render them liable to a
prosecution for *astrateia*. The orator seems to be
thinking of various categories of citizen who were
exempt from military service. In this category
can be placed members of the council (Lycurgus,
Against Leocrates 37), members of dramatic choruses
(Demosthenes, *Against Meidias* 15) and tax-collectors
[Demosthenes], *Against Neaera* 27).

ἐπειδὰν δὲ ταύτας λύσητε: 'and when you have repealed these', a temporal clause referring to the future, with the indefinite construction (G. 1434).

τηνικαῦτα: 'at that time', correlative to ἐπειδάν.

12. πρὶν ταῦτα πρᾶξαι: for πρίν with the infinitive in affirmative sentences, see G. 1469-71.

μὴ σκοπεῖτε τίς εἰπὼν τὰ βέλτισθ' ὑπὲρ ὑμῶν ὑφ' ὑμῶν ἀπολέσθαι βουλήσεται: 'don't look for someone who, in giving the best advice on your behalf, would be willing to be undone at your hands'. ἀπολέσθαι is here used as an equivalent to the passive of a verb meaning 'to ruin' and the orator rhetorically places the two prepositional phrases in juxtaposition.

τούτου μόνου περιγίγνεσθαι μέλλοντος: 'this alone being likely to result', genitive absolute. For the use of μέλλω with present or future infinitive, see G. 1254.

μηδὲν δ' ὠφελῆσαι τὰ πράγματα: 'and not improve the situation'.

ἀλλὰ καὶ εἰς τὸ λοιπὸν μᾶλλον ἔτ' ἢ νῦν τὸ τὰ βέλτιστα λέγειν φοβερώτερον ποιῆσαι: 'but for the future make it even more dangerous to give the best advice than it is now'. The comparative φοβερώτερον is here strengthened by a tautological μᾶλλον; cf. Plato, *Gorgias* 487B - αἰσχυντηροτέρῳ μᾶλλον τοῦ δέοντος ('more bashful than was fitting') and *Phaedo* 79E - ὁμοιότερον ἐστι ψυχὴ τῷ ἀεὶ ὡσαύτως ἔχοντι μᾶλλον ἢ τῷ μή.

καὶ λύειν . . . τοὺς νόμους δεῖ τούτους τοὺς αὐτοὺς ἀξιοῦν οἵπερ καὶ τεθήκασιν: 'and you must require those very same men who have made the laws to repeal them', a reference to Eubulus and his faction, who enacted the Theoric Law around 352 B.C. τεθήκασιν is the perfect tense of τίθημι, a verb which is used in the active voice of a lawgiver who makes laws on behalf of the city and in the middle of the people on whose behalf the laws are made (G. 1242.2); cf. the distinction between εἰρήνην ποιεῖν 'to bring about peace', used with reference to an individual negotiator acting on behalf of his city, and εἰρηνὴν ποιεῖσθαι 'to make peace', used of the city as a whole.

13. οὐ γάρ ἐστι δίκαιον τὴν μὲν χάριν ἣ πᾶσαν ἔβλαπτε τὴν πόλιν τοῖς τότε θεῖσιν (*sc*. τοὺς νόμους) ὑπάρχειν: 'for it is not right that the popularity (acquired by a law) which brought damage to the entire state should attach itself to those who at that time made the law', another reference to Eubulus. θεῖσιν is the dative plural of the aorist participle of τίθημι.

τὴν δ' ἀπέχθειαν δι' ἧς ἂν ἅπαντες ἄμεινον πράξαιμεν: 'and that the unpopularity (of those actions) by which we might all fare better', potential optative with ἄν; see G. 1327-8.

πρὶν δὲ ταῦτ' εὐτρεπίσαι: 'before you set this right'.

μηδαμῶς . . . μηδέν' ἀξιοῦτε τηλικοῦτον εἶναι παρ' ὑμῖν ὥστε τοὺς νόμους παραβάντα μὴ δοῦναι δίκην: 'don't expect anyone to be so influential among you as to break the law with impunity'. For consecutive ὥστε followed by the infinitive, see G. 1450.

εἰς προὖπτον κακόν: 'into manifest danger', an Attic contraction of the adjective πρόοπτον.

14. οὐ μὴν οὐδ' ἐκεῖνο γ' ὑμᾶς ἀγνοεῖν δεῖ: 'nor must you fail to recognise this point either'.

ἂν μὴ προσγένηται τὸ ποιεῖν ἐθέλειν τά γε δόξαντα προθύμως ὑμᾶς: (ἂν = ἐάν) 'unless there is added the willingness to implement enthusiastically your resolutions'. For ἐάν + subjunctive denoting a present general condition, see G. 1393.1 and 1431.1. The position of ὑμᾶς at the end of the sentence should indicate that it is meant to be emphatic but a contrast between the resolutions and the people who put them to the vote seems rather weak and it may be that the offending word ὑμᾶς is a later interpolation to the text; certainly it is deleted by many editors.

εἰ γὰρ αὐταρκῆ τὰ ψηφίσματ' ἦν ἢ ὑμᾶς ἀναγκάζειν ἃ προσήκει ἢ περὶ ὧν γραφείη (sc. τὰ ψηφίσματα) διαπράξασθαι: 'for if decrees were sufficient in themselves either to compel you to carry out your duty or to implement the purposes for which the proposals were made', a present unreal condition with an imperfect with ἄν in apodosis and an imperfect in the protasis (G. 1397). γραφείη is third person optative, second aorist passive of γράφω, used in a relative clause to denote repetition (G. 1392.2 and 1431.2).

οὔτ' ἂν ὑμεῖς πολλὰ ψηφιζόμενοι μικρά, μᾶλλον δ' οὐδὲν, ἐπράττετε τούτων: 'you would not be passing many decrees, and you would be implementing few, or rather none of them', where μικρά is used in place of ὀλίγα 'few'. With τούτων sc. ψηφισμάτων; the pronoun refers back to πολλὰ and thence to the unexpressed antecedent of περὶ ὧν.

οὔτε Φίλιππος τοσοῦτον ὑβρίκει χρόνον: 'nor would Philip have kept on insulting you over such a lengthy period of time'. ὑβρίκει is the pluperfect of ὑβρίζω, and ἄν is to be supplied from ἂν . . . ἐπράττετε in the previous clause. The pluperfect is rarely used in an unreal conditional clause but, when it does occur, it lays stress on the completion of the action or on the continuation of the result of the action for some time (G. 1397). Here the implication is that the effects of Philip's insults are still being felt in the present.

πάλαι γὰρ ἕνεκά γε ψηφισμάτων ἐδεδώκει δίκην: 'for long ago he would have paid the penalty, if decrees alone were what mattered', where the pluperfect with ἄν denotes 'he would have been and still would be now a suitably chastened individual'.

15. τὸ γὰρ πράττειν τοῦ λέγειν καὶ χειροτονεῖν ὕστερον ὂν τῇ τάξει, πρότερον τῇ δυνάμει καὶ κρεῖττόν ἐστι: 'for though in order of time action comes later than speeches and votes, in importance it comes in front and is superior'.

τοῦτ' οὖν δεῖ προσεῖναι, τὰ δ' ἄλλα ὑπάρχει: 'it is this then that must be added, for you already have everything else'. On the meaning of ὑπάρχω, see on ὑπηργμένων, *1st Olynthiac* 10 and on τῶν ὑπαρχόντων, *1st Olynthiac* 11 above.

καὶ γὰρ εἰπεῖν τὰ δέοντα παρ' ὑμῶν εἰσι . . . δυνάμενοι: 'for there are those among you who are able to tell you what you must do'.

καὶ γνῶναι πάντων ὑμεῖς ὀξύτατοι τὰ ῥηθέντα: 'you are yourselves the quickest of all at judging what has been said'. ῥηθέντα is used as the aorist participle passive of λέγω, from the same root as ἐρῶ, εἴρηκα, ῥῆσις, ῥῆμα and similar words.

καὶ πρᾶξαι δὲ δυνηθήσεσθε νῦν, ἐὰν ὀρθῶς ποιῆτε: 'and what is more, you will now be able to take action as well, if only you do your duty'. The combination καὶ . . . δὲ is used to denote emphasis, particularly in introducing the last item in a series (J.D. Denniston, *Greek Particles* 199-203); cf. *3rd Philippic* 70 - ἐγὼ νὴ Δί' ἐρῶ, καὶ γράψω δέ, ὥστ' ἂν βούλησθε χειροτονήσετε and *Against Callipus* 11 - πρὸς τὸν Ἀρχεβιάδην καὶ τὸν Ἀριστόνουν καὶ πρὸς αὐτὸν δὲ τὸν Κηφισιάδην. Here the orator intends to emphasise that his audience will not only be able to judge what has been said, but will now be able to take action as well. For ἐάν + subjunctive in future conditions, see *G.* 1403.

16. τίνα γὰρ χρόνον: note the series of nine successive rhetorical questions of varying lengths. For rhetorical questions in Demosthenes, see Introduction II 4 b, p.42.

οὐχ ἅπαντα μὲν ἡμῶν προείληφε τὰ χωρί' ἄνθρωπος· εἰ δὲ καὶ ταύτης κύριος τῆς χώρας γενήσεται, πάντων αἴσχιστα πεισόμεθα: 'has not the fellow taken from us already all our positions and if he becomes master of this territory also, shall we not suffer most ignominiously of all?'. τὰ χωρία refers to the various defensible places on the Macedonian seaboard captured by Philip in the course of his war with Athens, including Pydna, Methone, Potidaea and Amphipolis, mentioned elsewhere in the *Olynthiacs* (*1st Olynthiac* 5, 9 and 12; *2nd Olynthiac* 6 and 7). ἄνθρωπος: the word is here, as often, contemptuous. εἰ γενήσεται, future in the protasis of a conditional sentence containing a warning or an admonition; see on εἰ . . . προησόμεθα, 1st Olynthiac 12 above and G. 1405. ταύτης τῆς χώρας refers to the territory of the Chalcidian Confederacy, not to Attica. πεισόμεθα is the future tense of πάσχω and οὐ is to be supplied with it from οὐ . . . προείληφε in the preceding clause.

εἰ πολεμήσαιεν: 'if they were to go to war', a future condition in the less vivid form (G. 1408).

σώσειν ὑπισχνοῦμεθα: verbs of hoping, promising, threatening and swearing are usually followed by the accusative and future infinitive, when the reference is to the future (G. 1286).

οὐ βάρβαρος;: the people of Lower Macedonia are generally regarded in modern times as being of Greek descent, though in Upper Macedonia there probably was an admixture of Illyrian and Thracian blood. The Macedonian kings claimed descent from the royal family of Argos and, through it, from Heracles, Their claim to be Greek was challenged when Alexander I sought to compete in the Olympic Games, but the managers of the games accepted his candidature on the grounds of his Argive descent (Herodotus 5.22). Greeks in general, however, continued to regard Macedonians as barbarians and even an admirer of Philip such as Isocrates refers to Macedonians as a class intermediate between Greeks and barbarians (Philippus 107-8 and 154). Naturally Demosthenes persists in calling both Philip and the Macedonians in general barbarians (e.g. 3rd Olynthiac 24 below - ὑπήκουε δ' ὁ . . . αὐτοῖς βασιλεὺς, ὥσπερ ἐστὶ προσῆκον βάρβαρον Ἕλλησι; On the Embassy 305 - Αἰσχίνης . . . βάρβαρόν τε γὰρ πολλάκις καὶ ἀλάστορα τὸν Φίλιππον ἀποκαλῶν ἐδημηγόρει; On the Embassy 327 - Μακεδόνες καὶ βάρβαροι νῦν Ἀμφικτύονες εἶναι βιάζονται. Cf. the famous comparison at Third Philippic 30-1 between the Athenians and Spartans as legitimate sons of Greece and Philip who is a suppositious son, culminating in the words οὐ μόνον οὐχ Ἕλληνος ὄντος οὐδὲ προσήκοντος οὐδὲν τοῖς Ἕλλησιν, ἀλλ' οὐδὲ βαρβάρου ἐντεῦθεν ὅθεν καλὸν εἰπεῖν, ἀλλ' ὀλέθρου Μακεδόνος, ὅθεν οὐδ' ἀνδράποδον σπουδαῖον οὐδὲν ἦν πρότερον πρίασθαι.

οὐχ ὅ τι ἂν εἴποι τις: 'is he not whatever anyone might choose to call him?', potential optative with ἄν (*G.* 1327ff.).

17. πάντ' ἐάσαντες καὶ μόνον οὐχὶ συγκατασκευάσαντες αὐτῷ: 'having let all these places go and practically assisted him in consolidating his control over them'.

τότε τοὺς αἰτίους οἵτινες (sc. εἰσι) τούτων ζητήσομεν: literally, 'shall we not enquire about those resposible who they are', i.e. 'shall we not enquire into the identity of those responsible'; cf. on *1st Olynthiac* 21, ἄξιον δ' ἐνθυμηθῆναι . . . τὰ πράγματ' ἐν ᾧ καθέστηκε above.

οὐ γὰρ αὐτοί γ' αἴτιοι φήσομεν εἶναι: 'for we shall never say that we ourselves are responsible'. For the nominative and infinitive construction in indirect statement when the subject of both clauses is the same, see *G.* 927.

οὐδὲ γὰρ ἐν τοῖς τοῦ πολέμου κινδύνοις οὐδεὶς ἑαυτοῦ κατηγορεῖ: 'for nobody blames himself in the dangers of war either'.

καὶ πάντων μᾶλλον: 'and anybody rather (than himself)'.

ἥττηνται δ' ὅμως διὰ πάντας τοὺς φυγόντας δήπου: 'and yet they are defeated, I should imagine because of the fugitives taken as a whole', i.e. 'because of the fugitives collectively'.

εἰ δὲ τοῦτ' ἐποίει ἕκαστος, ἐνίκων ἄν: 'for if each individual had been doing this, they would have won the victory'. The imperfect tenses in the sentence denote, not unreality in the present, but unreality in the past extended over a period of time; see *G.* 1397.

18. καὶ νῦν: 'similarly on the present occasion'.

οὐ λέγει τις τὰ βέλτιστα: note the series of short hypothetical statements that follow one another paratactically, without connectives. For *asyndeton* in Demosthenes, see Introduction II 4 f (v) and (xiv).

ἀναστὰς ἄλλας εἰπάτω: 'let someone else stand up and speak'. ἀναστάς is 2nd aorist participle, with intransitive meaning, from ἀνίστημι 'I cause to stand up'. εἰπάτω is the third person singular aorist imperative; the second aorist εἶπον is generally preferred in Attic to the first aorist εἶπα, except in the second person of the indicative and imperative. The form εἰπάτω occurs elsewhere in Demosthenes only at *On the Embassy* 57 - ἀναστὰς . . . εἰπάτω (as here), *Against Leptines* 113, and the (probably spurious) *First Epistle* 14.

ταῦτα ποιεῖτ᾽ ἀγαθῇ τύχῃ: 'do this and good luck to you'. The phrase ἀγαθῇ τύχῃ (dative of accompanying circumstances) is common in inscriptions, especially at the beginning of a speaker's motion in an Athenian decree. So, e.g. Meiggs and Lewis 52 (Athenian Regulations for Chalcis, 446/5 B.C. lines 40-1 - Ἀντικλῆς εἶπεν· ἀγαθῇ τύχῃ τῇ Ἀθηναίων· ποιεῖσθαι τὸν ὅρκον Ἀθηναίους καὶ Χαλκιδέας etc.; and Tod 123 (decree of Aristoteles, 378/7 B.C.), lines 7-8 - Ἀριστοτέλης εἶπεν· τύχῃ ἀγαθῇ τῇ Ἀθηναίων καὶ τῶν συμμάχων τῶν Ἀθηναίων; ὅπως ἂν Λακεδαιμόνιοι ἐῶσι τοὺς Ἕλληνας ἐλευθέρους etc.

οὐκέτι τοῦθ᾽ ὁ λέγων ἀδικεῖ, πλὴν εἰ δέον εὔξασθαι παραλείπει: 'this is no longer the fault of the speaker, unless when he ought to be praying he omits to do so'. δέον εὔξασθαι is an accusative absolute, used in an impersonal phrase (*G*. 1569). With παραλείπει, we are to supply the noun εὐχήν, to be extracted from the verb εὔξασθαι.

εἰς ταὐτὸ πάνθ᾽ ὅσα βούλεταί τις ἀθροίσαντ᾽ ἐν ὀλίγῳ: 'gathering together all that one wants in a short petition'. With ἐν ὀλίγῳ we are probably intended to supply λόγῳ or some such word, though it would be equally possible to give the phrase a temporal meaning ('in a short time') if the word to be understood were χρόνῳ.

ὅταν περὶ πραγμάτων προτεθῇ σκοπεῖν: 'whenever an investigation of practical policy is the proposal under debate'. προτεθῇ is third person aorist subjunctive of προτίθημι. 'I put forward as a subject for debate'. For the subjunctive with ἄν in relative and temporal clauses denoting repetition, see G. 1431.1.

ἂν μὴ συναμφότερ' ἐξῇ: (ἂν = ἐάν) 'if both are not simultaneously possible'. For ἐάν with subjunctive in general suppositions, see G. 1393.

19. εἰ δέ τις ἡμῖν ἔχει καὶ τὰ θεωρικὰ ἐᾶν καὶ πόρους ἑτέρους λέγειν στρατιωτικά: 'but if anyone is able to leave the festival monies alone and to name alternative sources for the military fund'.

εἴποι τις ἄν: the regular formula for introducing a hypothetical statement; cf. *3rd Olynthiac* 10 above, *2nd Philippic* 13 and *On the Crown* 220. In *1st Olynthiac* 14 and 19 above the formula used is ἄν τις εἴποι.

εἴπερ ἔστιν: note the accent; translate 'if it is possible'.

θαυμάζω εἰ τῷ ποτ' ἀνθρώπων ὃ γέγονεν ἢ γενήσεται, ἂν τὰ πάροντ' ἀναλώσῃ πρὸς ἃ μὴ δεῖ, τῶν ἀπόντων εὐπορῆσαι πρὸς ἃ δεῖ: 'I wonder if it has ever been or ever will be possible for anyone, if (ἂν = ἐάν) he spends what he has available on what is unnecessary, to have a surplus for what is necessary out of what he no longer has'. ἀναλώσῃ is aorist subjunctive of ἀναλίσκω 'I spend'. In ἃ μὴ δεῖ the negative μὴ is used instead of οὐ because the relative clause is generic (on conditional relative clause, see G. 1428 and 1610). In the phrase τῶν ἀπόντων εὐπορῆσαι, the genitive is that which follows verbs denoting fullness or its opposite (G. 1112).

μέγα τοῖς τοιούτοις ὑπάρχει λόγοις ἡ παρ' ἑκάστου βούλησις: 'the wish of each individual lies at the heart of such proposals as these'. For the meaning of ὑπάρχω see on ὑπηργμένων, *1st Olynthiac* 10 and on τῶν ὑπαρξόντων, *1st Olynthiac* 11 above.

ὃ γὰρ βούλεται τοῦθ' ἕκαστος καὶ οἴεται (sc. εἶναι), τὰ δὲ πράγματα πολλάκις οὐχ οὕτω πέφυκεν: 'for what each man wishes, that he also believes to be true, but reality is not often quite like that'. For the use of πράγματα to denote 'reality', 'practical policy' and similar ideas, cf. ὅταν περὶ πραγμάτων προτεθῇ σκοπεῖν, 3rd Olynthiac 18 above. πέφυκε is perfect tense of φύω 'I produce', used intransitively to mean 'I have come into being', 'I am by nature'.

20. ὁρᾶτ'... ὅπως καὶ τὰ πράγματα ἐνδέχεται καὶ δυνήσεσθ' ἐξιέναι καὶ μισθὸν ἕξετε: 'see in what ways the reality permits, and how you will be able both to campaign and to receive your pay'. All these subordinate clauses, despite the difference in tense, are dependant on ὅπως: for ἐξιέναι with the meaning of 'perform military service', see 1st Olynthiac 6 and 2nd Olynthiac 13, 24, 27 and 31.

οὕτοι σωφρόνων οὐδὲ γενναίων ἐστιν ἀνθρώπων: 'nor indeed is it the mark of men of understanding, nor of high-minded men either'. For the genitive, cf. 1st Olynthiac 1 - τῆς ὑμετέρας τύχης ὑπολαμβάνω and 1st Olynthiac 16 - παντὸς εἶναι and τοῦτ' εἶναι συμβούλου; cf. G. 1094.1.

ἐλλείποντάς τι δι' ἔνδειαν χρημάτων τῶν τοῦ πολέμου: 'to be deficient in military action because of a lack of pay', where τῶν τοῦ πολέμου is to be construed with ἐλλείποντάς τι and not with δι' ἔνδειαν χρημάτων. Note the use of the participle in the accusative, despite its reference to a noun in the genitive. The accusative is usual in such cases, and agrees grammatically with the unexpressed subject of the infinitive (G. 928.2); cf. 1st Philippic 47 - κακούργου ἐστι κριθέντ' ἀποθανεῖν, στρατηγοῦ δὲ μαχόμενον τοῖς πολεμίοις and On the Chersonese 46 - τί οὖν εὖ φρονούντων ἀνθρώπων ἐστι; εἰδότας ταῦτα καὶ ἐγνωκότας ... ῥᾳθυμίαν ἀποθέσθαι.

εὐχερῶς τὰ τοιαῦθ' ὀνείδη φέρειν: 'to endure these reproaches lightly'.

ἐπὶ μὲν Κορινθίους καὶ Μεγαρέας ... πορεύεσθαι: if Demosthenes is referring to specific incidents, they should belong to recent history and not to the fifth century, as older commentators believed. The

Megarian campaign is probably that of 350/49 B.C., which originated in the Megarian cultivation of land sacred to Demeter on the Attic border (Androtion fgt. 30J and Philochorus fgt. 155J). According to the ancient scholia, the expedition against Corinth took place when the Corinthians excluded Athenian competitors from the Isthmian Games (perhaps those of 350 B.C.) but we have no further knowledge of such an expedition, if it ever took place. It may well be the case that the orator is not thinking of any specific occasion, but is merely contrasting Athenian enthusiasm for campaigns against nearby relatively insignificant states with their reluctance to act against more distant, powerful enemies.

21. καὶ ταῦτ' οὐχ ἵν' ἀπέχθωμαί τισιν ὑμῶν τὴν ἄλλως προῄρημαι λέγειν: 'I have chosen to say this not for the idle purpose of making myself unpopular with certain persons among you'. ἀπέχθωμαι is second aorist subjunctive of ἀπεχθάνομαι 'I am hated', used with ἵνα in a final clause (G. 1365). τισιν ὑμῶν appears to refer to the group already mentioned in 12-13 above, namely Eubulus and his faction. τὴν ἄλλως is an adverbial accusative (G. 1060); cf. τὴν πρώτην, *3rd Olynthiac* 2 above ('in the first instance'), τὴν ἀρχὴν ('at first') and τρόπον τινα ('in some way'). ἄλλως, in addition to meaning 'otherwise', can also mean 'in vain'.

οὐ γὰρ οὕτως ἄφρων οὐδ' ἀτυχής εἰμ' ἐγὼ ὥστ' ἀπεχθάνεσθαι βούλεσθαι μηδὲν ὠφελεῖν νομίζων: 'for I am not so foolish or misguided as to desire to be hated, when I do not consider that I can be of any benefit'. For ὥστε with the infinitive in consecutive clauses, see G. 1449-50. μηδέν is a cognate accusative to be construed with the unexpressed noun implied in the verb ὠφελεῖν, 'to benefit in no way' (G. 1054).

ἀλλὰ δικαίου πολίτου κρίνω τὴν τῶν πραγμάτων σωτηρίαν ἀντὶ τῆς ἐν τῷ λέγειν χάριτος αἱρεῖσθαι: 'but I am of the opinion that it is the characteristic of an upright citizen to value the public well-being more highly than his own popularity as a speaker'. For the genitive δικαίου πολίτου (*sc.*εἶναι), cf. *1st Olynthiac* 16, παντὸς εἶναι and τοῦτ' εἶναι συμβούλου, and on

3rd Olynthiac 20 above οὐ σωφρόνων οὐδὲ γενναίων ἐστιν ἀνθρώπων (G. 1094).

ἐπὶ τῶν προγόνων ἡμῶν: ἐπί is here temporal, 'in the time of our ancestors'.

ὥσπερ ἴσως καὶ ὑμεῖς (sc. ἠκούσατε): 'just as you too may perhaps have heard'.

τούτῳ τῷ ἔθει καὶ τῷ τρόπῳ τῆς πολιτείας: 'this habit and manner of statesmanship'.

τὸν Ἀριστείδην ἐκεῖνον: 'the famous Aristeides', a statesman influential in the 480s but ostracised in 482 B.C. after his failure to defeat Themistocles' proposals to construct a large, modern navy. Recalled in 480, he distinguished himself at Salamis and in the winter of 478/7 worked out the details of and the tribute assessments for the Delian League.

Νικίαν: the cautious moderate statesman who was prominent from Pericles' death in 429 to his own death in 413 at the hands of the Syracusans after the defeat of the Sicilian Expedition.

τὸν ὁμώνυμον ἐμαυτῷ: Demosthenes son of Alcisthenes, whose most famous exploits were the defeat of the Peloponnesians and Ambraciots at Olpae in 426, and the capture of Pylos in Messenia in 425 B.C. Like Nicias, he was put to death by the Syracusans in 413. His oratorical abilities are nowhere else attested and in general he seems to have been more of a soldier than a statesman.

Περικλέα: the most famous politician in Athens from the 450s to his death in 429 B.C., best remembered for inspiring the great building programme on the Acropolis in the 440s and 430s which included the Parthenon and the Propylaea. His outstanding oratorical abilities are attested by Eupolis (fgt. 94), Plato (Phaedrus 269E) and Diodorus (12.38.2).

22. ἐξ οὗ δ' οἱ διερωτῶντες ὑμᾶς οὗτοι πεφήνασι ῥήτορες, "τί βούλεσθε;": 'but ever since these orators have appeared, who keep asking you, "What would you like?"'. πεφήνασι is the third person plural of πέφηνα, the

second perfect of φαίνω, with intransitive meaning
('I have appeared'), as contrasted with the first
perfect πέφαγκα, which is transitive, 'I have shown'.

"τί βούλεσθε; τί γράψω; τί ὑμῖν χαρίσωμαι;": for the
three questions typical of orators who court the
popularity of the people, Demosthenes may well have
departed from his normal tone of delivery and sought
to impersonate a typical example of the sort of
speaker he had in mind. The technical term for such
impersonation is *prosopopoiia* (see Introduction II 4 d,
p.43). For the use of the subjunctive in deliberative
questions ('How am I to please you?'), see G. 1358.

προπέποται τῆς παραυτίχ' ἡδονῆς καί χάριτος τὰ τῆς
πόλεως πράγματα: 'the interests of the city have
been pledged away in exchange for momentary pleasure
and gratification'. προπέποται is perfect passive
of προπίνω 'I drink to someone's health'. Since
the drinking vessel was often gifted subsequently
to the person pledged, who in turn would present the
drinker with a gift of his own (cf. *On the Crown* 296
- τὴν ἐλευθερίαν προπεπωκότες . . . Φιλίππῳ, 'having
given away their freedom to Philip'), the verb is
here used metaphorically with a genitive of price,
denoting the gift for which the drinking cup is
exchanged. The best manuscripts omit the words
ἡδονῆς καί.

καί τοιαυτί συμβαίνει, καί τὰ μὲν τούτων πάντα καλῶς
ἔχει, τὰ δ' ὑμέτερ' αἰσχρῶς: 'and the following
situation results, that their affairs all prosper,
while yours are in a disgraceful state'. τούτων
refers to the orators who court popularity by
flattering the audience.

23. σκέψασθ . . . ἅ τις ἂν κεφάλαι' εἰπεῖν ἔχοι τῶν τ' ἐπί
τῶν προγόνων ἔργων καί τῶν ἐφ' ὑμῶν: 'yet consider
what one might be able to say in summary form about
the achievements of the time of your ancestors and
about those of your day'. The adjective κεφάλαιος
means 'principal' but is usually found in the neuter
as a noun meaning 'chief point', 'salient feature',
'gist', 'summary', 'crowning act' or similar ideas.
ἂν ἔχοι is a potential optative (G. 1327). Parts of
this and the following section reappear with additions in the speech *On Syntaxis* 21ff.

ἔσται δὲ βραχὺς καὶ γνώριμος ὁ λόγος: 'my account will be short and familiar to you'.

οὐ γὰρ ἀλλοτρίοις ὑμῖν χρωμένοις παραδείγμασιν, ἀλλ' οἰκείοις . . . εὐδαίμοσιν ἔξεστι γενέσθαι: 'for it is possible for you still to become prosperous, if you follow the examples of your own city, and not those taken from other states'. χρωμένοις refers to ὑμῖν, which is to be construed with ἔξεστι; ἀλλοτρίοις . . . παραδείγμασι in turn depends upon χρωμένοις.

24. ἐκεῖνοι: 'the former set of people', i.e. 'your ancestors', as contrasted with οὗτοι, 'the latter', i.e. 'the orators of the present day'.

οἷς οὐκ ἐχαρίζονθ' οἱ λέγοντες οὐδ' ἐφίλουν αὐτούς: 'whom their orators did not seek to gratify and for whom they had no affection', where οὐδ' ἐφίλουν αὐτούς is equivalent to καὶ οὓς οὐκ ἐφίλουν. When two relative pronouns in different cases refer to the same antecedent, the second is usually replaced by a personal or demonstrative pronoun (G. 1040); cf. on *2nd Olynthiac* 4, ἃ δὲ καὶ χωρὶς τούτων ἔνι . . . καὶ μεγάλ' . . . κατ' ἐκείνου φαίνοιτ' ἂν ὀνείδη . . . ταῦτ' εἰπεῖν πειράσομαι, above.

πέντε μὲν καὶ τετταράκοντ' ἔτη τῶν Ἑλλήνων ἦρξαν ἑκόντων: the 45 year period which the orator has in mind is a round figure for the years between the foundation of the Delian League in 477 to the outbreak of the Peloponnesian War in 431 B.C. τῶν Ἑλλήνων refers not to the Greeks as a whole but to the members of the Delian League. The position of ἑκόντων at the end of the clause is intended to emphasise the willingness which, though undoubtedly present at the time of the League's creation, had evaporated in some cases long before the end of the 45 year period. The literary evidence indicates that a series of revolts took place (Naxos ca. 469, Thasos ca. 464, Euboea in 446, Samos and Byzantium in 440 B.C.), while the epigraphical evidence points to more widespread unrest. Thucydides more correctly states that the allies were willing members of the League at the outset (1.96.1 - παραλαβόντες δ' οἱ Ἀθηναῖοι τὴν ἡγεμονίαν ἑκόντων τῶν συμμάχων), as do other references in the orators (e.g. Isocrates, *On the Peace* 30 - παρ' ἑκόντων τῶν Ἑλλήνων τὴν ἡγεμονίαν

ἐλάβομεν and *Areopagiticus* 17 - παρ' ἑκόντων τῶν
'Ελλήνων τὴν ἡγεμονίαν ἔλαβον; Dinarchus, *Against
Demosthenes* 37 - 'Αριστείδην καὶ Θεμιστκλέα . . .
τοὺς φόρους εἰς ἀκρόπολιν ἀνενεγκόντας παρ' ἑκόντων
καὶ βουλομένων τῶν 'Ελλήνων).

πλείω δ' ἢ μύρια τάλαντ' εἰς τὴν ἀκρόπολιν ἀνήγαγον:
according to Pericles in Thucydides 2.13.3, the
largest amount of treasure that had ever been
accumulated on the Acropolis at any one time was 9700
talents. The figure came to be rounded upwards to
10,000 talents, the regular sum in the Reserve Fund
in fourth century writers (so Ephorus, fgt. 196J =
Deodorus 12.40.2; Isocrates, *On the Peace* 69 and
Antidosis 234).

ὑπήκουε δ' ὁ ταύτην τὴν χώραν ἔχων αὐτοῖς βασιλεύς:
'the king who possesses this territory paid them
tribute', clearly a reference to Macedonia, despite
its absence from the speech since 17 above. During
the Pentecontaetia the kings of Macedonia were
Alexander I (ca.495 - ca.452) and Perdiccas II (ca.
452 - 413 B.C.). Demosthenes is guilty of rhetorical
exaggeration in claiming that Macedonia was ever
tributary to Athens, but the allegation was commonplace in the fourth century and later; cf. [Demosthenes],
On Halonesus 12 - ἐφ' ἡμῖν γὰρ ἦν ἡ Μακεδονία καὶ
φόρους ἡμῖν ἔφερον and *On the Letter of Philip* 16 -
τῶν ἐν Μακεδονίᾳ βασιλευσάντων κἀκεῖνοι μὲν 'Αθηναίοις
φόρους ἤνεγκαν ; Arrian, *Anabasis* 7.9.4 - ὡς ἀντὶ τοῦ
φόρους τελεῖν 'Αθηναίοις . . . παρ' ἡμῶν . . . ἐκείνους
τὴν ἀσφάλειάν σφισι πορίζεσθαι. The Macedonian kings
in the period were in fact concerned mainly with
preserving their independence by playing off Athenians
against Peloponnesians. Perdiccas kept switching his
alliance from one to the other and, though he was the
inferior partner when allied to Athens, at no time
did he ever pay tribute.

ὥσπερ ἐστὶ προσῆκον βάρβαρον 'Ελλησι: (*sc.* ὑπακούειν)
'as is fitting for a barbarian to be subject to Greeks'.
On the barbarism of Macedonia and its kings, see on
οὐ βάρβαρος, *3rd Olynthiac* 16 above.

πολλὰ δὲ καὶ καλὰ καὶ πεζῇ καὶ ναυμαχοῦντες ἔστησαν
τρόπαια: e.g. at the Eurymedon (ca.468 B.C.) and
off Salamis in Cyprus (450) against Persia, at
Cecryphaleia (457) and off Aegina (459) against the
Peloponnesians, and at Oenophyta (457) against the
Boeotians. ἔστησαν here is the first aorist of

ἴστημι, with transitive meaning, 'they erected'.

αὐτοὶ στρατευόμενοι: Demosthenes is unable to resist making the point that these victories were won in the fifth century, when it was normal for the Athenians to fight in person, instead of relying on mercenaries, as in the orator's own day. For his continual advice to send citizen troops into the field, see *1st Olynthiac* 6, *2nd Olynthiac* 13 and 30, *3rd Olynthiac* 34 below, *1st Philippic* 19 and *On the Chersonese* 21 and 23.

μόνοι δ' ἀνθρώπων κρείττω τὴν ἐπὶ τοῖς ἔργοις δόξαν τῶν φθονούντων κατέλιπον: 'and alone of men they left behind them a reputation for achievement that is too powerful for envy'. For ἐπί with the dative after δόξαν, cf. *1st Olynthiac* 11 - τὴν ἐπὶ τοῖς πεπραγμένοις ἀδοξίαν ('the ignominy arising from what has been done'). τῶν φθονούντων is the genitive of comparison (G. 1153) after κρείττω, meaning literally 'more powerful than for people to envy it', i.e. 'too powerful to be an object of envy'.

25. ἐπὶ μὲν 'Ελληνικῶν: 'in the affairs of Greece', 'in the sphere of Greek affairs'.

ἔν τε τοῖς κοινοῖς καὶ ἐν τοῖς ἰδίοις: 'in both public and private life'.

οἰκοδομήματα καὶ κάλλη τοιαῦτα καὶ τοσαῦτα κατεσκεύασαν ἡμῖν . . . ὥστε μηδενὶ τῶν ἐπιγιγνομένων ὑπερβολὴν λελεῖφθαι: 'they created for us buildings and objects of beauty of such quality and quantity that the ability to surpass them has been bequeathed to none of their successors'. The plural of abstract nouns normally denotes specific concrete instances or manifestatations of the idea expressed by the abstract. Hence κάλλη indicates 'particular examples of beauty', 'beautiful objects'. For ὥστε with the infinitive expressing result, see G. 1449-50. λελεῖφθαι is perfect infinitive passive of λείπω, used to denote an act that is already completed (G. 1272).

ἱερῶν καὶ τῶν ἐν τούτοις ἀναθημάτων: 'temples and

objects of dedication within them', where ἀναθημάτων denotes both the cult image of the god and objects dedicated by private individuals. The most outstanding examples of temples built during the Pentecontaetia are the Parthenon with Pheidias' cult statue of Athene Parthenos, the Hephaestaeum, and the temple of Ares in Athens, the temple of Poseidon at Sounion, and the temple of Nemesis at Rhamnous with its cult image by Agoracritus of Paros.

καὶ σφόδρ' ἐν τῷ τῆς πολιτείας ἤθει μένοντες: 'and strongly attached to the spirit of the constitution'. μένοντες is here used as an adjective, meaning 'true to'.

26. Ἀριστείδου: see 21 above.

Μιλτιάδου: a statesman who began his career as ruler of the Athenian settlement in the Thracian Chersonese in succession to his brother Stesagoras (ca.515 B.C.). In 493 he was obliged to return to Athens after incurring the hostility of Darius, his nominal suzerain, and is best remembered for his part in defeating the Persians at the battle of Marathon in 490. In 489 B.C. he led an unsuccessful expedition against the island of Paros but, on receiving a serious wound in the course of the campaign, returned to Athens. He was immediately prosecuted by Xanthippus the father of Pericles on a charge of deceiving the people and was condemned to pay a huge fine. Being unable to pay, he was put in prison, where he died of his wound shortly afterwards.

εἴ τις ἄρ' οἶδεν ὑμῶν: 'if indeed anyone of you does actually know', where the particle ἄρα is used to suggest that the hypothesis is in fact unlikely to be true.

ὁρᾷ τῆς τοῦ γείτονος οὐδὲν σεμνοτέραν οὖσαν: 'he sees that it is in no way more impressive than that of the man next door'. For the use of the accusative and participle after a verb of seeing, hearing etc., see G. 1588. Note the change from ὥστε with the infinitive in the previous sentence (οἰκοδομήματα τοιαῦτα καὶ τοσαῦτα . . . κατεσκεύασαν . . . ὥστε λελεῖφθαι),

denoting the result which the leading verb aims at
or tends to produce, to ὥστε with the indicative
(ὁρᾷ), indicating an action that really is produced
('so that everyone actually does see'); see G. 1449-
50, and cf. Thucydides 3.21.3 - πύργοι ἦσαν . . .
ὥστε πάροδον μὴ εἶναι παρὰ πύργον, ἀλλὰ δι' αὐτῶν
μεσῶν διῇσαν, 'there were towers . . . built so that
there should be no way through past them (result
aimed at), but so that people actually passed through
the middle of them (result actually produced)'.

οὐ γὰρ εἰς περιουσίαν ἐπράττετ' αὐτοῖς τὰ τῆς πόλεως:
'for public affairs were not being conducted by them
with a view to their own private gain'. The use of
the dative of the agent, in place of ὑπό with the
genitive, is common in prose only with the perfect
and pluperfect passive (G. 1186), and in Demosthenes
occurs usually when the verb is πράττω or λέγω.
Demosthenes does occasionally extend the use of the
dative of the agent to the aorist (e.g. *For Phormio* 3
- ἅπαντα τὰ πραχθέντα τούτῳ, *Against Pantaenetus* 6 -
τὰ μὲν δὴ πραχθέντα τούτοις, *3rd Against Aphobus* 11 -
τὰ τούτῳ ῥηθέντα), but with the imperfect the idiom
occurs only here. Since it is accompanied by the
phrase εἰς περιουσίαν, the dative could be seen as
being to some extent a dative of advantage (G. 1165).

ἐκ δὲ τοῦ τὰ μὲν Ἑλληνικὰ πιστῶς, τὰ δὲ πρὸς τοὺς θεοὺς
εὐσεβῶς, τὰ δ' ἐν αὐτοῖς ἴσως διοικεῖν μεγάλην εἰκότως
ἐκτήσαντ' εὐδαιμονίαν: 'and in consequence of their
dealing in a spirit of loyalty with the conduct of
Greek affairs, in a spirit of piety towards the gods,
and in a spirit of equity among themselves, they
rightly attained prosperity'. The infinitive διοικεῖν
is to be taken with ἐκ τοῦ at the beginning of the
sentence as an articular infinitive (G. 1546). The
adverb ἴσως, which normally means 'perhaps', is here
to be used in its literal meaning of 'equally', in
order to preserve the symmetrical construction of
these successive and emphatic adverbs (πιστῶς, εὐσεβῶς,
ἴσως).

27. χρωμένοις οἷς εἶπον προστάταις: for χρωμένοις τοῖς
προστάταις οὓς εἶπον, 'having as leaders those whom
I mentioned'. A relative pronoun in the accusative
is usually attracted into the case of an antecedent

in the genitive or dative, but here the antecedent is in turn attracted into the relative clause ('attraction and assimilation', *G*. 1038); cf. *Against Eubulides* 37 - τούτῳ γίγνονται τέτταρες παῖδες ἐκ μὲν ἧς τὸ πρῶτον ἔσχε γυναικὸς (= ἐκ γυναικὸς ἥν τὸ πρῶτον ἔσχε).

νυνὶ δὲ πῶς ἡμῖν ὑπὸ τῶν χρηστῶν τῶν νῦν τὰ πράγματ' ἔχει: 'but how do matters stand now, thanks to these worthy statesmen of the present', where χρηστός is ironical.

οἷς - τὰ μὲν ἄλλα σιωπῶ, πόλλ' ἂν ἔχων εἰπεῖν, ἀλλ' ὅσης ἄπαντες ὁρᾶτ' ἐρημίας ἐπειλημμένοι: 'to whom - I omit the rest, though there is much that I might mention - but you all see what a clear field we had obtained'. The relative οἷς may refer either to ἡμῖν or to ὑπὸ τῶν χρηστῶν in the previous sentence but, in either case, it is left without a construction when the parenthesis is inserted and the sentence then resumes just as if the relative had never been used in the first place. Such a disruption in the construction of a sentence is called *anacoluthon* (see Introduction II 4 e (ii) and cf. on εἶτ' οὐκ αἰσχύνεσθε., *1st Olynthiac* 24 above). τὰ μὲν ἄλλα σιωπῶ is an instance of *parasiopesis*, a claim to be suppressing information which (in contrast to *paraleipsis*) is *not* mentioned (see Introduction II 4 e (iv)). The particle ἂν is used with the participle ἔχων in place of a potential optative ('although I might say many things', *G*. 1308). ὅσης . . . ὁρᾶτ' ἐρημίας ἐπειλημμένοι is a further example of attraction and assimilation (see on χρωνένοις οἷς εἶπον προστάταις above) and represents ἐπειλημμένοι τοσαύτης ἐρημίας ὅσην ὁρᾶτε. ἐρημία is a metaphor derived from the public games, denoting 'an absence of competitors', 'a clear field'. ἐπειλημμένοι is perfect participle middle, from ἐπιλαμβάνω.

Λακεδαιμονίων μὲν ἀπολωλότων: the reference is to Sparta's defeats at the hands of the Thebans at Leuctra (371) and Mantinea (362 B.C.), as a result of which she lost the hegemony of Greece. ἀπολωλότων (genitive absolute) is the participle of the intransitive second perfect ἀπόλωλα ('I am undone') from ἀπόλλυμι 'I destroy', 'I lose'. This verb also has a transitive first perfect ἀπολώλεκα, 'I have lost or destroyed', used in 28 below.

Θηβαίων δ' ἀσχόλων ὄντων: 'the Thebans having no time', i.e. because of their involvement in the Sacred War against Phocis since 356 B.C.

τῶν δ' ἄλλων οὐδενὸς ὄντος ἀξιόχρεω περὶ τῶν πρωτείων ἡμῖν ἀντιτάξασθαι: 'and of the others there being nobody capable of ranging himself against us for the supremacy', another genitive absolute. For the infinitive after adjectives denoting ability or fitness, see G. 1526. τὰ πρωτεῖα means literally 'the first prize', thus continuing the public games metaphor begun with ἐρημία.

ἔξον δ' ἡμῖν καὶ τὰ ἡμέτερ' αὐτῶν ἀσφαλῶς ἔχειν καὶ τὰ τῶν ἄλλων δίκαια βραβεύειν: 'and it being in our power to have our possessions in safety and to be umpires of the rights of others'. The impersonal ἔξεστι is here used in the accusative absolute construction (G. 1569). βραβεύω, 'I serve as a judge', from βραβεύς 'referee', 'umpire', again continues the metaphor from the games.

28. χώρας οἰκείας: 'our own territory', 'the territory that belongs to us', i.e. Pydna, Methone, Amphipolis and Potidaea, the cities repeatedly mentioned by Demosthenes as Athenian possessions taken by Philip (see on οὐχ ἅπαντα μὲν ἡμῶν προείληφε τὰ χώρια ἄνθρωπος, 3rd Olynthiac 16 above).

πλείω δ' ἢ χίλια καὶ πεντακόσια τάλαντ' ἀνηλώκαμεν εἰς οὐδὲν δέον: 'and we have spent more than 1500 talents on unnecessaries'. ἀνηλώκαμεν is the perfect of ἀναλίσκω 'I spend'. The figure of 1500 talents is also given by Aeschines (On the Embassy 71) as the sum frittered away by Chares in the course of this same war.

οὓς δ' ἐν τῷ πολέμῳ συμμάχους ἐκτησάμεθα, εἰρήνης οὔσης ἀπολωλέκασιν οὗτοι: 'those present day statesmen of ours have lost in peace time the allies we acquired during the war'. By the allies acquired during the war, Demosthenes refers to the members of the Second Athenian Confederacy, recruited in 378/7 B.C.: the war in question is not that currently being waged against Philip, but the war of 378-371 B.C. against Sparta. Among allies subsequently lost were the

Euboeans and Acarnanians (370), the Byzantines (ca. 363) and the Chians, Rhodians and Coans who broke away at the time of the Social War (357-5 B.C.). Strictly speaking, Athens was at war with Philip throughout the period 357-46 B.C., and so was not at peace when she lost Chios, Rhodes and Cos, but the orator probably means that Athens was at peace with both Sparta and Thebes at the time. He may also be distorting the truth to magnify the incompetence of the politicians whom he is attacking. On ἀπολωλέκασι, see on Λακεδαιμονίων μὲν ἀπολωλότων, *3rd Olynthiac* 27 above.

ἐχθρὸν δ᾽ ἐφ᾽ ἡμᾶς αὐτοὺς τηλικοῦτον ἠσκήκαμεν: 'we have trained against ourselves an enemy of such great strength', a further continuation of the public games metaphor.

29. ἀλλ᾽ ὦ τᾶν: 'but, my good sir', introducing an imaginary objection made by one of Eubulus' partisans; cf. on ἀλλ᾽, ὦ τᾶν, οὐχὶ βουλήσεται, *1st Olynthiac* 26 above.

εἰ ταῦτα φαύλως τά γ᾽ ἐν αὐτῇ τῇ πόλει νῦν ἄμεινον ἔχει: 'if we are in a sorry plight in these respects (i.e. in respect of our foreign policy), our domestic affairs at least are in a better state'.

καὶ τί ἄν εἴπειν τις ἔχοι: 'why, what would one be able to mention', a potential optative with ἄν (G. 1327ff.). καί followed by an interrogative very often conveys a nuance of contempt, surprise or disbelief (Denniston, *Greek Particles* 310).

τὰς ἐπάλξεις ἃς κονιῶμεν: 'the battlements which we are whitening'. κονιάω means 'I cover in lime or plaster (κονία)'. This and the two following phrases contain Demosthenes' contemptuous summary of the achievements of Eubulus' administration, which concentrated on what the orator considers to be petty domestic improvements at the expense of strengthening Athens' position abroad.

καὶ κρήνας καὶ λήρους: 'and the fountains and the follies', where λήρους gives us Demosthenes' personal opinion of Eubulus' public works programme. The word refers not merely to the fountains, but also to the road works and to the whitewashing of the fortifications, and is selected because of its use to indicate something that is imposing but useless.

ἀποβλέψατε δὴ πρὸς τοὺς ταῦτα πολιτευομένους: 'come and take a look rather at the men who made these things the aim of their policy'. δὴ is used with the imperative in emotional contexts to add a note of urgency to the command.

ἐκ πτωχῶν πλούσιοι . . . ἐξ ἀδόξων ἔντιμοι . . . τὰς ἰδίας οἰκίας τῶν δημοσίων οἰκοδομημάτων σεμνοτέρας: note the rhetorical juxtaposition of antonyms. The scholiasts at this point give a list of statesmen to whom Demosthenes may be referring, but as such charges are commonly brought against politicians of every age, he may be thinking of Eubulus' followers in general and may not have any specific individual in mind.

εἰσὶ κατεσκευασμένοι: periphrastic perfect middle of κατασκευάζω; see on ἂν ἦτ' ἀπηλλαγμένοι, 1st Olynthiac 8 above.

ὅσῳ δὲ τὰ τῆς πόλεως ἐλάττω γέγονεν, τοσούτῳ τὰ τούτων ηὔξηται: 'the more the city's fortunes have declined, the more have these men's fortunes increased'. ἐλάττω is a comparative adjective with no positive in use in Attic prose, used as a comparative of μικρός. ηὔξηται is perfect middle of αὐξάνω 'I increase'. For ὅσῳ . . . τοσούτῳ with comparative adjectives or adverbs, see on ὅσῳ γὰρ ἑτοιμότατ' . . . τοσούτῳ μᾶλλον, 2nd Olynthiac 12 above, and G. 1184.

30. τί δή ποθ' ἅπαντ' εἶχε καλῶς τότε, καὶ νῦν οὐκ ὀρθῶς: since καλῶς is contrasted with οὐκ ὀρθῶς and τότε with νῦν, we have here an example of *chiasmus* (see Introduction II 4 f(iv)). For the meaning of ποτε with an interrogative pronoun, see on σκοπεῖσθ' εἰς τί ποτ' ἐλπὶς ταῦτα τελευτῆσαι, 1st Olynthiac 14 above.

δεσπότης τῶν πολιτευομένων: 'master of the politicians', where the participle is masculine.

κύριος ἁπάντων τῶν ἀγαθῶν: 'controller of all good things', where the adjective ἀγαθῶν is neuter.

ἀγαπητὸν ἦν παρὰ τοῦ δήμου τῶν ἄλλων ἑκάστῳ καὶ τιμῆς καὶ ἀρχῆς καὶ ἀγαθοῦ τινος μεταλαβεῖν: 'it was sufficient for each of the others to receive from the people his share of honour or power or some other benefit'.

31. ἐκνενευρισμένοι: perfect participle middle of ἐκνευρίζω, 'I cut (someone's) sinews' (from νεῦρον 'sinew'), used metaphorically to mean 'weakened' or 'enervated', whether physically or, as here, mentally or morally.

περιῃρημένοι χρήματα, συμμάχους: 'deprived of funds and allies'. περιῃρημένοι is perfect participle passive of περιαιρέω 'I take away'. In the active this verb is usually construed with the genitive of the person and accusative of the thing but in the passive it can be used personally with an object of the thing taken away. The better manuscripts read χρήματα, συμμάχους, while the inferior ones have χρήματα καὶ συμμάχους. If καί is omitted, we have an example of *asyndeton* (see Introduction II 4 f(v)), which is common only when at least three words are linked together. However instances of two nouns in asyndeton occur elsewhere in Demosthenes, e.g. *On the Crown* 67 - τὴν χεῖρα τὸ σκέλος πεπηρωμένον; *On the Crown* 94 - δόξαν εὔνοιαν παρὰ πάντων ἐκτᾶσθε and *On the Embassy* 220 - Εὔβοιαν Ὠρωπὸν ἀποδώσειν.

ἐν ὑπηρέτου καὶ προσθήκης μέρει γεγένησθε: 'you have found yourselves in the category of underlings and appendages'.

ἀγαπῶντες ἐὰν μεταδίδωσι θεωρικῶν ὑμῖν ἢ Βοηδρόμια πέμψωσιν οὗτοι: 'being content if these people give you your share of the festival monies or arrange a procession at the Boedromia'. μεταδίδωσι is a subjunctive denoting a general supposition (G. 1393). The Boedromia was a minor festival of Apollo from which the month Boedromion (roughly September) derived its name but we have no other evidence that a procession formed part of this festival.

τὸ πάντων ἀνδρειότατον: 'the most manly thing of all', ironical (see Introduction II 4 f(viii)).

τῶν ὑμετέρων αὐτῶν χάριν προσοφείλετε: 'on top of everything else you thank them for what is your own', where the prefix of προσοφείλω denotes 'in addition', 'besides'.

ὑμᾶς ἐπάγουσιν ἐπὶ ταῦτα: 'they lead you on (i.e. 'entice you') to these things'.

καὶ τιθασεύουσι χειροήθεις αὐτοῖς ποιοῦντες: 'and in doing so they make you tame and accustomed to the hand'. τιθασεύω 'I domesticate', the verbal form from the adjective τιθασός 'tame', is a metaphor derived from the training of wild animals to become submissive household pets.

32. νεανικόν: an adjective meaning literally 'youthful', used frequently in a good sense, as here, to mean 'active', 'spirited', 'vigorous', but also in the bad sense of 'hot-headed', 'impetuous'.

ὁποῖ' ἄττα γὰρ ἂν τὰ ἐπιτηδεύματα τῶν ἀνθρώπων ᾖ, τοιοῦτον ἀνάγκη καὶ τὸ φρόνημ' (sc. αὐτοὺς) ἔχειν: 'for whatever men's habits may be, such must inevitably be the character they have', a conditional relative clause with ἂν and the subjunctive (G. 1428 and 1431). ἄττα is a purely Attic alternative form of τινά, the neuter plural of the indefinite pronoun τις. The belief that habit affects a man's character appears elsewhere in Greek literature: see especially the discussion at the beginning of Book 2 or Aristotle's *Nicomachean Ethics*, culminating in the words τὰ μὲν δίκαια πράττοντες δίκαιοι γινόμεθα, τὰ δὲ σώφρονα σώφρονες, τὰ δ' ἀνδρεῖα ἀνδρεῖοι (*Ethics* 1103a).

ταῦτα μὰ τὴν Δήμητρ' οὐκ ἂν θαυμάσαιμ' εἰ μείζων εἰπόντι ἐμοὶ γένοιτο παρ' ὑμῶν βλάβη τῶν πεποιηκότων αὐτὰ γενέσθαι: 'by Demeter, I should not be surprised if greater harm at your hands were to befall me for saying this than to befall those who had brought it about', a future condition in the less vivid form (G. 1408). The word μά ('by') is used with the accusative in oaths to indicate the divinity by whom one swears, when the sentence is negative (in affirmative sentences νή is used instead). There is some dislocation in this sentence of the natural word order: ταῦτα at the beginning is the object of εἰπόντι, and μείζων is to be taken with βλάβη. τῶν πεποιηκότων is a genitive of comparison (G. 1153), equivalent to ἢ τοῖς πεποιηκόσι.

33. ἐὰν . . . ἀπαλλαγέντες τούτων τῶν ἐθῶν ἐθελήσητε στρατεύεσθαι . . . ἴσως ἂν . . . τέλειόν τι καὶ μέγα κτήσαισθ' ἀγαθόν: 'if you were willing to get rid of those habits and take the field . . . then perhaps you might obtain some conclusive and significant advantage', a mixed condition, having a protasis in the form of a future condition in the vivid form, with ἄν + subjunctive, and a protasis in the form of a potential optative with ἄν. For examples of this type of mixed condition, see G. 1421.2. ἀπαλλαγέντες is second aorist participle passive of ἀπαλλάττω 'I free one thing from another', 'I remove something from something else'; the genitive here is a genitive of separation (G. 1117).

καὶ ταῖς περιουσίαις ταῖς οἴκοι ταύταις ἀφορμαῖς ἐπὶ τὰ ἔξω τῶν ἀγαθῶν χρήσησθε: 'and if you use those domestic surpluses as a means towards obtaining advantages abroad'. For the adverb οἴκοι, see on τὰ οἴκοι, 1st Olynthiac 18 above. ἀφορμή means 'resources', 'starting point' and is here used predicatively after περιουσίαις. For ἀφορμή, cf. 1st Olynthiac 23 - ἀφορμὴ τοῦ κακῶς φρονεῖν ('the starting point for folly') and 2nd Olynthiac 22 - πλείους ἀφορμὰς εἰς τὸ τὴν παρὰ τῶν θεῶν εὔνοιαν ἔχειν ὁρῶ ὑμῖν ἐνούσας ('I see that we have more numerous means open to us for attaining the favour of the gods').

ἴσως ἄν, ἴσως: an example of the figure of speech called *anadiplosis* (see Introduction II 4 f(xi)). The repetition of ἴσως also occurs at *On the Chersonese* 77.

ἃ τοῖς ἀσθενοῦσι παρὰ τῶν ἰατρῶν σιτίοις διδομένοις ἔοικε: 'which are like the foods given by doctors to invalids'. The word ἀσθενοῦσι, though found in all manuscripts, is deleted as a gloss by some scholars, on the grounds that it does not appear in the similar passage in the collection of Demosthenes' *Exordia* (53.4). The article τοῖς in that case would have to be construed with σιτίοις, 'like the foods administered by doctors'. For other examples of simile in the *Olynthiacs*, see Introduction II 4 f(ii).

καὶ γὰρ ἐκεῖν' οὔτ' ἰσχὺν ἐντίθησιν οὔτ' ἀποθνῄσκειν ἐᾷ: 'for the foods neither impart strength to the patient nor allow him to die'. Both ἐκεῖν' in this clause and ταῦθ' at the beginning of the next refer to words in the previous sentence, ἐκεῖν' to σίτια and ταῦθ' to λήμματα. Where οὗτος and ἐκεῖνος are contrasted, ἐκεῖνος normally means 'the one that is more remote' (i.e. 'the former') while οὗτος means 'the one that is nearer' (i.e. 'the latter'). The orator here uses the words with the usual meaning reversed, because ταῦθ' refers to the item that is uppermost in his mind, the λήμματα, whereas σίτια are only brought in as an illustration and the item is not uppermost in his mind.

οὔτε τοσοῦτ' ἐστὶν ὥστ' ὠφέλειαν ἔχειν τινὰ διαρκῆ, οὔτ' ἀπογνόντας ἄλλο τι πράττειν ἐᾷ: 'neither are they of such a size as to have any permanent beneficial effect, nor do they allow one to reject them and to turn to something else'. For ὥστε with the infinitive in a consecutive clause, see G. 1450.

ἀλλ' ἔστι ταῦτα τὴν ἑκάστου ῥᾳθυμίαν ἡμῶν ἐπαυξάνοντα: 'but they only increase the apathy of each one of you'. ἔστι . . . ἐπαυξάνοντα is a periphrasis for ἐπαυξάνει. The periphrastic use of the verb 'to be' with the present participle generally occurs only when the participle has the force of an adjective, e.g. *On the Embassy* 36 - καὶ πάντ' ἀναδεχόμενος καὶ εἰς αὑτὸν ποιούμενος τὰ τούτων ἁμαρτήματ' ἐστί ('he is a person of the sort who takes upon himself and adopts all their misdeeds'). In the present passage, however, the periphrastic form is probably intended to provide a symmetrical parallel to τοσοῦτ' ἐστιν in the previous clause.

34. οὐκοῦν σὺ μισθοφορὰν λέγεις; φήσει τις: '"do you then mean payment for military service?", someone will ask'. φήσει τις is used here to introduce a question from an imaginary member of the audience in place of the more usual ἄν τις εἴποι or εἴποι ἄν τις. For hypothetical questions in Demosthenes, see Introduction II 4 d, p.42. Since payment was usual at Athens for military service, the questioner must be asking whether Demosthenes is suggesting that monies from the Theoric Fund should be diverted to pay only those on military service and that those not involved should receive nothing.

καὶ παραχρῆμά γε τὴν αὐτὴν σύνταξιν (sc. λέγω) ἁπάντων: 'Yes (γε), and I also advocate forthwith the same system for everything'. For the meaning of this phrase, cf. *1st Olynthiac* 20 above - καὶ μίαν σύνταξιν εἶναι τὴν αὐτὴν τοῦ τε λαμβάνειν καὶ τοῦ ποιεῖν τὰ δέοντα, where the orator expresses the opinion that state payments should only be made to those who are actually performing some service for the state and, by implication, that theoric distributions as such should cease. ἁπάντων could be either masculine ('for everybody') or neuter ('for everything'); in the present context, where Demosthenes is thinking of the various state payments and services, the latter interpretation is more likely.

ἵνα τῶν κοινῶν ἕκαστος τὸ μέρος λαμβάνων, ὅτου δέοιθ᾽ ἡ πόλις, τοῦθ᾽ ὑπάρχοι: 'so that each, while receiving his proportion of the public funds, might be this, namely whatever the state might require', i.e. 'might be whatever he is required to be in accordance with the needs of the state'. ὅτου (= οὗτινος) δέοιθ᾽ is an indefinite or conditional relative clause (G. 1431.2): the mood is optative by way of assimilation to the optative in the clause on which it is dependent (G. 1439). The use of the optative ὑπάρχοι in a final clause which is apparently in primary sequence is highly irregular. Where this construction is found, the clause on which the optative depends usually implies a reference to the past just as much as to the present, e.g. Lysias 20.21 - οἴχονται ἵνα μὴ δοῖεν δίκην, where οἴχονται is virtually equivalent to a past tense such as ἀπῆλθον. In Demosthenes the construction appears in three other passages (*Against Androtion* 11, *Against Timocrates* 145 and 147) and in all three instances the final clause with the optative depends on a phrase (οὗτος ὁ νόμος . . . κεῖται, τοῦτο τὸ γράμμα . . . γέγραπται and τοῦτον τὸν τρόπον ἔχει ὁ νόμος) where the orator is thinking of a law and has in mind not so much the present force of the law as the intention of the legislator at the time in the past when the law was formulated. In the present passage, we would have to suppose, if the analogy is relevant, that Demosthenes is referring less to the time in the present when he is making his suggestion than to the time in the past when he first evolved this way of thinking. Scholars who find this interpretation strained generally prefer to amend the text and adopt in preference to τοῦθ' ὑπάρχοι the reading τοῦτο παρέχῃ (subjunctive), which is found in some manuscripts of Dionysius of Halicarnassus, *Isaeus* 13, where this passage is quoted. The translation would then be 'so that each man may provide by way of service whatever the state may require'. However even in the text of Dionysius of Halicarnassus the majority of manuscripts read παρέχοι (optative).

ἔξεστιν ἄγειν ἡσυχίαν· οἴκοι μένειν βελτίων (*sc.* ἐστιν): literally 'it is possible to keep the peace; he is better off staying at home'. Here and throughout the rest of 34 we have instances of *asyndeton* (the omission of connectives, see Introduction II 4 f(v)), and the placing alongside one another of parallel clauses in *parataxis* (see Introduction II 4 f(xiv)). Syntactically the first of each pair of paratactic clauses (ἔξεστιν ἄγειν ἡσυχίαν / συμβαίνει τι τοιοῦτον οἷον καὶ τὰ νῦν / ἐστι τις ἔξω τῆς ἡλικίας ἡμῶν) is equivalent to a hypothetical clause ('if it were possible to keep the peace' / 'supposing that some sort of condition like the present were to arise' / 'if there is anyone outside military age'). For οἴκοι, see on τὰ οἴκοι *1st Olynthiac* 18 and on καὶ ταῖς περιουσίαις ταῖς οἴκοι at *3rd Olynthiac* 33 above.

τοῦ δι' ἔνδειαν ἀνάγκῃ τι ποιεῖν αἰσχρὸν ἀπηλλαγμένος: 'free from the necessity of doing anything dishonourable through poverty', i.e. since he would be in receipt of state payments for performing some useful peacetime occupation such as attendance at the *ecclesia* or jury service. ἀπηλλαγμένος is perfect

participle passive of ἀπαλλάττω: for the meaning
and construction of this verb, see on 33 above.

στρατιώτης αὐτὸς ὑπάρχων ἀπὸ τῶν αὐτῶν τούτων λημμάτων:
'it is better for him to serve as a soldier in person,
in receipt of payments derived from those very same
sums', where βελτίων ἐστι is to be supplied from the
previous sentence.

ἔξω τῆς ἡλικίας: 'outside the age', sc. for military
service, i.e. aged 60 or over.

ὅσ' οὗτος ἀτάκτως νῦν λαμβάνων οὐκ ὠφελεῖ, ταῦτ' ἐν
ἴσῃ τάξει λαμβάνων πάντ' ἐφορῶν καὶ διοικῶν ἃ χρὴ
πράττεσθαι: 'let him receive, under a parallel
regulation, for overseeing and managing everything
that needs to be done, what he now receives under
no system at all and with no benefit to the state'.
ἀτάκτως means 'irregularly', 'under no ordinance',
i.e. without having to perform any particular
function, a reference to the theoric payments. The
adverb is intended to provide a contrast with ἐν
ἴσῃ τάξει, meaning 'on the basis of a system parallel
to that under which those on active service are paid'.
Demosthenes is expressing the view that state payments
should be made only to those who serve the state in
some useful capacity. Men in their sixtieth year
were already obliged to serve the state as *diaitetai*
or public arbitrators, whose official function was
to try to effect a reconciliation between two pros-
pective litigants, in return for which they received
a fee (*parastasis*) of one drachma per case.

35. ὅλως: 'in short', 'in a word'; cf. its use at *2nd
Olynthiac* 7 and 14 above.

οὔτ' ἀφελὼν οὔτε προσθεὶς πλὴν μικρῶν: 'neither taking
away nor adding anything, apart from a small amount',
i.e. the orator's proposal will ensure that the amount
allocated to the citizens in state payments will not
differ to any extent from that spent under the existing system. ἀφελὼν is the second aorist participle
of ἀφαιρέω 'I take away'; προσθεὶς is the similar
form from the verb προστίθημι 'I add'.

τὴν ἀταξίαν ἀνελὼν εἰς τάξιν ἤγαγον τὴν πόλιν: 'by removing the lack of a system, I have brought the state to order'. The orator uses the aorist because he is looking back to the general formulation of his proposal concerning state payments which has been gradually evolving from as far back as 11 above.

τοῦ λαβεῖν, τοῦ στρατεύεσθαι, τοῦ δικάζειν: 'for receiving payments, for performing military service, for sitting on juries'.

τοῦ ποιεῖν τοῦθ' ὅ τι καθ' ἡλικίαν ἕκαστος ἔχοι (sc. ποιεῖν) καὶ ὅτου καιρὸς εἴη: 'for doing whatever each one according to his age is able to do and what the occasion requires'. Since the tense of the main verb (ἤγαγον) puts the sentence into historic sequence, the conditional relative sentences require the optative mood (G. 1431.2).

οὐκ ἔστιν ὅπου μηδὲν ἐγὼ ποιοῦσι τὰ τῶν ποιούντων εἶπον ὡς δεῖ νέμειν: 'in no case have I for my part ever proposed that we must give the dues of those who act to those who do nothing'. οὐκ ἔστιν ὅπου (literally 'there is no case in which') is used idiomatically to mean simply 'in no case'. The orator separates the subject ἐγὼ from its verb (εἶπον) to give it greater emphasis and for the same reason separates the participle ποιοῦσι from its object (μηδέν). μή is used in place of οὐ with the participle when the phrase is generic, i.e. μηδὲν ποιοῦσι is equivalent to a conditional relative clause (see G. 1413, 1563.5 and 1612).

οὐδ' αὐτοὺς μὲν ἀργεῖν: (sc. εἶπον) 'nor have I ever proposed that we ourselves should remain idle'. ἀργέω means 'I am at rest', 'I have nothing to do', 'I am unemployed', very often used in the bad sense, 'I am indolent'.

ὅτι δ' οἱ τοῦ δεῖνος νικῶσι ξένοι, ταῦτα πυνθάνεσθαι: 'and be told that so-and-so's mercenaries are winning a victory'. For the indefinite pronoun ὁ δεῖνα, see on μὴ ἃ ἂν ὁ δεῖν' ἢ ὁ δεῖν' εἴπῃ, 2nd Olynthiac 31 above.

36. ἀλλὰ καὶ ὑμᾶς ὑπὲρ ὑμῶν αὐτῶν ἀξιῶ πράττειν ταῦτ' ἐφ' οἷς ἑτέρους τιμᾶτε: 'but I do require you to do on your behalf that for which you honour others'.

καὶ μὴ παραχωρεῖν τῆς τάξεως ἣν ὑμῖν οἱ πρόγονοι τῆς ἀρετῆς μετὰ πολλῶν καὶ καλῶν κινδύνων κτησάμενοι κατέλιπον: 'and not to desert the position of dignity which your ancestors won and bequeathed to you through many glorious perils'. The orator here uses a military metaphor, derived from the notion of a soldier deserting his assigned place in the ranks. τῆς ἀρετῆς is a descriptive genitive depending on τῆς τάξεως ('in the position of merit') but, in order to avoid the awkwardness of a double genitive, Demosthenes puts the words into the relative clause, thus making the relative pronoun ἣν the grammatical antecedent.

εἴρηχ': 'I have said', from the root of ῥῆσις, ῥῆμα, ἐρρήθην etc., and doing duty for the perfect tense of λέγω.

ὑμεῖς δ' ἕλοισθ' ὅ τι καὶ τῇ πόλει καὶ ἅπασι συνοίσειν ὑμῖν μέλλει: 'may you choose whatever is likely to be best for the city and for you all'. ἕλοισθ' is the second person plural second aorist middle of αἱρέω, in the meaning of 'choose'. Here the optative is used in a principal clause to express a wish for the future (G. 1507). συνοίσειν is future infinitive of the impersonal verb συμφέρει 'it is expedient', 'it is of benefit'. When a conditional relative clause is dependent on a verb in the optative mood, it regularly itself takes the optative by assimilation, when the reference is to the future (G. 1439). But when the reference is to the present rather than to the future, the verb resists assimilation. Here the retention of μέλλει in preference to the assimilated μέλλοι indicates that the orator is thinking of the situation as it is at present, 'may you choose whatever is now at the present moment likely to be of benefit'; cf. the concluding words of the *1st Philippic* - νικῴη δ' ὅ τι πᾶσαν μέλλει συμοίσειν. It is characteristic of Demosthenes to end a public oration with a phrase of happy omen and, in particular, with a wish (cf. the ends of the *1st Olynthiac* and *1st*, *2nd* and *3rd Philippics*).

VOCABULARY

In the following vocabulary, the genitive and gender of nouns are provided only for those belonging to the third declension. Nouns of the first and second declension are indicated by *(1)* and *(2)* respectively.

The principal parts of verbs are given only in cases where some doubt might arise, and only those parts actually found in the *Olynthiacs* are listed. Principal parts are given a separate entry only in cases where the stem differs substantially from that of the present.

The feminine and neuter forms of adjectives are given only in the case of those belonging to the third declension. Adverbs are normally listed under the adjective from which they are derived.

ABBREVIATIONS

acc.:	accusative case	*masc.*:	masculine gender
act.:	active voice	*mid.*:	middle voice
adj.:	adjective	*neut.*:	neuter gender
adv.:	adverb	*num.*:	numeral
aor.:	aorist tense	*opt.*:	optative mood
comp.:	comparative degree	*part.*:	participle
conj.:	conjunction	*pass.*:	passive voice
dat.:	dative case	*perf.*:	perfect tense
fem.:	feminine gender	*plur.*:	plural number
fut.:	future tense	*poss.*:	possessive
gen.:	genitive case	*prep.*:	preposition
imperf.:	imperfect tense	*pron.*:	pronoun
impers.:	impersonal	*sing.*:	singular number
indef.:	indefinite	*subj.*:	subjunctive mood
indic.:	indicative mood	*superl.*:	superlative degree
inf.:	infinitive mood	*trans.*:	transitive
interrog.:	interrogative	*verb. adj.*:	verbal adjective
intrans.:	intransitive		

A

ἀγαθός (adj.): good.
ἀγαπάω (+ acc. or dat.): be content with.
ἀγαπητός (adj.): acceptable, to be acquiesced in.
ἀγγέλλω (aor. pass. ἠγγέλθην): announce.
ἀγνοέω: be ignorant of.
ἀγνώμων -ονος (adj.): lacking in judgment; adv. ἀγνωμόνως, senselessly.
ἀγορά (1): market(place).
ἄγω (aor. ἤγαγον): lead, bring; keep, observe.
ἀγών -ῶνος (masc.): contest, struggle.
ἀδεής -ές (adj.): secure; adv. ἀδεῶς, without fear, with impunity, in security.
ἀδικέω: (trans.) wrong, injure; (intrans.) be wrong.
ἄδικος (adj.): unjust; adv. ἀδίκως, unjustly.
ἀδοξία (1): dishonour, ignominy, ill repute.
ἄδοξος (adj.): ignoble, obscure.
ἀεί (adv.): always.
ἀήθης -ες (adj. + gen.): unaccustomed (to).
ἆθλον (2): prize, reward.
ἀθροίζω (aor. ἤθροισα): collect, gather.
ἀθυμία (1): despondency.
ἄθυμος (adj.): despondent, disheartened.
ἀθῷος (adj.): unpunished, unscathed.
αἵρεσις -εως (fem.): choice.
αἱρέω (aor. εἷλον, aor. mid. εἱλόμην, perf. mid. ᾕρημαι): (act.) take; (mid.) choose.
αἴρω (aor. pass. ἤρθην): raise.
αἰσθάνομαι: perceive, learn.
αἰσχρός (adj; superl. αἰσχιστος): base, shameful, disgraceful; adv. αἰσχρῶς, basely.
αἰσχύμη (1): shame, disgrace.
αἰσχύνω: shame, dishonour; (mid.) be ashamed.
αἰτιάομαι: accuse.
αἴτιος (adj. + gen.): responsible (for), guilty (of).
ἀκαιρία (1): lack of opportunity.
ἀκέραιος (adj.): pure, inviolate.
ἀκίνδυνος (adj.): safe, free from danger; adv. ἀκινδύνως: without danger, in safety.
ἀκούω (aor. ἤκουσα, perf. ἀκήκοα): hear.
ἀκρασία (1): incontinence, wantonness.
ἀκριβής -ές (adj.): accurate, exact; adv. ἀκριβῶς, precisely, correctly.
ἀκρόπολις -εως (fem.): citadel.
ἀλήθεια (1): truth.
ἀληθής -ές (adj.): true.
ἀλλά (conj.): but.
ἀλλήλους -ων -οις (pron.): one another.
ἄλλοθεν (adv.): from another place.
ἄλλοθι (adv.): elsewhere.
ἄλλος (adj.): other; adv. ἄλλως, in other ways, in other respects; in vain; ἄλλως τε καί: especially.
ἀλλότριος (adj.): belonging to another; foreign.
ἀλυσιτελής -ές (adj.): unprofitable, inexpedient.
ἁμαρτάνω: do wrong, make a mistake.
ἄμαχος (adj.): invincible.
ἀμείνων -ον (comp. adj.): better (used as comp. of ἀγαθός: good).

ἀμέλεια *(1)*: negligence, neglect.
ἀμελέω *(+ gen.)*: neglect, disregard.
ἀμύνω *(fut.* ἀμυνῶ*)*: *(act.)* ward off; *+ dat.*, defend; *(mid. tr.)* punish, *(mid. intr.)* defend oneself.
ἀμφότερος *(adj.)*: both.
ἀναβάλλω: *(act.)* throw up; *(mid.)* postpone, defer.
ἀναγκάζω: compel.
ἀναγκαῖος *(adj.)*: necessary.
ἀνάγκη *(1)*: necessity, compulsion.
ἀνάγω *(aor.* ἀνήγαγον*)*: take up, bring up.
ἀναδέχομαι *(aor.* ἀνεδεξάμην*)*: take up, undertake.
ἀνάθημα -ατος *(neut.)*: dedication, offering.
ἀναιρέω *(fut.* ἀναιρήσω*, aor.* ἀνεῖλον*)*: *(act.)* take up; destroy, abolish; *(mid.)* take up for oneself, win, undertake.
ἀναλίσκω *(aor.* ἀνήλωσα*, perf.* ἀνήλωκα*)*: spend, waste.
ἀνάστασις -εως *(fem.)*: removal, uprooting.
ἀναχαιτίζω: upset, overturn, unseat.
ἀνδραποδίζω *and (more frequently)* ἀνδραποδίζομαι: enslave.
ἀνδραποδισμός *(2)*: enslavement.
ἀνδρεῖος *(adj.)*: manly, brave.
ἄνευ *(prep. + gen.)*: without.
ἀνήρ, ἀνδρός *(masc.)*: man.
ἀνθέω: blossom, flourish.
ἄνθρωπος *(2)*: man, human being; (contemptuous), fellow.
ἀνίστημι *(aor.* ἀνέστην*)*: *(trans. tenses)* erect, set up; *(intrans. tenses and mid.)* stand up.
ἀνόητος *(adj.)*: foolish, senseless.

ἄνοια *(1)*: folly, stupidity.
ἀνταίρω *(aor.* ἀντῆρα*)*: rise up against.
ἀντέχω: hold out, resist.
ἀντί *(prep. + gen.)*: in place of, in return for.
ἀντιλαμβάνω *(aor.* ἀντέλαβον*, verb. adj.* ἀντιληπτέος*)*: *(act.)* take in return; *(mid., + gen.)* take hold of, apply oneself to.
ἀντίρροπος *(adj.)*: balancing, counterpoising.
ἀντιτάττω *(aor.* ἀντέταξα*)*: *(act.)* set up in opposition; *(mid. + dat.)* set oneself up against.
ἀνυπέρβλητος *(adj.)*: unsurpassable.
ἄνω *(adv.)*: up, upwards.
ἀξία *(1)*: worth, merit, reputation.
ἀξιόπιστος *(adj.)*: credible.
ἄξιος *(adj. + gen.)*: worthy (of); *adv.* ἀξίως, worthily.
ἀξιόχρεως -ων *(adj.)*: notable, memorable.
ἀξιόω *(+ inf.)*: require, ask; think worthy.
ἀπαγγέλλω *(aor. pass.* ἀπηγγέλθην*)*: announce.
ἀπαγορεύω *(perf.* ἀπείρηκα*)*: *(+ dat.)* forbid; bid farewell to.
ἀπαιτέω: ask back.
ἀπαλλάττω *(aor. pass.* ἀπηλλάγην*, perf. pass.* ἀπήλλαγμαι*)*: *(act.)* free, remove; *(mid. and pass. + gen.)* get rid of, be released from.
ἅπαξ *(adv.)*: once.
ἅπας, ἅπασα, ἅπαν *(adj.)*: all, every.
ἀπειλέω *(+ dat.)*: threaten.
ἄπειμι: be absent.
ἀπελαύνω: drive away.
ἀπεχθάνομαι *(aor.* ἀπηχθόμην*)*: be hated.
ἀπέχθεια *(1)*: hatred,

antagonism, unpopularity.
ἀπιστέω (+ dat.): distrust.
ἄπιστος (adj.): suspect, unreliable, untrustworthy; adv. ἀπίστως, unreliably.
ἁπλοῦς -ῆ -οῦν (adj.): single, simple; adv. ἁπλῶς, simply, absolutely; in short.
ἀπό (prep. + gen.): from.
ἀποβλέπω (aor. ἀπέβλεψα): look at, pay attention to.
ἀπογιγνώσκω (aor. ἀπέγνων): give up, renounce.
ἀποδίδωμι (fut. ἀποδώσω): give back, assign; (+ dat. and inf.) allow.
ἀποθνῄσκω: die.
ἀποκλίνω (aor. ἀπέκλινα): turn away, decline.
ἀπόλλυμι (aor. mid. ἀπωλόμην, trans. perf. ἀπολώλεκα, intrans. perf. ἀπόλωλα): (act.) destroy, lose; (mid.) perish, be ruined.
ἀπορέω: be in doubt, be in difficulties, be at a loss, be helpless.
ἀπορία (1): difficulty, perplexity; (+ gen.) lack, deficiency (of).
ἀπόρρητος (adj.): unspoken, secret.
ἀποστέλλω (aor. ἀπέστειλα): send, despatch.
ἀποστερέω (+ gen.): deprive (of).
ἀπόστολος (2): naval expedition.
ἀποτρίβω: rub off, wipe out, obliterate.
ἀπουσία (1): absence.
ἀποφαίνω: (act.) declare; (mid. with or without γνώμην) give an opinion.
ἀπωθέω: push away, thrust back.
ἀργέω: be idle, be inactive.
ἀργύριον (2): silver.

ἀρέσκω (+ dat.): please.
ἀρετή (1): merit, valour, excellence.
ἁρπάζω (aor. ἥρπασα): seize, snatch.
ἀρρώστημα -ατος (neut.): illness, sickness.
ἀρχαῖος (adj.): ancient; used as noun in neut. pl., τὰ ἀρχαῖα: principal, capital.
ἀρχή (1): beginning; principle; rule; magistracy, political office.
ἄρχω (aor. ἦρξα): begin; rule.
ἀσελγής -ές (adj.): wanton, licentious.
ἀσθενέω: be sick.
ἀσθενής -ές (adj.): weak, feeble; adv. ἀσθενῶς, feebly.
ἀσκέω: train.
ᾆσμα -ατος (neut.): song.
ἄσμενος (adj.): glad.
ἀσφάλεια (1): safety.
ἀσφαλής -ές (adj.): safe; adv. ἀσφαλῶς, safely.
ἄσχολος (adj.): busy, engaged.
ἀτακτέω: be disorderly, undisciplined.
ἄτακτος (adj.): disorderly, irregular; adv. ἀτάκτως, irregularly, under no system.
ἀταξία (1): disorder, irregularity.
ἄτοπος (adj.): strange.
ἀτυχής -ές (adj.): unfortunate.
αὖ (adv.): again (sometimes used pleonastically with πάλιν).
αὐξάνω and αὔξω (aor. ηὔξησα aor. pass. ηὐξήθην, perf. pass. ηὔξημαι): increase, magnify.
αὐτάρκης -ες (adj.): (self) sufficient.
αὐτόματος (adj.): spontaneous, of one's own accord.
αὐτόνομος (adj.): independent.
ἀφαιρέω (aor. ἀφεῖλον): take away.

ἀφανής -ές (adj.): hidden, secret.
ἀφίημι (aor. ἀφῆκα, inf. ἀφεῖναι): release, set free, acquit; let slip.
ἀφίστημι (trans. aor. ἀπέστησα, intrans. aor. ἀπέστην): (act.) remove, set aside; cause to revolt; (mid. and intrans. tenses of act.) be separated from, be removed from; revolt.
ἀφορμή (1): starting point, origin; grounds; opportunity; (plur.) resources.
ἄφρων -ον (adj.): foolish, senseless.

B

βαδίζω: walk, go, proceed.
βάρβαρος (2'): barbarian.
βασιλεύς -έως (masc.): king.
βέβαιος (adj.): firm, reliable; adv. βεβαίως, reliably.
βέλτιστος (adj.): best (used as superlative of ἀγαθός, good).
βελτίων -ον (adj.): better, preferable (used as comp. of ἀγαθός, good).
βῆμα -ατος (neut.): orator's platform.
βία (1); force, might.
βίος (2): life.
βλαβή (1): harm, damage.
βλάπτω: injure, harm.
βοάω (fut. βοήσομαι): shout.
βοηδρομιών -ῶνος (masc.): third month of Attic year, roughly equivalent to September.
βοήθεια (1): help, assistance.
βοηθέω (+ dat.): assist, send help to, come to aid of.
βοηθός (as adj.): assisting, auxiliary; (as noun): helper.
βουλεύω, βουλεύομαι: take counsel, deliberate.
βουλή (1): counsel, deliberation.
βούλησις -εως (fem.): wish.
βούλομαι (+ inf.): wish.
βραβεύω: (trans.) arbitrate, pass judgement on; (intrans.) be a judge or umpire.
βραχύς -εῖα -ύ (adj.): short.

Γ

γείτων -ονος (masc.): neighbour.
γελάω (aor. pass. ἐγελάσθην): laugh.
γελοῖος (adj.): amusing, comic.
γενναῖος (adj.): noble; high-minded.
γεωργέω: (trans.) cultivate; (intrans.) be a farmer.
γίγνομαι (fut. γενήσομαι, aor. ἐγενόμην, perf. γέγονα and γεγένημαι): become.
γιγνώσκω (aor. ἔγνων, perf. ἔγνωκα): come to know, become aware of.
γνώμη (1): opinion; disposition, inclination.
γνώριμος (adj.): well known, familiar.
γράφω (fut. γράψω, aor. ἔγραψα, aor. pass. ἐγράφην): write; (of laws) propose.

Δ

δαιμόνιος (adj.): superhuman, miraculous.
δανείζω: (act.) lend; (mid.) borrow.
δαπανάω: spend.
δέδοικα (perf. with pres. meaning; aor. ἔδεισα): be afraid.

δεῖ (impers.): it is necessary; (+ gen.) there is need of. Part. frequently used as adj. δέον: fitting, proper and as noun τὸ δέον, τὰ δέοντα: one's duty.
δεῖγμα -ατος (neut.): proof, evidence.
δείκνυμι and δεικνύω (fut. δείξω, aor. ἔδειξα, verb. adj. δεικτέος): show.
δεῖνα (gen. δεῖνος): such a one, so and so (always with article).
δεινός (adj.): terrible; clever, skilful.
δέκα (num.): ten.
δέος -ους (neut.): fear.
δεσπότης (1): lord, master.
δεῦρο (adv.): hither, to this place.
δέω (+ gen.): lack. More frequently in mid. δέομαι (+ gen.): need, be in want of; beg, ask.
δῆλος (adj.): clear, obvious.
δημηγορέω: speak in public, address assembly, harangue.
δῆμος (2): people.
δημόσιος (adj.): public (dat. sing. fem, δημοσίᾳ often used adverbially: at public expense, in public, as a community). Used also as noun: public slave (employed in various capacities, esp. as executioner).
δήπου: doubtless, surely, presumably.
διά (prep.): (+ acc.) on account of; (+ gen.) by means of.
διαβάλλω: slander.
διάκειμαι: be disposed, fixed, positioned.

διαλέγομαι (+ dat.; aor. διελέχθην): converse with.
διαλλαγή (1): reconciliation.
διαλλάττω (perf. pass. διήλλαγμαι): reconcile, (pass.) be reconciled.
διαλύω: destroy, terminate, break off.
διανέμω: distribute, assign.
διαπράττω and διαπράττομαι (aor. mid. διεπραξάμην): accomplish, achieve.
διαρκής -ές (adj.): adequate, sufficient; lasting.
διατίθημι (aor. mid. διεθέμην): (act.) arrange, manage; (mid.) dispose of.
διατρίβω: spend time; waste time.
διάφορος (+ gen.): different (from). As noun, τὸ διάφορον: difference.
διαψεύδω (perf. mid. διέψευσμαι): (act.) deceive; (mid.) be deceived, be mistaken.
διδάσκω: teach, instruct.
δίδωμι (fut. δώσω, aor. ἔδωκα with inf. δοῦναι and part. δούς, perf. δέδωκα): give.
διεξέρχομαι (perf. διεξελήλυθα): go through; come to end of; describe.
διέρχομαι (aor. διῆλθον, perf. διελήλυθα): pass, elapse.
διερωτάω: ask constantly.
διίστημι (intrans. perf. διέστηκα, with inf. διεστάναι): (act.) separate, set apart; (mid. and intrans. tenses of act.): stand apart, be at variance.
δικάζω: (trans.) judge; (intrans.) serve as juror.
δίκαιος (adj.): just, upright. Often as noun τὸ δίκαιον: justice; adv. δικαίως, rightly.
δίκη (1): lawsuit; penalty,

punishment.
διό, διόπερ (conj.): wherefore.
διοικέω: manage, administer, govern.
διχῇ (adv.): in two ways.
δοκέω (aor. ἔδοξα): seem, think. Often impers., δοκεῖ: it seems good to, it is resolved.
δοκιμάζω: examine, scrutinise, put to the test.
δόξα (1): opinion, reputation; glory.
δοῦλος (2): slave.
δουλόω: enslave.
δύναμαι (fut. δυνήσομαι, aor. ἐδυνήθην): be able.
δύναμις -εως (fem.): power, ability, effectiveness, force.
δυνατός (adj.): powerful; capable; possible.
δύο (gen. and dat. δυοῖν): two.
δύσμαχος (adj.): difficult to fight against.
δυσχερής -ές (adj.): disagreeable, annoying, difficult.

E

ἐάω (+ inf.): allow, permit; (+ acc.) leave alone.
ἐγγύθεν (adv.): (from) nearby, at close quarters.
ἔγκλημα -ατος (neut.): charge, accusation, grounds of complaint.
ἐθέλω (+ inf.): be willing to. Often negative, οὐκ ἐθέλω: refuse.
ἔθος -ους (neut.): custom, habit.
εἰ (conj.): if; whether.
εἶδον: saw (used as aor. of ὁράω).
εἰκότως: reasonably (see under ἔοικα).
εἴκω (+ dat.): yield.
εἷλον: took (used as aor. of αἱρέω).
εἰμί (fut. ἔσομαι): be; (impers.) be possible.
εἶπα, εἶπον: said (used as aor. of λέγω).
εἰρήνη (1): peace.
εἰς (prep. + acc.): to, into, against.
εἷς, μία, ἕν (num.): one.
εἰσφέρω: pay, contribute (esp. with reference to the eisphora or property tax).
εἶτα (adv.): then, next.
ἐκ, ἐξ (prep. + gen.): from, out of; as a result of, in consequence of.
ἕκαστος (adj.): each.
ἑκάτερος (adj.): each (of two).
ἑκατομβαιών -ῶνος (masc.): first month of Attic year, corresponding roughly to July.
ἐκβαίνω (aor. ἐξέβην): turn out.
ἐκβάλλω (aor. ἐξέβαλον): expel.
ἔκδηλος (adj.): clear, plain.
ἐκεῖ (adv.): there.
ἐκεῖθεν (adv.): from that place.
ἐκεῖνος (adj. and pron.): that.
ἐκεῖσε (adv.): to that place.
ἐκλαλέω: blurt out, divulge.
ἐκνευρίζω (perf. pass. ἐκνενεύρισμαι): cut sinews of; weaken, enfeeble.
ἐκπέμπω (aor. ἐξέπεμψα): send forth.
ἐκπολεμέω: involve, embroil in war.
ἐκπολεμόω (+ dat.): make an enemy of.
ἐκφέρω (aor. ἐξένεγκα): carry out, bring out.
ἐκφεύγω (perf. ἐκπέφευγα): flee, escape.
ἑκών -οῦσα -όν (adj.): willing.

ἐλάττων -ον (comp. adj.):
less, lesser, inferior.
ἐλέγχω: convict.
ἐλεύθερος (adj.): free.
ἔλλειμα -ατος (neut.):
defect.
ἐλλείπω (fut. ἐλλείψω):
(trans.) leave undone;
(intrans.) fail, fall
short, be deficient.
ἐλπίζω: hope, expect.
ἐλπίς -ίδος (fem.): hope.
ἐμβαίνω: embark.
ἐμβάλλω (aor. ἐνέβαλον):
throw into, place into.
ἐμπειρία (1): experience.
ἔμπειρος (adj. + gen.):
experienced, skilled
(in).
ἐμπόδισμα -ατος (neut.):
hindrance, obstacle.
ἐμποδών (adv.): (+ dat.)
in the way of; (+ inf.)
presenting a hindrance in,
i.e. preventing one from.
ἐμπόριον (2): market.
ἐν (prep. + dat.): in.
ἐναντίος (adj. + dat.):
opposite to, contrary to,
hostile to; adv. ἐναντίως,
contrariwise.
ἐνδεῖ (impers. verb + gen.):
there is need of, there is
lack of.
ἔνδεια (1): lack, need.
ἐνδέχομαι: admit, allow of;
be possible.
ἔνειμι (+ dat.): be within,
be present in; be possible.
ἕνεκα (prep. + gen.): on
account of, for the sake
of.
ἐνθάδε (adv.): here.
ἐνθένδε (adv.): from this
place.
ἐνθυμέομαι: think, reflect.
ἔνι (for ἔνεστι): it is
possible.
ἐνιαυτός (2): year.
ἔνιοι (adj.): some.

ἐνοχλέω (+ dat.): bother,
trouble, annoy.
ἐνταῦθα (adv.): here,
there.
ἐντίθημι: put, place in;
instil in.
ἔντιμος (adj.): honoured;
prominent, eminent.
ἐξαιρέω (aor. ἐξεῖλον):take
out; take away; capture;
destroy.
ἐξαπατάω: deceive.
ἐξελέγχω (perf. pass.
ἐξελήλεγμαι, fut. pass.
ἐξελεγχθήσομαι): put to
the test, refute, convict.
ἐξέρχομαι (inf. ἐξιέναι,
Part. ἐξιών, perf.
ἐξελήλυθα): march out
(esp. on military exped-
ition).
ἔξεστι (fut. ἐξεσται,
imperf. ἐξῆν; + dat.):
it is possible.
ἐξετάζω (aor. ἐξέτασα, fut.
pass. ἐξετασθήσομαι):
examine, estimate.
ἑξήκοντα (num.): sixty.
ἔξω: (adv.) outside, abroad;
(prep. + gen.) outside,
beyond.
ἔοικα (+ dat.): be like,
resemble; seem (as impers.)
ἔοικε: it seems, it is
fitting; perf. part. ἐοικώς,
εἰκώς used adjectivally:
fitting, seemly; adv.
εἰκότως, naturally,
reasonably.
ἑορτή (1): festival.
ἐπάγω: lead on.
ἐπαινέω (fut. ἐπαινέσομαι):
praise.
ἔπαινος (2): praise.
ἐπαισθάνομαι: perceive.
ἔπαλξις -εως (fem.): battle-
ment, parapet.
ἐπανίημι (aor. ἐπανῆκα, part.
ἐπανείς -έντος): give up,
abandon.

ἐπανορθόω: set up again, restore; correct.
ἐπαυξάνω: increase, augment.
ἐπεί, ἐπειδή (conj.): when; since.
ἐπέρχομαι (aor. ἐπῆλθον): attack; approach; come upon; come into one's head, occur to.
ἐπί (prep.): (+ acc.) to, towards; against; in search of; (+ gen.) on; in the time of; (+ dat.) on, over, at.
ἐπιβαίνω (aor. ἐπέβην): set foot in.
ἐπιγίγνομαι: come after, succeed.
ἐπιεικής -ές (adj.): reasonable, seemly.
ἐπιθυμέω (+ gen.): desire, long for.
ἐπικλίνω (aor. ἐπέκλινα): turn, cause to incline.
ἐπιλαμβάνω and ἐπιλαμβάνομαι (+ gen.): lay hold of; obtain.
ἐπιορκέω: break one's oath, commit perjury.
ἐπίορκος (adj.): false to one's oath, perjured.
ἐπισκευάζω: repair.
ἐπισκοτέω (+ dat.): cast a shadow over.
ἐπισφαλής -ές: precarious, insecure, unstable.
ἐπιτάττω (+ dat.): order, instruct.
ἐπιτήδευμα -ατος (neut.): practice, pursuit, habit.
ἐπιτιμάω (+ dat.): censure, find fault with.
ἐπιχειρέω (+ dat.): attack.
ἔργον (2): work, deed, action, business, task.
ἐρημία (1): desolation, solitude.
ἐρίζω (+ dat.): quarrel with, strive against.
ἐρρωμένος (adj., properly perf. part. pass. of ῥώννυμι): strong, powerful; adv. ἐρρωμένως, resolutely.
ἔρχομαι (aor. ἦλθον): come, go.
ἐρῶ (fut.) and εἴρηκα (perf.): say, speak (used as fut. and perf. of λέγω).
ἕτερος (adj.): one of two; other, another.
ἔτι (adv.): still, yet.
ἕτοιμος (adj.): ready; adv. ἑτοίμως: readily.
ἔτος -ους (neut.): year.
εὖ (adv.): well.
εὐδαιμονία (1): happiness, prosperity.
εὐδαίμων -ον (adj.): successful, prosperous.
εὐεργεσία (1): benefaction.
εὐεργέτημα -ατος (neut.): benefaction, good deed.
εὐήθεια (1): simplicity, senselessness.
εὐήθης -ες (adj.): simple, foolish.
εὐθύνα (1): scrutiny, accounting; investigation (esp. of a magistrate's conduct).
εὐθύς (adv.): immediately.
εὔλογος (adj.): reasonable.
εὔνοια (1): favour, good will.
εὐπορέω: be wealthy, have plenty.
εὔπορος (adj.): wealthy; easy.
εὐπραξία (1): success, prosperity.
εὑρίσκω (fut. εὑρήσω): find, discover.
εὐσεβής -ές (adj.): pious; adv. εὐσεβῶς, devotedly, piously.
εὐτρεπής -ές (adj.): ready; adv. εὐτρεπῶς, well

prepared; in good order.
εὐτρεπίζω: prepare, make ready.
εὐτυχέω: be fortunate.
εὐχερής -ές (adj.): unconcerned, unflinching; adv. εὐχερῶς, easily, with equanimity.
εὔχομαι (aor. ηὐξάμην): pray.
ἐφίστημι (intr. perf. ἐφέστηκα): (act.) set over; (mid. and intrans. tenses of act.) be set over; be in charge of.
ἐφόδιον (2) (more frequently plur. ἐφόδια): supplies, provisions.
ἐφοράω: oversee, supervise.
ἐφορμέω (+ dat.): lie in wait for; stand by and observe.
ἔχθρα (1): hatred, hostility.
ἐχθρός (2): enemy.
ἔχω (fut. ἕξω and σχήσω, imperf. εἶχον): have; (+ adv.) be, (+ inf.) be able to.
ἕως (conj.): while; as long as; until.

Z

ζάω: live.
ζηλόω: strive after.
ζημία (1): penalty, punishment.
ζημιόω: punish, penalise.
ζητέω: seek.

H

ἡγεμών -όνος (masc.): leader.

ἡγέομαι: (+ gen.) rule; (+ dat.) lead; (with acc. or acc. and inf.) believe.
ἤδη (adv.): already, by now; forthwith.
ἡδονή (1): pleasure.
ἡδύς -εῖα -ύ (adj.): sweet, pleasant.
ἦθος -ους (neut.): character.
ἥκιστος (superl. adj.): least (adv. ἥκιστα).
ἥκω (fut. ἥξω): have come.
ἡλικία (1): age; prime of life (οἱ ἐν ἡλικίᾳ: men of military age).
ἡλίκος (adj.): as, correlative to τηλικόσδε and τηλικοῦτος; how great (indirect interrog.).
ἡμέρα (1): day.
ἡμέτερος (poss. adj.): our.
ἡνίκα (conj.): when.
ἡσυχία (1): rest, leisure, inactivty.
ἡττάομαι: be inferior; be defeated.

Θ

θαρρέω: have confidence.
θάτερον: either of two (= τὸ ἕτερον).
θαυμάζω (aor. ἐθαύμασα): marvel, be amazed.
θαυμαστός (adj.): marvellous, admirable.
θαυματοποιός (2): worker of miracles, juggler, conjuror.
θεάομαι: see.
θεῖος (adj.): divine, sent from the gods.
θέλω: wish, be willing.
θεός (2): god.
θεωρέω: see.
θεωρικός: pertaining to the spectators at festivals; in neut. as noun τὸ θεωρικόν, fund from which money was distributed to provide

entrance fees for state festivals (see Introduction, Appendix B).
θνήσκω (perf. τέθνηκα, part. τεθνεώς): die.
θόρυβος (2): disturbance, turmoil, uproar.
θρυλέω: talk about, have on one's lips.

I

ἰατρός (2): doctor.
ἴδιος (adj.): one's own, personal, peculiar, private; dat. sing. fem. ἰδίᾳ, as adv.: in private; on one's own account; for oneself.
ἱερός (adj.): sacred.
ἱκανός (adj.): adequate, sufficient.
ἵνα (conj.): in order that.
ἴσος (adj.): equal, fair; adv. ἴσως, equally; (more frequently) perhaps.
ἵστημι (aor. ἔστησα): set up, erect.
ἰσχυρός (adj.): strong.
ἰσχύς -ύος (fem.): strength.
ἰσχύω: be strong, prevail.

K

καθαιρέω (aor. pass. καθῃρέθην): take down, pull down, lay low.
καθείργνυμι, καθείργω (aor. καθεῖρξα): shut in, confine.
καθέλκω: pull down, launch.
κάθημαι: sit.
καθίζω (aor. καθῖσα and ἐκάθισα): give seat to; set up, establish.
καθίστημι (fut. καταστήσω, aor. κατέστησα, intrans. perf. καθέστηκα): (act.) set up, establish (mid. and intrans. tenses of act.) be established, be situated.
καθυφίημι and mid. καθυφίεμαι (aor. mid. καθυφείμην): surrender, abandon.
καίπερ (+ part.): although.
καιρός (2): time; season, opportunity; crisis.
καίτοι: and yet.
κακοδαιμονία (1): possession by evil spirit.
κακός (adj.): bad; adv. κακῶς, badly.
κάλλος -ους (neut.): beauty; object of beauty.
καλός (adj.): good, beautiful, splendid; adv. καλῶς, well.
καρπόω: (act.) bear fruit; (mid.) enjoy.
κατά (prep.): (+ acc.) during, in the course of; in accordance with; to the degree of; by (used distributively, e.g.κατὰ συμμορίας: in symmories); (+ gen.) against.
κατακούω (+ gen.): hear, obey.
καταλείπω (aor. κατέλιπον): leave, bequeath.
καταλλαγή (1): compact, reconciliation.
καταρρέω: flow down; sink, fall in ruin.
κατασκευάζω (aor. κατεσκεύασα, perf. κατεσκεύακα; perf. mid. κατεσκεύασμαι): provide, furnish, prepare.
καταστρέφομαι (fut. καταστρέψομαι, aor. κατεστρεψάμην): subdue.
κατέχω (fut. καθέξω): hold on to.
κατηγορέω (+ gen.): accuse.
κατορθόω: (trans.) erect; bring to success; (intrans.

and mid.) succeed,
prosper.
κάτω (*adv.*): down,
downwards.
κάτωθεν (*adv.*): from below;
beneath.
κελεύω: order.
κενός (*adj.*): empty,
fruitless.
κεφάλαιον *(2)*: gist,
main point.
κινδυνεύω: (*trans.*)
endanger; (*intrans.*) take
risks.
κίνδυνος *(2)*: danger.
κινέω: move, disturb.
κλείω (*perf. pass.* κέκλειμ-
μαι): shut.
κοινός (*adj.*): common,
general; *in neut.* (τὸ
κοινὸν, τὰ κοινα): state,
league, confederacy;
public affairs.
κολάζω: punish.
κόλαξ -ακος (*masc.*):
flatterer.
κομιδῇ (*adv.*): exactly;
entirely; just so.
κομίζω (*fut.* κομιῶ): (*act.*)
provide, convey; (*mid.*)
recover, win back.
κονιάω: cover with
plaster.
κόπτω: cut; strike; pound,
batter, wear out.
κορδακισμός *(2)*: lewd
dancing.
κρατέω (+ *gen.*): rule,
conquer, make oneself
master of.
κράτιστος (*superl. adj.*):
best, strongest (*used as
superl. of* ἀγαθός).
κρείττων -ον (*comp. adj.*):
better, preferable (*used
as comp. of* ἀγαθός).
κρήνη *(1)*: spring,
fountain.
κρίνω (*aor.* ἔκρινα):

judge, determine.
κριτής *(1)*: judge.
κτάομαι (*aor.* ἐκτησάμην,
perf. κέκτημαι): acquire;
(*in perf. tenses*)possess.
κτῆμα -ατος (*neut.*):
(*sing.*) acquisition;
(*plur.*) possessions.
κτῆσις -εως (*fem.*):
acquisition.
κύριος (+ *gen.*): having
control over, master of.
κωλύω: prevent.

Λ

λαμβάνω (*aor.* ἔλαβον, *aor.
pass.* ἐλήφθην): take,
accept.
λαμπρός (*adj.*): brilliant,
distinguished.
λανθάνω: (*act.* + *part.*) do
something without being
detected; escape notice;
(*mid.*)forget.
λέγω (*fut.* ἐρῶ, *aor.* εἶπα
and εἶπον, *perf.* εἴρηκα,
perf. pass. εἴρημαι, *aor.
pass.* ἐρρήθην): say, speak;
mean.
λείπω (*perf. pass.* λέλειμμαι):
leave.
λῆμμα -ατος (*neut.*): gain,
profit.
λῆρος *(2)*: trifle, trumpery.
λῃστής *(1)*: robber, brigand.
λίαν (*adv.*): too much, to
excess.
λιμήν -ένος (*masc.*):
harbour.
λογίζομαι: reckon, calculate.
λογισμός *(2)*: calculation.
λόγος *(2)*: word, speech;
account; argument; reason,
excuse.
λοιδορία *(1)*: abuse.
λοιπός (*adj.*): remaining,
left over; future.

λυπέω: distress, vex.
λυσιτελέω: profit, benefit; often impers. λυσιτέλει (+ dat.): it is of advantage (to).
λύω: loose, release; repeal, annul.

M

μά (+ acc.): no by . . . (in negative oaths).
μαιμακτηριών -ῶνος (masc.): fifth month of Attic year, corresponding roughly to November.
μάλα (adv.): much, exceedingly; comp. μᾶλλον: more, rather; superl. μάλιστα: most of all; indeed.
μάταιος (adj.): vain, to no purpose.
μέγας, μεγάλη, μέγα (comp. μείζων, superl. μέγιστος): great, large.
μέθη (1): drunkenness.
μεθύσκω (aor. pass. ἐμεθύσθην): intoxicate; aor. part. pass. μεθυσθείς used as adj.: drunk.
μείζων -ον: comp. of μέγας (q.v.).
μέλλω (+ inf.): intend, be likely to, be about to; delay, postpone. Frequently used in part. τὸ μέλλον and τὰ μέλλοντα as noun: the future.
μέμφομαι: blame, criticize.
μέντοι (particle): however.
μένω: remain.
μερίς -ίδος (fem.): part; contribution.
μέρος -ους (neut.): part, share; rank, category; ἐν μέρει and κατὰ μέρος: in turn.
μεστός (+ gen.): full (of).

μετά (prep.): (+ acc.): after; (+ gen.) with.
μεταβολή (1): change, conversion.
μεταγειτνιών -ῶνος (masc.): second month of Attic year, corresponding roughly to August.
μεταδίδωμι (+ gen.): give a share (in).
μεταλαμβανω (+ gen.; aor. μετέλαβον): have a share in.
μετάστασις -εως (fem.): change, alteration.
μέτειμι (+ dat.): be among. Usually impers.
μέτεστι (+ dat. of person and gen. of thing): partake of, share in.
μετέχω (+ gen.): share in, participate in.
μέχρι: (conj.) until; (prep. + gen.) up to, as far as.
μηδαμῶς (adv.): by no means.
μηδείς, μηδεμία, μηδέν (adj. and pron.) nobody, nothing.
μήν, μηνός (masc.): month.
μικρός (adj.): small, little.
μιμέομαι: imitate.
μιμνήσκω (perf. mid. μέμνημαι, aor. pass. ἐμνήσθην): (act.) remind; (mid.) call to mind; (perf. mid.) remember.
μῖμος (2): actor, performer of mimes.
μισέω: hate.
μισθός (2): pay, wages.
μισθοφορά (1): pay, wages.
μνημονεύω: mention, call to mind.
μόγις (adv.): scarcely, with difficulty.
μόνος (adj.): alone, only.
μοχθηρία (1): baseness, wickedness; poor condition.
μύριοι (num. adj.): ten

thousand.
μυστήριον *(2)*: mystery, secret rite; *in plur.* Eleusian mysteries.

N

ναυμαχέω: fight at sea, fight naval battle.
ναῦς, νεώς *(fem.)*: ship.
νεανικός *(adj.)*: spirited, vigorous, impetuous.
νέμω: distribute, assign.
νικάω: prevail, conquer.
νομίζω *(aor.* ἐνόμισα*)*: think, consider, believe.
νομοθέτης *(1)*: lawgiver.
νόμος *(2)*: law.
νοῦς, νοῦ *(masc.)*: mind.
νῦν, νυνί *(adv.)*: now, at the present moment.

Ξ

ξένος *(adj.)*: foreign. *As noun*, foreigner; foreign soldier, mercenary.

O

ὁδός *(2 fem.)*: way, road, path.
οἶδα *(fut.* εἴσομαι, *imperf.* ᾔδη*)*: know.
οἰκεῖος *(adj.)*: one's own, belonging to oneself, private; domestic.
οἰκία *(1)*: house.
οἰκοδόμημα -ατος *(neut.)*: building.
οἴκοι *(adv.)*: at home.
οἶκος *(2)*: house, home.
οἶμαι, οἴομαι *(aor.* ᾠήθην*)*: think, suppose.
οἷος *(adj.)*: such as *(often as correlative to* τοιοῦτος*)*; *(+ inf.)*: fit to, able to (οἷος τ᾽ εἰμί: I can); *in neut.* οἷον: as, for instance.
οἴχομαι: be gone, depart.
ὀκνέω: be reluctant, hesitate; *(+ inf.)* shrink from, fear to.
ὀλίγος *(adj.)*: little, small; *(in plur.)* few.
ὀλιγωρέω *(+ gen.)*: neglect, despise.
ὅλος *(adj.)*: whole, entire; *adv.* ὅλως, on the whole, in general; in a word; altogether.
ὅμοιος *(adj.)*: equal; *adv.* ὁμοίως, equally.
ὅμορος *(adj.)*: neighbouring, adjacent.
ὁμώνυμος *(+ dat.)*: having same name (as).
ὅμως *(adv.)*: yet, nevertheless.
ὄνειδος -ους *(neut.)*: reproach, blame, disgrace.
ὀνομάζω *(aor.* ὠνόμοσα*)*: name, mention.
ὀξύς -εῖα -ύ *(adj.)*: sharp, keen.
ὅπλον *(2)*: implement; *(in plur.)* weapons.
ὅποι *(adv.)*: to what place.
ὁποῖος *(adv.)*: *(interrog.)* of what kind; *(indef.)* of whatever kind.
ὅπως *(conj.)*: how; in order that.
ὁπωσδήποτε *(adv.)*: somehow or other.
ὁράω *(imperf.* ἑώρων, *aor.* εἶδον*)*: see.
ὀργή *(1)*: anger, passion.
ὀρθός: straight, correct; *adv.* ὀρθῶς, rightly.
ὀρχέομαι: dance.
ὅσος *(adj.)*: *(interrog.)* how great, how much; *(relative)* as great, as much.
ὁστισοῦν, *neut.* ὁτιοῦν: any-

body, anything at all;
(freq. with negative)
οὐδὲν ὁτιοῦν: nothing
whatsoever.
ὅτε (conj.): when; since.
ὅτι (conj.): that; because.
οὐδείς, οὐδεμία, οὐδέν (adj.
and pronoun): no-one,
nothing.
οὐδέποτε (adv.): never.
οὐκέτι (adv.): no longer.
οὐκοῦν (particle): therefore.
οὗτος, αὕτη, τοῦτο (pron.
and adj.): this; adv.
οὕτως, thus, in this
way.
οὕτω(ς) (adv.): so, to
such an extent.
ὀφείλω: owe; (+ inf.) be
bound to.
ὀφλισκάνω (perf. ὤφληκα):
incur, bring on oneself;
acquire a name for.

Π

πάλαι (adv.): long ago.
πάλιν (adv.): again.
πανοῦργος: (adj.) bad,
wicked; (noun) scoundrel.
παντάπασι (adv.): in all
ways, completely.
πανταχοῦ (adv.): everywhere.
πάνυ (adv.): very much.
πάρα (prep.): (+ acc.)
contrary to; throughout; (+ gen.) from;
(+ dat.) in, among.
παραβαίνω (aor. παρέβην):
transgress.
παράδειγμα -ατος (neut.):
example, precedent.
παραδίδωμι (fut. παραδώσω,
aor. παρέδωκα, aor.
part. παραδούς -όντος):
hand over; betray.
παράδοξος (adj.): unexpected.
παρακρούω: (act.) strike
aside; (mid.) cheat,
deceive, mislead.
παραλαμβάνω: receive,
take over.
παραλείπω (fut. παραλείψω):
omit, pass over.
παραπίπτω (perf. παραπέπτωκα): fall one's way.
παραπλήσιος (adj.): nearly
equal, about the same;
adv. παραπλησίως: almost
equally.
παρασκευάζω (aor. παρεσκεύασα, aor. pass.
παρεσκευάσθην): prepare,
make ready.
παρασπάω: draw aside,
divert, detach.
παραυτίκα (adv.):
immediately; for the
moment.
παραχρῆμα (adv.): forthwith;
at the moment; frequently
in phrase ἐκ τοῦ παραχρῆμα:
on the spur of the moment.
παραχωρέω (+ gen.): retreat,
withdraw (from).
πάρειμι (+ dat.): be present
(at); take part (in). Part.
παρών used as adj.: present; and in neut. as noun,
τὸ πάρον, τὰ πάροντα: the
present.
παρέρχομαι (aor. παρῆλθον):
come forward to speak.
παρέχω (aor. παρέσχον):
(act.) provide, offer;
cause, render; (mid.)
exhibit, show.
παρίστημι (fut. παραστήσω):
(act.) set beside, present;
(mid.) bring over to one's
side forcibly, reduce;
(intrans. usage in both
act. and mid.) stand beside;
come into one's mind, occur
to.
παρόμοιος (+ dat.): similar

(to), like.
παροξύνω (fut. παροξυνῶ, aor. pass. παρωξύνθην): rouse, stimulate, spur on.
παρρησία (1): freedom of speech; frankness.
παρωθέω (perf. pass. παρέωσμαι): thrust aside.
πᾶς, πᾶσα, πᾶν (adj.): all, every.
πάσχω (fut. πείσομαι, aor. ἔπαθον, perf. πέπονθα): suffer, undergo, experience.
πατρίς -ίδος (fem.): native land.
πεζέταιρος: foot companion (technical name used of infantry-men serving in Macedonian army).
πεζός: (adj.) on foot; (noun) land force, army. In dat. fem. πεζῇ as adv.: on foot, by land.
πείθω (perf. pass. πέπεισμαι, aor. pass. ἐπείσθην): persuade.
πειράω, πειράομαι (+ inf.): try.
πέμπω (aor. ἔπεμψα): send, despatch; organise procession (at a festival).
πεντακόσιοι (num. adj.): five hundred.
πέντε (num.): five.
περαίνω: accomplish, perform.
περί (prep.): (+ acc.) around; (with name of person, οἱ περί . . . ; those in the company of . . . ; (+ gen.): about, concerning.
περιαιρέω (perf. pass. περιῄρημαι): take away, remove, deprive; (in pass. + acc.) have something removed.
περιγίγνομαι (+ gen.): be superior to, get the better of; be the result or consequence of.
περίειμι (+ gen.; fut. περιέσομαι): be superior to, surpass; be left over; survive. As impers., περίεστι: the result is.
περιίστημι (fut. mid. περιστήσομαι, intrans. aor. περιέστην, part. περιστάς): (act.) place around; (mid.) stand around, surround. Also in mid., with intrans. meaning: come round, turn out.
περιουσία (1): abundance, surplus; profit.
πικρός (adj.): harsh, unpleasant; adv. πικρῶς: harshly.
πιστεύω (+ dat.): trust, believe.
πιστός (adj.): loyal, faithful, trustworthy; adv. πιστῶς, loyally.
πλεονεκτέω: be greedy for more; (+ gen.) gain advantage over.
πλεονεξία (1): covetousness, aggrandisement; advantage.
πλέω: sail.
πλήν (adv. and prep. + gen.): except.
πλησίον (adv. and prep. + gen.): near; ὁ πλησίον: one's neighbour.
πλοῖον (2): boat, vessel.
πλούσιος (adj.): rich.
πόθεν (interrog. adv.): whence, from where?
ποιέω: do, make.
ποιητής (1): maker; composer, poet.
πολεμέω (+ dat.): make war on, fight against.

πολέμιος *(2)*: enemy.
πόλεμος *(2)*: war.
πολιορκέω: besiege.
πόλις -εως *(fem.)*: city.
πολιτεία *(1)*: constitution (esp. free constitution, as opposed to monarchy); political life.
πολιτεύω and (more frequently) πολιτεύομαι: be a citizen, take part in politics, pursue a political career; (+ *acc.*): administer, make part of one's policy.
πολίτης *(1)*: citizen.
πολλάκις *(adv.)*: often.
πολύς, πολλή, πολύ *(comp.* πλείων, *superl.* πλεῖστος): much; (*in plur.*) many.
πονηρία *(1)*: baseness, wickedness.
πόνος *(2)*: toil, labour.
πορεύω: *(act.)* convey; *(mid.)* go, journey.
πόρος *(2)*: way; means of providing, provision; source.
πόσος *(interrog. adj.)*: how much?
ποτε *(indef. adv.)*: at some time, ever; πότε *(with accent, interrog. adv.)*: when?
πότερος *(interrog. adj.)*: which of two? *neut.* πότερον *used as adv.*: whether.
πρᾶγμα -ατος *(neut.)*: thing, matter, affair, business; trouble, bother.
πρᾶξις -εως *(fem.)*: deed, action.
πράττω *(fut.* πράξω, *aor.* ἔπραξα, *perf. mid.* πέπραγμαι, *aor. pass.* ἐπράχθην): *(trans.)* do,
perform, transact; *(intrans.)* fare.
πρέσβεια *(1)*: embassy.
πρεσβεύομαι: serve as ambassador, negotiate, send an embassy.
πρεσβευτής *(1)* (*pl.* πρέσβεις -εων): ambassador, envoy.
πρίν: *(adv.)* formerly, previously; *(conj.)* before.
πρό *(prep. + gen.)*: before; in front of; on behalf of.
προάγω *(aor.* προήγαγον): *(act.)* bring forward; *(mid.)* persuade, win over.
προαιρέω *(perf. mid.* προῄρημαι): *(act.)* bring forth; *(mid.)* prefer, choose.
πρόγονος *(2)*: ancestor.
προέρχομαι *(perf.* προελήλυθα): advance, proceed.
προέχω (+ *gen.*): be superior (to), surpass.
προήκω: have reached, come to.
προθυμία *(1)*: zeal, enthusiasm.
πρόθυμος *(adj.)*: eager, enthusiastic; *adv.* προθύμως: eagerly.
προίημι *(fut.* προήσω, *aor. mid.* προείμην, *subj.* προῶμαι): *(act.)* send forth; *(mid.)* give up, let go, abandon, neglect.
προκινδυνεύω: run risk before; be first to incur danger.
προλαμβάνω *(aor.* προὔλαβον, *perf.* προείληφα): take in advance, capture beforehand.
προπίνω *(perf. pass.* προπέπομαι): drink up; give freely; squander.
πρός *(prep.)*: (+ *acc.*) to, towards; with reference to,

in the light of; (+ gen.)
before, in the name of;
by (in oaths); (+ dat.)
at, beside, near; in
addition to.
προσγίγνομαι (aor. προσ-
εγενόμην): be added.
προσδεῖ (impers. verb +
gen.): there is still
need of.
προσεδρεύω: sit beside
(esp. with notion of
paying attention to).
πρόσειμι (+ dat.; fut.
προσέσομαι): be added
(to).
προσέχω (+ dat.; fut.
προσέξω): turn one's
mind to, pay attention
to.
προσήκω (+ dat.): belong
(to). Often impers.
προσήκει: it concerns, it
is fitting.
προσθήκη (1): addition,
additional factor; super-
numerary, extra (of
people).
προσκαθέζομαι (fut.
προσκαθεδοῦμαι): sit down
before, besiege.
προσλαμβάνω: take in
addition; win over.
προσνέμω (perf. mid.
προσνενέμημαι): assign,
allocate.
προσοφείλω: be still in
debt, owe in addition.
προσπολεμέω: wage war
against.
προστάτης (1): (political)
leader.
προστίθημι (aor. προσέθηκα,
subj. προσθῶ, part.
προσθείς): add or apply
one thing to another.
πρότερος (comp. adj.):
former, previous; superior;
adv. πρότερον, before, in
the past; superl. πρῶτος
(q.v.).
προτίθημι (aor. pass.
προὐτέθην): set before.
προτρέπω: encourage,
urge.
πρόοπτος (adj., contracted
from πρόοπτος): foreseen,
manifest.
πρόφασις -εως (fem.):
pretext, excuse.
πρωτεῖον (2): first place;
first prize.
πρῶτος (adj.): first.
πταῖσμα -ατος (neut.):
fall, slip, stumble.
πταίω: trip, stumble.
πτωχός (adj.): poor; as
noun: beggar.
πυνθάνομαι: enquire.
πώποτε (adv.): ever.
πῶς (adv.): (interrog.)
how? in what way?; πως
(without accent, indef.)
somehow, in some way.

Ρ

ῥᾴδιος (adj.; comp. ῥᾴων,
superl. ῥᾷστος): easy.
ῥᾳθυμέω: be idle.
ῥᾳθυμία (1): indifference;
indolence, inactivity.
ῥαΐζω: recover (from
illness).
ῥῆγμα -ατος (neut.):
break, fracture.
ῥητός (adj.): said, spoken;
(in combination with
ἀπόρρητος, q.v.) open.
ῥήτωρ -ορος (masc.):
orator, spokesman.
ῥοπή (1): turning (of the
pan of a balance);
weighing (on a pair of
scales).
ῥώμη (1): strength.
ῥώννυμι (perf. mid.
ἔρρωμαι): strengthen;
perf. part. pass.

ἐρρωμένος (used as adj.):
strong, powerful; adv.
ἐρρωμένως, resolutely.

Σ

σαθρός (adj.): unsound.
σαφής -ές (adj.): clear;
adv. σαφῶς, clearly.
σεμνός (adj.): revered;
magnificent, majestic.
σθένος -ους (neut.):
strength.
σιτίον (2): food.
σιωπάω: (trans.) keep
silent about; (intrans.)
be silent.
σκῆψις -εως (fem.):
excuse, pretext.
σκοπέω (aor. ἐσκεψάμην,
perf. ἔσκεμμαι): view,
consider, examine.
στασιάζω: be at
variance; be rent with
faction.
στενός (adj.): narrow. As
noun, τὸ στενόν: confined
space.
στρατεία (1): campaign,
expedition.
στράτευμα -ατος (neut.):
army.
στρατεύω, στρατεύομαι:
serve as a soldier,
campaign.
στρατηγέω: be general.
στρατηγός (2): general,
commander.
στρατιώτης (1): soldier.
στρατιωτικός (adj.):
military; neut. plur. τὰ
στρατιωτικά as noun:
military funds.
στρατόπεδον (2): camp.
στρέμμα -ατος (neut.):
twist, sprain.
συγκατασκευάζω (aor.
συγκατεσκεύασα): help in
providing, assist in
establishing.
συγκροτέω: knock together;
weld, put into shape.
συγκρύπτω (aor. συνέκρυψα):
hide, conceal.
συζάω: live together with.
συλάω: pillage, plunder.
συμβαίνω (aor. συνέβη):
agree, come to terms;
happen, occur; συμβαίνει
(impers.): it happens.
συμβουλεύω (+ dat.): (act.)
advise; (mid.) deliberate.
σύμβουλος (2): adviser.
συμμαχία (1): alliance.
συμμαχικός (adj.): pertaining to an alliance; τὸ
συμμαχικόν, τὰ συμμαχικά
(neut. as noun): alliance;
the forces or members of
an alliance.
σύμμαχος (2): ally.
συμμορία (1): symmory,
division of Athenian
people for liturgical
purposes.
συμπλέκω (aor. pass.
συνεπλάκην): plait
together, mix, entangle;
(pass.) grapple with, come
to grips with.
συμπονέω: work together.
συμφέρω (+ dat.; fut.
συνοίσω): be useful (to).
συμφερει (impers.) it is
of interest to, it is of
advantage to.
συμφορά (1): circumstance,
event; misfortune,
disaster.
συναίρω (aor. mid. συνηράμην):
(act.) raise up together;
(mid.) help in bearing,
join in undertaking.
συναμφότερος (adj.): (sing.)
combined with, in combin-
ation with; (plur.) both
together.
συναναλίσκω (aor. συνανήλωσα):
lose together, lose some-

thing along with something else.
σύνειμι (+ dat.): associate (with).
συνεισβάλλω: join in invading.
συνεχής -ές (adj.): continuous; adv. συνεχῶς, constantly.
συνίημι: understand.
συνίστημι (intrans. aor. συνέστην): (act.) combine, put together, organise, establish; (mid. and intrans. tenses of act.) band, league together.
σύνοιδα: be aware of, be conscious of.
συνοράω (aor. συνεῖδον): perceive, understand.
σύνταξις -εως (fem.): set-up, system, organisation, structure.
σφαλερός (adj.): slippery, unreliable.
σφόδρα (adv.): very, exceedingly.
σχεδόν (adv.): almost, approximately.
σχολάζω: be at leisure.
σώζω (fut. σώσω, aor. ἔσωσα, perf. σέσωκα, aor. pass. ἐσώθην): save, preserve.
σῶμα -ατος (neut.): body.
σωτηρία: safety, salvation, preservation.
σώφρων -ον (adj.): sensible, prudent, decent.

T

ταλαιπωρέω: be distressed, endure hardship.
τάλαντον (2): talent, Attic weight and sum of money.
ταμίας (1): treasurer, steward.
τᾶν: form of address, only in phrase ὦ τᾶν: my good sir, my good friend.
τάξις -εως (fem.): rank, order, position; system.
ταπεινός (adj.): low, humble.
ταράττω (perf. pass. τετάραγμαι): disturb, confuse.
ταχύς -εῖα -ύ (adj.): quick, fast (comp. θάττων, superl. τάχιστος); adv. ταχέως: quickly (superl. τάχιστα).
τειχίζω: fortify.
τεῖχος -ους (neut.): wall; fort.
τέλειος (adj.): perfect, complete.
τελευταῖος (adj.): last, final. Neut. τὰ τελευταῖα as adv.: finally.
τελευτάω: end.
τελευτή (1): end.
τέταρτος (num. adj.): fourth.
τετταράκοντα (num.): forty.
τέως (adv.): for a time, in the meantime (correlative to ἕως).
τηλικοῦτος (adj.): so great, of such a size or importance.
τηνικαῦτα (adv.): then, at that time.
τιθασεύω: tame, domesticate.
τίθημι (aor. ἔθηκα, opt. θείην, part. θείς; perf. τέθηκα, aor. mid. ἐθέμην): put, place; make; reckon.
τιμάω: honour.
τιμή (1): honour; political office.
τιμωρέω: (act. + dat.) avenge; (act. and mid. +

acc.): punish, take
vengeance on.
τίς, τί: (accented) who?
what? (interrog.)
(unaccented) someone,
something (indef.).
τοιοῦτος (adj.): of such
a kind.
τόκος (2): interest.
τολμάω (+ inf.): dare,
have courage to.
τόπος (2): place.
τοσοῦτος (adj.): so large,
so much.
τότε (adv.): at that time.
τρέπω (fut. τρέψω): turn.
τριάκοντα (num.): thirty.
τριακόσιοι (num. adj.):
three hundred.
τριηραρχέω: serve as treir-
arch, contribute to cost
of maintaining a trireme.
τριηρής -ους (fem.):
trireme, warship.
τρίτος (num. adj.): third.
τρόπαιον (neut.): trophy.
τρόπος (2): way, method;
custom; attitude.
τροφή (1): nourishment,
maintenance.
τυγχάνω (aor. ἔτυχον):
(+ part.) happen to;
(+ gen.) hit upon,
obtain; impers., τυγχάνει:
it happens.
τυραννικός (adj.): belonging to a tyrant or
tyranny.
τυραννίς -ίδος (fem.):
tyranny, monarchy,
despotism.
τύραννος (2): tyrant.
τύχη (1): chance, fortune,
luck.

Υ

ὑβρίζω (perf. ὕβρικα): be
arrogant, be insolent.

ὕβρις -εως (fem.):
arrogance, insolence.
ὑβριστής (1): man of
violence, bully.
ὑμέτερος (poss. adj.):
your.
ὑπακούω (+ dat.): obey.
ὑπάρχω (aor. ὑπῆρξα, perf.
mid. ὑπῆργμαι): begin;
underlie; exist, be.
Frequently used in neut.
part. τὰ ὑπάρχοντα, τὰ
ὑπηργμένα of things
already existing: present
circumstances; one's record
etc. (see notes ad locc).
ὑπέρ (prep.): (+ acc.)
above, beyond; (+ gen.)
on behalf of, for the sake
of.
ὑπερβολή (1): excess;
superiority; means of
surpassing.
ὑπερεκπλήττω (perf. pass.
ὑπερεκπέπληγμαι): (act.)
astonish, terrify greatly;
(mid, and pass.) be
terribly afraid of; be
increasingly amazed at.
ὑπηρέτης (1): servant.
ὑπισχνέομαι (aor. ὑπεσχόμην):
promise.
ὑπό (prep.): (+ gen.) by,
by means of, because of;
(+ dat.) under.
ὑποδέχομαι (aor. ὑπεδεξάμην):
receive, admit.
ὑπόθεσις -εως (fem.): basic
principle, conception,
premise.
ὑπολαμβάνω: take up; understand, suppose.
ὑπολείπω: (act.)leave;
(mid.) remain.
ὑπόλοιπος (adj.): remaining,
left over.
ὑπομένω (aor. ὑπέμεινα):
endure, tolerate.
ὑπομιμνήσκω (aor.
ὑπέμνησα): remind.

ὑποστέλλω (aor. ὑπέστειλα):
draw back; (mid.) shrink
from.
ὑποτίθημι (aor. mid.
ὑπεθέμην, inf.
ὑποθέσθαι): (act.)
suggest; (mid.) propose
for discussion; assume
as a starting point.
ὕστερος (adj.): behind,
next, later; neut.
ὕστερον as adv.:
afterwards.

Φ

φαίνω (fut. φανῶ, intrans.
perf. πέφηνα, aor. pass.
ἐφάνην, fut. pass.
φανήσομαι): (act.) show;
(mid. and intrans. perf.)
appear; (+ inf.) seem to.
φανερός (adj.): clear,
manifest, obvious.
φάσκω: assert, allege.
φαῦλος (adj.): mean,
shoddy, worthless; adv.
φαύλως, badly.
φενακίζω (perf. πεφενάκικα):
cheat, deceive.
φέρω: carry, bear,
endure.
φεύγω (aor. ἔφυγον): flee,
avoid.
φημί (fut. φήσω): say.
φθονέω (+ dat.): envy,
bear malice.
φιλέω: love, show
affection for.
φιλία (1): friendship.
φιλοπραγμοσύνη (1):
restlessness, meddle-
someness.
φίλος (adj.): dear; (as
noun) friend.
φιλοτιμία (1): ambition;
rivalry, jealousy.
φοβέομαι: fear.
φοβερός (adj.): terrible,
formidable.
φόβος (2): fear.
φράζω (aor. ἔφρασα):
speak, tell, say.
φρονέω: have sense; think,
intend.
φρόνημα -ατος (neut.):
spirit, mind, purpose.
φροντίζω: think; pay
attention to; provide
for.
φροντίς -ίδος (fem.):
thought.
φύλαξ -ακος (masc.):
guard, guardsman.
φυλάττω (fut. φυλάξω, aor.
ἐφύλαξα): guard,
preserve, keep.
φύσις -εως (fem.): nature.
φύω (intrans. aor. ἔφυν,
intrans. perf. πέφυκα):
(act.) produce; (mid. and
intrans. tenses of act.):
be born, grow; (intrans.
perf.) be by nature; be.
φωνή (1): voice.
φωράω: detect, discover.

Χ

χαίρω (+ dat.): rejoice,
delight (in).
χαλεπός (adj.): difficult,
hard, disagreeable; adv.
χαλεπῶς: with
difficulty.
χαρίζομαι (+ dat.; aor.
ἐχαρισάμην): favour,
please, gratify.
χάρις -ιτος (fem.):
favour; thanks,
gratitude; delight;
popularity.
χειροήθης -ες (adj.):
tame, docile.
χειροτονέω: vote (by show
of hands).
χείρων -ον (comp. adj.):
worse, inferior; χείριστος

(superl. adj.) worst.
χίλιοι (num. adj.): one thousand.
χράομαι (+ dat.; fut. χρήσομαι, aor. ἐχρησάμην, perf. κέχρημαι): use, enjoy, make the most of; have to deal with.
χρή (fut. χρῆσται, imperf. χρῆν): it is necessary.
χρῆμα -ατος (neut.): (sing.) thing; (plur.) money.
χρήσιμος (adj.): useful, profitable.
χρηστός (adj.): useful; good.
χρόνος (2): time.
χώρα (1): land, territory.
χωρέω: go, proceed.
χωρίον (2): place; walled settlement, township.
χωρίς (prep. + gen.): without, apart from.

Ψ

ψεύδω (act.) cheat, mislead; (mid.) lie.
ψηφίζομαι (aor. ἐψηφισάμην, perf. ἐψήφισμαι): vote, decree.
ψήφισμα -ατος (neut.): decree.

Ω

ὥρα (1): time, season.
ὡς (conj.): that; when; since.
ὥσπερ (adv.): just as, as if.
ὥστε (conj.): so that, with the result that.
ὠφελέω: help, assist.

ὠφελία (1): help, assistance, benefit.

PAEONIA
R. Strymon
R. Axios
ILLYRIA
MACEDONIA
Philippi
CHALCIDICE
Amphipolis
THASOS
Pella
Aegae
Methone
Pydna
Olynthos
THERMAIC GULF
EPEIROS
THESSALY
MAGNESIA
Pherai
Crannon
Pagasae
HALONNESOS
AMBRACIA
Crocus Field
Halus
Lamia
Thermopylai
SKYROS
ACARNANIA
Elatea
EUBOIA
Chaeronea
Amphissa
Delphi
BOEOTIA
Chalcis
Thebes
Megara
ACHAIA
Sicyon
Athens
ELIS
Corinth
Paeania
Olympia
ARCADIA
Argos
Megalopolis
Messene
Sparta
MELOS
CAPE TAENARUM

THRACE
MACEDONIA
CHALCIDICE
THESSALY
MAGNESIA
R. Axius
R. Strymon
R. Haliacmon
R. Peneus
MT. PANGAION
Amphipolis
Eion
Abdera
Doriscus
SERRIUM
THASOS
SAMOTHRACE
IMBROS
LEMNOS
TENEDOS
HALONNESUS
SCYROS
SCIATHUS
PEPARETHUS
Pella
Methone
Pydna
Apollonia
Acanthus
ACTE
Olynthus
Mecyberna
Poteidaea
THERMAIC
GULF
Aphytis
Torone
SITHONIA
PALLENE
Mende
Scione
Pherae
Crannon
Pagasae
Pharsalus
Crocus Field
Halus
Lamia